TEEN READ WEEK™
and
TEEN TECH WEEK™

Tips and Resources
for YALSA's Initiatives

Edited by Megan Fink
for the Young Adult Library Services Association

A division of the
American Library Association

Chicago
2011

MEGAN FINK is middle school librarian and advisor at Charlotte Country Day School, in Charlotte, North Carolina. A former Teen Read Week committee chair, Fink worked in children's publishing before earning her MLS at the University of North Carolina and has written multiple articles for *Young Adult Library Services*, ILoveLibraries.org, *BookLinks*, and the Charlotte Observer.

Teen Tech Week and Teen Read Week: Tips and Resources for YALSA's Initiatives/edited by Megan Fink for the Young Adult Library Services Association. Supported by a Carnegie-Whitney Award from the American Library Association.

The paper used in this publication meets the minimum requirements of American National Standard for Information Sciences—Permanence of Paper for Printed Library Materials, ANSI Z39.48-1992. ♾

Library of Congress Cataloging-in-Publication Data

Teen Read Week and Teen Tech Week : tips and resources for YALSA's initiatives / edited by Megan Fink.
   pages cm—(Best of YALS series)
 Articles originally published in the journal Young adult library services.
 Includes bibliographical references.
 ISBN 978-0-8389-8559-5 (alk. paper)
 1. Young adults' libraries—United States. 2. Libraries and teenagers—United States. 3. Young adults' libraries—Activity programs—United States. 4. Young adults' libraries—Information technology—United States. 5. Teenagers—Books and reading—United States. I. Fink, Megan. II. Young Adult Library Services Association. III. Young adult library services.
 Z718.5.T44 2011
 027.62'6—dc22   2010048780

ISBN-13: 978-0-8389-8559-5

Printed in the United States of America

15 14 13 12 11   5 4 3 2 1

CONTENTS

PART II: TEEN TECH WEEK™

FIVE: BEST PRACTICES FOR TEEN TECH WEEK

SIX: CELEBRATING TEEN TECH WEEK IN CHALLENGING SITUATIONS

SEVEN: TEEN TECH WEEK PROGRAMMING

EIGHT: MARKETING, OUTREACH, AND PROMOTION FOR TEEN TECH WEEK

APPENDIXES

FOREWORD

Welcome to the very first volume in YALSA's Best of *YALS* series. Drawing on years of expertise shared through *Young Adult Library Services*, our professional journal, this work represents the first in a series of subject guides for practicing librarians.

This book is yet another milestone for our no-longer-fledgling division. YALSA is now more than fifty years old—middle-aged and all grown up by some accounts. Teen library services have come a long way in that time, but teen services still show the potential for significant growth. As past president of the fourth-largest division of ALA, I'm delighted to have been asked to introduce this new venture. This series will address various subjects that support teen service providers as they provide excellent customer service to teens.

For this inaugural volume, editor Megan Fink has selected the best articles from the eight volumes of *YALS*, focusing on YALSA's teen reading and technology initiatives to support young adult services at public libraries and school librarians as they plan for these events, with articles on collection development, programming, budget restrictions, and other important topics. Articles have been edited and updated as necessary. For example, audiobooks are rarely available on cassette anymore, so mentions of tapes have been edited to include CDs, MP3s, or Playaways.

Serving Teens, One Customer at a Time

Good customer service can be described as a four-legged stool. To be strong and stable, libraries need to have all four legs firmly planted on the ground. Each leg represents one piece of the overall service model—materials, trained staff, designated spaces, and programming suitable for the targeted population. So, how are young adult services doing out in the field? In 2007 YALSA worked with the Public Library Association to add a series of questions to the annual Public Library Data Service (PLDS) Statistical Report in order to track young adult service trends in public libraries. In conjunction with the Harris Interactive poll conducted for the American Library Association that same year, we have a baseline snapshot of our progress. It is fair to say that public libraries routinely offer some teen or YA materials to their customers, with 90 percent of respondents to the PLDS report indicating that they do so. They also provide at least shelving and a couple of seats as a designated "teen" area. We also know that more than 50 percent of all public libraries have hired a designated teen or young adult staff person to focus service on this population. So that leaves programming, the fourth leg of our stool. Here a whopping 90 percent of the surveyed public libraries indicated that they offer young adult programming!

And there is even more good news. . . . YALSA, a forward-thinking organization that recognized that teen librarians needed support, created two national initiatives: Teen Read Week™ and Teen Tech Week.™ In fact, more than ten years ago, YALSA realized that teen librarians and staff serving teens needed identifiable age-appropriate ways to program—something for staff to easily hang their hats on to the way that children's librarians and staff use storytimes and summer reading to serve their young customers and families. Hence, Teen Read Week was born—a designated week each fall to highlight available teen materials and to raise the profile of teens who read for fun. It's been successful and has spawned additional projects such as the Teens' Top Ten list, in which teens vote for their favorite books during August and September, with the results announced to kick off Teen Read Week. Every fall teens are involved in a wide variety of activities that lead back to those wonderful materials, and it is no surprise that surveys indicate that teens read. In fact, the Harris Interactive poll showed that of those asked who use the library regularly (about 70 percent or so), more than three-quarters of the responding teens said that they checked materials out for personal use, not just for school assignments.

But that's not all teens do, and YALSA's second national initiative, set each spring, focuses on another activity teens do well: use technology of all kinds. Teens are often the early adapters of new technology, from video gaming and MySpace pages to YouTube postings, texting, and a host of technologies in between. YALSA developed Teen Tech Week as a time to deliberately and publicly celebrate something so many teens are so good at—using technology.

So keep reading through this excellent comp-ilation. It is the first in a series of books that will bring you proven resources for serving your teens. Whether you are that mature, experienced, and highly trained teen librarian with years of programming success under your belt or that new staff person designated as the one to add value to your library by offering teen programs, you'll find great ideas and blueprints to help you make sure that your fourth leg of the stool is all quality!

Enjoy trying out these ideas and strategies, but then be sure to share your variations on these programs so the next generation of staff can build on your success, just as you are going to do with the ones highlighted in this volume.

—Judy T. Nelson, Youth Services Director
Pierce County Library System

BOOKS AND TECHNOLOGY: READING'S FUTURE

CYNTHIA LEITICH SMITH

The sparking, sparkling conversation of books takes place on the page, on the screen, and in person. For teens around the country, libraries are at the heart of that dialogue.

We're past fretting that books and technology compete. Over the past several years, we've seen how well they compliment and reinforce one another.

Teen Read Week and Teen Tech Week are celebrations of that exciting reality.

When I first began publishing books like *Rain Is Not My Indian Name* (HarperCollins, 2001), I struck out on the Internet to send a message that contemporary Native heroes belonged in today's stories for young readers. By embracing technology to do so, I sent the message that we're all part of the past, present, and future of books.

Since that time, I've built a children's and YA literature website that attracts more than two million visitors annually, launched two children's and YA book blogs at five sites, and began regularly skipping across social networks to highlight new releases, encourage new voices, and connect, connect, connect.

Since I've begun publishing books like *Tantalize* and *Eternal* (both Candlewick) for the YA audience, teens have been seeking me out in return. I've made a point of responding to every teen that has sent me a message, even on days when it takes an hour or three.

The interaction matters—if the reader is motivated enough to reach out, then I want to do whatever I can to validate their enthusiasm and steer them to more books that they'll enjoy, no matter who the author.

Among other initiatives, Teen Read Week and Teen Tech Week take efforts like that—ongoing outreach by individual authors to the national level, be it in real space or virtual, and springing from state to state, city to city, neighborhood to neighborhood, and laptop to cell phone—all of it under the guidance of rock-star media professional.

When I say "rock star," I'm speaking from the perspective of a grown-up kid who's a library success story. Growing up, my mama took me every Saturday morning to the public library, and then as I continued on to school, the library there became a frequent destination as well. Along with my grandfather and a great aunt, it was librarians who encouraged me in my writing, my studies, my dreams. . . . I became the first person in my family to graduate from college, then went onto law school, and became a full-time writer. None of that would've happened if I hadn't largely grown up in the library.

In conjunction with programs like Teen Read Week and Teen Tech Week, I'm honored to stand with librarians and offer even more support to the latest generation of young readers. It's vitally important to raise them up. And it's equally key to remind the world that they deserve the very best in library services. To reach out, appreciate, and sound off, year after year, celebration after celebration! ■

ACKNOWLEDGMENTS

I would like to thank the American Library Association's Publications Committee for their support by giving us the Carnegie-Whitney grant for this project.

A special thank you to RoseMary Honnold, Sarah Flowers, and Valerie Ott—editors of *Young Adult Library Services* during the time these issues were published.

This compilation would not be possible without the cooperation and hard work of the YALSA staff, including Beth Yoke, executive director; Eve Gaus, program officer for continuing education; Nichole Gilbert, program officer for conferences and events; Stephanie Kuenn, communications specialist; and Letitia Smith, program coordinator for membership.

Finally, my immense gratitude goes to the authors, without whom YALSA would not have this book and its contents. Thank you to Linda Braun, Shonda Brisco, Elizabeth Burns, Jane Charles, Mary K. Chelton, Francisca Goldsmith, Erin Helmrich, Sandra Hughes-Hassell, Kim Herrington, Patrick Jones, Elizabeth Kahn, Carla Land, Jodi Lockbee, Darcy Lohmiller, Katherine Makens, Iona Malanchuk, Cynthia Matthias, C. D. McLean, Judy Michaelson, Christy Mulligan, Walter Dean Myers, Judy Nelson, Charli Osborne, Ann Peachcek, Cathy Rettberg, Kimberlee Ried, Beth Saxton, Jami Schwarzwalder, Julie Scordato, Cynthia Leitich Smith, Camden Tadhg, Vikki Terrile, Jennifer Velasquez, and the Technology for Young Adults Committee.

—Megan Fink
September 2010

PART I

TEEN READ WEEK™

TEEN READ WEEK—MORE THAN JUST FOR THE FUN OF IT

Megan Fink, with contributions from Walter Dean Myers and Elizabeth Kahn

Teen Read Week and Teen Tech Week are an annual opportunity for librarians to beat the drum of reading and highlight the importance of teen literacy to the world. This *YALS* collection features articles that focus on the planning, programming, and marketing and promotion of the library in conjunction with YALSA's national literacy and technology turnkey programs.

Teen Read Week began in 1998 with a simple theme: Read for the Fun of It. Since then, YALSA has developed a subtheme each year for librarians to use to build programs, special events, and resources to attract teens to their library and promote reading as a fun, free activity that teens can do anytime, anywhere. Teen Read Week is celebrated the third week of October each year, and librarians and educators can find the latest information on this year's celebration at www.ala.org/teenread.

Teens are reading in a variety of formats, including online, audiobooks, and e-readers. Their experiences in the library can cultivate them into becoming lifelong readers. In addition to showing teens the pleasures of reading, libraries and librarians can use Teen Read Week to respond to the ever-growing educational needs of the community. One of the recent studies of literacy by the American College Test found that greater literacy skills in high school led to better achievement in math, science, and social studies, and that higher levels of literacy contributed to greater college enrollment and higher grades in all college courses.[1] Thus, secondary educators have begun to look at literacy skills as a key indicator of how on track students are to graduate from high school ready for college and work. Yet a whopping 69 percent of eighth-graders and 65 percent of twelfth-graders read below proficiency as measured by the National Assessment of Educational Progress.[2]

OPENING DOORS: A TEEN READ WEEK SUCCESS STORY

ELIZABETH KAHN

In 2007, during my second year as librarian at Patrick F. Taylor Science & Technology Academy in Jefferson, Louisiana, I decided to enhance the school's celebration of Teen Read Week. The library book group and I sat down to plan daily activities during lunch to entice non-library users into the library, and TRW that year was a big success in my library.

So when I saw YALSA's Best Teen Read Week Contest in 2008, in which my school could win a visit from YA author Tiffany Trent, I knew that I had to take a chance and apply. I was very surprised when I received the call in January 2008 that we had actually won. The event was planned for Teen Tech Week. It was going to be the anchor for our library's celebration. Working with Tiffany's publishers at Mirrorstone, the school was sent enough copies of her first book for every student and teacher at school. This meant that the students would have an opportunity to read Tiffany's work before she arrived.

The day of her visit was a whirlwind of activity. Two assemblies were planned in the morning. I think the students were won over when Tiffany showed a picture of herself surrounded by bear cubs. After each assembly, the students had a chance to get their book signed. The library book group was invited to share a catered lunch with the author.

In the afternoon, Tiffany gave a writing seminar for students in a science-fiction class. Tiffany visit had a lasting effect on the students at Taylor. I saw students all over school reading *In the Serpent's Coils*. For weeks afterward, I would have students in the library who wanted a copy of her second book. One of my students told me a few days after the event, "It's not my genre of choice, but after I saw the author who was so enthusiastic, I decided to read [her] book. I really enjoyed it."

I want the students at Taylor to read, and this special event got more of them reading. ■

A MOUNTAIN OF BOOKS

WALTER DEAN MYERS

Summers in Harlem: Basketball in the playground across the street, stickball between the sewers around the corner, and handball against the church wall. When it rained or when it was too hot for other kids to play ball (it was never too hot for me!), I would make the trek to the George Bruce Branch of the New York Public Library. At some point in my life, I made the decision to read all of the books in the library. I quickly realized that there was literally a mountain of books to tackle. But once a week, I would try to get to the library and carefully select the four books I was allowed to take out at a time.

Books filled my time nicely. They amused me. Some books I even found delightful. Despite my being unaware of it at the time, they were also telling me some interesting things about myself. To begin with, I was not nearly as unique a person as I had thought. There were other people who wondered if they were attractive or not, and others who felt alone in the world. Some of the books told me that there were people who lived in foreign lands who sometimes despaired of their lives and their chances for success. Other books told me of people who had lived long before me who worried about the same problems that I had felt could only have been mine. By the time I was fifteen, I was beginning to realize that the singular viewpoint of my life was only a small part of a much larger world.

I was also learning more mundane things. A biography of a Chinese philosopher poet told me how he struggled to achieve but also how he traveled through China and how the government worked there. A novel translated from the French told me how difficult life was in Paris in 1819 and led me to finding that city on the map.

In years to come, I would also discover that the secondary things I had found in books would be part of my casual conversation with other people who read and that the books experienced by others would be the basis of new friendships.

My summer reading added greatly to the person I was during those summers. I was not only a ballplayer, an athlete, but I had developed an entirely new dimension. As important as sports were to me, and they remained that important for years, the new dimensions provided by the books I read eventually became even more vital to my life. I have never climbed that entire mountain of books, but I have used so many of those books to enrich and expand all of the seasons of my life. ■

What can libraries do to support educators and schools in this campaign? They can get involved in initiatives like Teen Read Week, which encourages teens to read for fun and become regular library users. Multiple studies show that reading comprehension, vocabulary, and reading speed improve with more time spent on independent reading and these in turn lead to improved academic performance.[3]

The programming and best practices of libraries across the country in this collection—aimed at helping librarians plan successful Teen Read Week celebrations—promote reading as a worthwhile activity and a pleasurable experience. As librarians, we can provide a community that encourages and promotes reading as a worthwhile and valuable pursuit. We can collaborate with the local community by reaching out to parents, teens, and teachers to work with us on encouraging teens to read and on making Teen Read Week a big deal in our libraries.

Repeated studies have shown that teens need recommendations and encouragement about reading, and "that the support of peers who value reading is a factor of major significance among adolescents who are being motivated to read."[4] Libraries are the catalyst for many students beginning a lifelong reading habit, and libraries can cultivate reading groups among teens. Using the best practices, collection development advice, programming tools, and marketing tips in this volume, you can let your library shine as a forum for readers, with passionate librarians as the indefatigable guardians of the literate future.

NOTES

1. Bob Wise, "Adolescent Literacy: The Cornerstone of Student Success," *Journal of Adolescent & Adult Literacy* 52, no. 5 (2009): 369–75.

2. Ibid.

3. Joseph Sanacore and Anthony Palumbo, "Middle School Students Need More Opportunities to Read across the Curriculum," *Clearing House* 83, no. 5 (2010): 180–85.

4. Diane Lapp and Douglas Fisher, "It's All about the Book: Motivating Teens to Read," *Journal of Adolescent & Adult Literacy* 52, no. 7 (2009): 556–61.

TEEN READ WEEK
BEST PRACTICES

IN THIS CHAPTER, you'll see a sampling of ideas, history, and advocacy that librarians have used across the country to create inviting celebrations. The articles in this chapter offer helpful tips for getting teens involved, collection development, and including adult services staff in your event each year.

POWERING UP WITH PRINT: TEN BEST PRACTICES
Patrick Jones

On a tour through Kansas to promote *New Directions for Library Services to Young Adults* (ALA Editions, 2002), librarians from mostly smaller school and public libraries shared with me their best practices, many of them low or no cost, to promote reading and libraries to teenagers. Among them are the following:

- Buhler High School in Hutchinson positioned a magazine rack near computers to display new books.
- Derby Public Library hosted a mystery night for teens on a Friday after closing. They purchased a script from Double Dog Press, had prizes and refreshments, and decorated the library.
- Goodland High School created a coffeehouse environment with teens reading from their own poetry or their favorite published pieces. The school's English teacher collaborated on the event.

- Hutchinson Public Library uses teen advisory board members to choose magazines for the library's collection.
- Johnson County Library outside Kansas City recruited teen bands to perform at an end-of-the-year, after-hours summer reading program party. Adults and younger children weren't allowed at the event, which attracted more than one hundred teens.
- Liberal Public Library staff cleaned the library's basement to create a teen area. Open from 3–6 p.m. after school, it's filled with teen materials, comfy chairs, and computers. Teens have decorated the walls and have helped to make the space more attractive to teens.
- Marysville Public Library created a weekly "Lunch Bunch" book discussion group. Teens bring a sack lunch, and the library furnishes chips, soda, and, of course, books.

This article originally appeared in the Fall 2003 issue of *YALS*.

- Salina Public Library's Teen Summer Reading program rewarded teens who had read the most pages with incentives such as a DVD player. The library also created a YA advisory board, which produces library ads for broadcast on the local cable affiliate.

- Sterling High School Library celebrated Teen Read Week by having teens decorate their lockers to promote a favorite book.

- Wichita Public Library staff took pictures of teens reading, posting the pictures near the library entrance.

These programs are a just a snapshot of what's being done across the country. Below are ten recurring themes and trends as librarians share their success stories about connecting young adults and libraries.

1. **Put the books with the teens.** When teens enter a library, particularly boys, they make a beeline for the computers. Some go to chat rooms or blogs, others send e-mails, while many surf the Internet, gathering information not for school, but for themselves. In other words, teens use computers to either build their personal cultures or to explore their interests—or both. But while they are on the computers, where are the titles that might help them in their quest? You guessed it: on a shelf half a room away. Place books near the computers, printers, and copiers. Place them on tables and chairs where teens gather. Place books by the phone, checkout desk, and other high teen traffic areas. The worst that can happen is that the books don't get checked out or need to be reshelved. The best—and I hear this from librarians everywhere—is that the books get checked out.

2. **Buy the right stuff.** YALSA's selected booklists (www.ala.org/yalsa/booklists) are a start. Other lists can be culled from your library's most circulated, most reserved, and most lost or stolen teen titles. Consider also conducting formal and informal surveys of teens to learn their interests, favorite books, and other collection-building tips. Also, because many books that teens want to read aren't usually shelved in the young adult section (*The Coldest Winter Ever* by Sister Souljah and *A Child Called*

It by Dave Pelzer are two titles that come to mind), cross-sell titles in other parts of the library in your young adult collection. Customers, not customs, should drive collection development.

3. **Make space.** One of the most gratifying developments in young adult services has been the creation of amazing young adult spaces in public libraries, with libraries in Phoenix and Los Angeles being prime examples. While the great ones have done amazing things, so have smaller school and public libraries. The "Dream YA Spaces" column that ran in *Voice of Youth Advocates* highlighted how libraries have revitalized teen services through room makeovers. The most successful libraries have given over the task of creating an exciting space for teens to teen volunteers or patrons, with great results.

4. **Involve teens in selection.** A customer-driven collection means the customer has done the selecting, and there are many models to do this with teens. Some librarians meet their teen advisory groups at bookstores and shop together. Others hold monthly Breakfast Clubs where teens review sources and make suggestions over juice, coffee, and bagels. The most successful programs place certain collection functions fully in the hands of teens. After establishing limits and explaining policies, libraries have let teens select music, graphic novels, anime, DVDs, magazines, fantasy, and science fiction. This practice not only gives libraries a better selection than most any professional could do in these areas; they also empower and involve young people.

5. **Let readers react.** For some teens, sharing the reading experience is as important as the experience itself, and librarians have developed some creative ways to help them do so. Some have torn a page from Amazon.com, allowing teens to review books on their website and even create lists of favorites. But the vehicle for sharing doesn't have to be high-tech. Book discussion groups are all the rage, partly because of Oprah, partly because librarians realize reading can be a social activity. Other libraries post teen reviews on bulletin boards. To embrace

books, teen readers must find value in the experience. Offering opportunities for teens to share and respond to their reading adds value.

6. **Booktalk, booktalk, booktalk.** Circulation stats don't lie: Selling books to teens via booktalks is still an efficient and effective method. A plethora of print and Internet resources explain how to conduct a booktalk. Publishers like Scholastic and vendors like NoveList even offer booktalks to customers. YALSA regularly offers an online course on improving your booktalking. At its most basic, a booktalk is a librarian or, even better, a school and public librarian together, in front of a group of teens, selling them on titles. Technology increases the experience by providing the opportunity to project the covers or sample pages onto a screen, in particular from nonfiction and graphic formats. Regardless of the technology involved, the taxonomy is the same: Don't tell, sell.

7. **Make reading opportunities.** Teen Read Week, poetry contests, art contests, summer reading games, read-a-thons. There isn't enough space here to list all of the creative, innovative, and traditional programming options I learned as a YALSA Serving the Underserved trainer. What most programming ideas have in common is pretty simple: They are built on a basic understanding of the developmental needs of teenagers, setting realistic objectives, and then creating excitement. One of the missing pieces of young adult programming lies in measuring outcomes as numbers as opposed to experiences, a difference in quantity versus quality. For example, a teen book discussion group with forty in attendance might look like a success on paper. In reality, however, because most teens didn't get a chance to talk, it's a failure. While there are exceptions, there seems to be an inverse ratio between quality and quantity in teen programming. While the occasional concert at the library (successfully done in Houston and Salt Lake City) pads the stats, it is primarily programs where teens have a chance to interact that go furthest in promoting reading, libraries, and asset building. Teen Read Week provides a framework for creating such programs, and teen summer reading programs continue to grow in number.

8. **Understand that it's much more than books.** Two decades ago, most young adult areas were merely collections of paperback reprints and series. But the explosion in formats has led, dare I say, to a redefinition of what reading and libraries mean to teens. Teen reading no longer equals young adult literature. It is graphic novels, picture books, comic books, magazines, online reading, nonfiction of all shapes and sizes, cult favorites, best sellers, and, yes, even classics. Yet with all of these formats battling for the attention of readers who prefer something other than narrative, the young adult novel is probably as strong as at any time in history. With the Printz Award as the prize, the voices emerging in the field are outstanding.

9. **Create nurturing partnerships.** Even for school librarians, working with teachers continues to be a challenge, in particular in the "teach to the test" landscape. But success is possible. School librarians have made great strides in moving beyond only working with English teachers to harvest relationships with others on the teaching curriculum, such as coaches and those who guide teens during after-school activities.

10. **Ensure appropriate staff attitudes.** All of this means nothing, however, if staff don't get it. Young adult librarians can knock themselves out forty hours a week, doing all of the above, only to have it undermined by a director, security guard, clerk, or librarian from hell. If we truly want to power teens up with print, the place to begin is in the library with staff training. Staff must understand the importance of connecting young adults and libraries, of seeing the library's big-picture role in youth development, and of serving teens as vital present and future customers. You can't power up any teen with print if you can't get them in the door or to listen to your message.

There is a great deal of progress, to be sure, but the work isn't over. The work of the DeWitt Wallace–Reader's Digest Fund for Public Libraries as Partners in Youth Development has provided libraries with models for rethinking services to teens. But the term "underserved" still applies to teens in most libraries.

While there has been some growth nationally in the number of libraries hiring full-time young adult librarians, the hiring hasn't kept pace with other library specialty areas—and it certainly hasn't kept pace with the number of teens using libraries. For every teen participating in a young adult volunteer program, book discussion group, or Teen Read Week event, many more either don't use libraries or have negative experiences associated with them. However, by using best practices such as these and by building on a strong foundation of youth development, we can continue to connect young adults and libraries.

PERSPECTIVES ON PRACTICE: YOUNG ADULT COLLECTIONS ARE MORE THAN JUST YOUNG ADULT LITERATURE

Mary K. Chelton

It is interesting to see how things change over fifty years. When I started out in YA services in 1963, the service standards of that era dictated that YA collections should be 80 percent adult books, in part because of what was published by adult and juvenile departments of trade publishers, and also because the goal of YA services was (and still is) to facilitate the transition to adulthood and adult interests, while serving the needs of the present. Everything was just books then; and programs were only supposed to promote the book collection. I remember an article by Dick Moses, specifics long forgotten, where he argued that programs in and of themselves were good for kids and that they did not need to promote anything beyond the learning/event/ experience of the moment. These ideas probably seem quaint to current librarians serving young adults, but they are perhaps a reminder that today's adolescents are inherently interested in varied multimedia formats.

Granted, YA literature—meaning "books published *for* young adults," as opposed to my preferred definition, "any books young adults select independently on their own"—has changed remarkably. It is now more sophisticated in subject matter and style, thanks in large part to the Michael L. Printz Award, which a great many fine adult authors seem to be writing for and lusting after. The realities that television journalism forces us to face daily, the popularity of the highly irreverent Comedy Central shows with young people, the ubiquity of the Internet, and the awareness of school shootings (most terribly typified by Columbine) have all contributed to a more sophisticated content in YA literature.

Richard Peck once spoke at a meeting I organized, pointing out to a group of YA librarians mired in sixties nostalgia that we were living in the YA post-Vietnam era. We are now in the YA world of the post-Columbine/ Internet era, and despite all the adult protests about content and filters and indecency, it will be hard to shut the door again.

That said, however, it is important to reiterate in this context that a YA collection that is just print these days is inadequate, even worse if it's only fiction. The research coming out on boys' reluctance to read—or to even admit to being readers—has a lot to do with a (dare I say, female) bias toward narrative fiction on the part of teachers and librarians. Even adult librarians are finally admitting that nonfiction can be enjoyable to readers, and everyone should know by now that the *Guinness Book of World Records* is not just a "reference book" where kids are concerned. *Guinness* and other almanac-type books should be staples in YA collections.

Patrick Jones, God bless him, has been exhorting for years that kids like magazines and that boys like wrestling. A few years ago, YALSA began partnering with World Wrestling Entertainment on the WrestleMania Reading Challenge, and wrestling stars have appeared at ALA conferences. But Patrick's point about magazines still needs to be taken into consideration. Libraries often view young adults only as students and magazines as grist for research and that need to be indexed to be purchased; however, many titles also match YA personal interests and hobbies. Admittedly, beyond developmental concerns—the "Am I normal?" sexuality and relationship topics, for example—these personal interests are varied and can be mercurial, but

This article originally appeared in the Winter 2006 issue of YALS.

it is important to have materials that represent them. This is an ideal area for youth participation to help in deciding which titles to get. Patrick also makes a good point when he suggests buying magazines in multiple copies from independent wholesalers, as we do with paperbacks, rather than subscribing to them through library magazine vendors. That way, when interest wanes, you're not stuck with unexpired subscriptions to magazines nobody wants, and you can simply change titles.

Librarians serving YAs in schools should know by now that audiobooks help many kids with reading. Given all the great actors narrating audiobooks, I consider this format the equivalent of being read to by experts. From a public library perspective, though, many kids prefer music to existing audiobook formats, although MP3s, CDs, and downloadable audio may make them more attractive. The real problem is that most are not available in a format for iPods, the player of choice for young adults. The other problem is that there is often a categorical segregation of who buys which formats in public libraries, and it is important to figure out how best to get YA interests represented in the selection process without causing some sort of "turf war" within the library.

Ideally—audiobooks, however purchased and in whatever format—should be part of YA collections, with YA input into format and title decisions.

To return to the subject of print for a moment, though, public libraries should subscribe to local school and youth-produced or -oriented newspapers as a matter of course. (I used to roll them and put them into a spray-painted wine rack on top of lower shelves as a display/housing solution.) School yearbooks are also popular, both with kids in the particular school as well as friends from other schools, and older kids love to look at junior high photos in amused relief at how much better they look, if for nothing else. I doubt that school libraries could budget and justify having these items from other schools, but it is an idea for consideration.

Another print format to include is pamphlets, which should not be buried in the vertical file, but displayed so that kids can find them. Some of the best written, least formidable, most succinct, and up-to-date health education materials are produced in this format, either for school nurses, doctors' offices, or clinics. It is silly not to take advantage of them, preferably in multiple copies.

Graphic novels are also must-buy items for contemporary YA collections, not only because of their overwhelming popularity with the age group, but also because boys, in particular, like them. YALSA's Great Graphic Novels for Teens committee will not only help novice selectors in this area, but also gives an aura of respectability to this format for libraries.

It almost goes without saying that a good contemporary YA collection includes music and DVDs, but another question is why should it also not include computer games and CD-ROMS of popular reference works? I am aware of all the security concerns about these items and the problem of plagiarism, but the same problems existed, and still exist, for print, but that has never been advanced as an argument not to include books. It might be argued that public libraries cannot duplicate formats for YA, but what I am suggesting is buying and placing YA-interest items in the YA collection in the first place and exclusively there if only one copy of an item is purchased, if the public library has a separate YA collection.

Obviously, whatever selections are made are within an adopted selection policy, preferably with YA input to both policy and selection. It is important to remember, regardless of whether the YA collection is the entire collection or a separate part of a larger collection, that young adults are its intended audience. I have come to loathe the word "appropriate" because I am finding librarians continually using it as code to mean "something kids will like but won't make adults mad." Trying to create a collection that is of real interest to young adults will likely upset somebody, so it would be smarter to learn to manage intellectual freedom than to constantly second-guess potentially upset adults. The point to remember is that YA collections now include much more than simply YA literature, and it is our duty to keep up with the changing trends and reflect them in our libraries' collections.

BREAK ON THROUGH TO THE OTHER SIDE: GET ADULT SERVICES STAFF TO BUY INTO TEEN READ WEEK

Carla Land

Getting ready for Teen Read Week means planning activities that will get teens involved in reading. For many school librarians, this means working with principals to get schoolwide programs going, working the theme into the curriculum, or even getting student aides to do something other than check books out to other students. Many public librarians work with school librarians to hold awesome Teen Read Week programs or do their own programming to promote teen reading. But for some public librarians, Teen Read Week can mean something else altogether.

As many public librarians know, it can be difficult to get a teen program going in a library branch. Money spent on teen programs is often scrutinized ("You spent how much for only nine attendees?"). Inevitably there is a staff member who writes it off entirely ("We don't want teenagers in the library!"). Often there is an invisible wall between the youth and adult services departments—crossover programming can be rare and in some libraries isn't even encouraged. Teen Read Week is an opportunity for us to change this! It's a chance to get these two sides of the library working together to create something that your teen patrons will remember, even if it's just that the library staff are pretty cool. The easiest place to start is introducing your adult services staff to the Alex Awards. The Alex Awards are given annually by YALSA to adult books that appeal to young adults. A current list of winners can be found on YALSA's awards page (http://www.ala.org/yalsa/booklists/alex). Talk with adult services staff about doing a book display using these titles or hosting a book discussion group that is either geared for or can include teens. Offer to help in any way you can to promote and plan the event or to curb unruly behavior, and let your teens wow the adult staff with their maturity.

Each year Teen Read Week uses a different theme for librarians to use as a turnkey. Themes have ranged from "Get Graphic!"—which promoted graphic novels—to "Read Beyond Reality," promoting sci-fi, fantasy, and other out-of-this-world titles. Most library staffs have at least one or two voracious readers who are passionate about whatever that year's theme may be. Asking these people to compile a list of favorites that would be good for teens is a great way to introduce them to readers' services for teens. I also recommend having a list handy for other staff needing a little help in finding adult titles for teens who are ready to move on from young adult collections. Don't get discouraged if you run into roadblocks or don't get the outpouring of support you were hoping for. It may take some time to convince the other side that library services to teens is a good thing, and some staff may never be convinced. However, using Teen Read Week to try and break the barrier can be effective if done in non-intrusive ways, and it could open the doors for other shared programs and ideas in the future.

This article originally appeared in the Summer 2009 issue of *YALS*.

T W O
PROGRAMMING FOR
TEEN READ WEEK

FROM THE GENESIS of a book club organized by university librarians for sixth-graders to planning events on the cheap, these Teen Read Week programming ideas can be used to highlight your collection and celebrate reading at any time of year.

ACADEMIC LIBRARIANS ORGANIZE A SIXTH-GRADE READING CLUB

Iona R. Malanchuk

A group of academic librarians at the University of Florida (UF) in Gainesville offered their collective expertise and energy to a group of middle school students. In an attempt to assist in the national effort to promote literacy and reading for pleasure, they organized a successful parent-child reading club. Knowing that there are many compelling novels for young adults available at the nearest public or school library, these UF academic librarians wanted to introduce middle school students to unforgettable stories and characters, and for kids to experience the great escape that a good book provides. Armed with the knowledge that "decades of research draw a strong connection between parental reading to and with a child and the child's subsequent success with literacy,"[1] they invited parents, who were strongly encouraged to attend. Parents participated in the monthly club meetings consistently and with gratitude. As a result, an additional benefit was the opportunity for these young adults and their parents to spend some uninterrupted time talking over the concerns that young people have but don't readily discuss with their own parents.

The Initial Concept

It all began with one librarian's idea of having her colleagues in the university library assist with a reading club for middle school students and their parents. Because it is well known that "reading for enjoyment is the key to developing literacy,"[2] the university librarians decided to participate directly in the national effort to increase literacy among young adults by reaching beyond the university gate. In essence, they agreed with Richard Dougherty, former director of the University of Michigan Libraries, when he admonished academic librarians for not getting involved with outreach efforts to the youths in their communities: "College and university librarians have

This article originally appeared in the Summer 2006 issue of *YALS*.

for too long sat on the sidelines. They have resisted the opportunity or responsibility to reach out and become more involved with young people in their community."[3] It seems logical to tap the inherent desire to promote reading for pleasure that exists among most librarians. In addition, academic librarians' involvement in outreach programs in support of public school students meets the service criteria of most university tenure and promotion requirements.

The timing was perfect since a meeting of the University of Florida Librarians Tenure and Promotions Support Group was about to be held. The organizing staff development officer agreed to have this idea presented to the entire group of tenured and untenured librarians. The meeting was attended by many new, younger librarians on the tenure track, as well as a number of experienced tenured librarians who spoke of the various requirements for tenure and promotion at the University of Florida, creating the perfect forum to introduce this new idea for meeting the required service component of the tenure and promotions criteria. These librarians were well aware that the president and provost of the university had recently stated that helping children and families in Florida was a priority, and that service to the community was considered a valuable contribution of university faculty. All the librarians expressed an interest in volunteering to organize and run a young adult reading club. They agreed to help in any way they could, despite the fact that the details and logistics of such a program were just being developed. Their enthusiastic response to promoting reading and working with young people—so typical of library professionals—was just the beginning.

The Response of Middle School Students and Parents

The supportive and grateful administration of a nearby school responded positively to the idea of well-educated university librarians volunteering their time and energy to help their middle school students. Although it was decided that all written communication with the sixth-grade students and their parents should happen through the language arts teachers, the school administrators and the teachers themselves were relieved that the university librarians were more than ready and willing to invest the time and energy into this new venture. The middle school teachers were already serving on various after-school committees; and with their full schedules, they relished the idea of other educators assisting them.

Because the faculty and administration of the school were immediately supportive of the idea, a number of middle school students and parents were then asked about their interest in participating in a reading club: If the book club met at night, would the students be able to attend once a month? Would the students want their parents to join them? Would the students be embarrassed if their parents wanted to contribute to the discussions or state an opposing viewpoint? Would the parents be interested in reading one YA novel each month? Would they be able to schedule a two-hour meeting to discuss the book every month, making arrangements for their other family members?

The sixth-graders were overwhelmingly in favor of having a parent participate with them. The parents were equally enthusiastic about the idea. However, while there were many verbal commitments, when a questionnaire was developed and distributed (through the language arts teachers) to approximately 112 families, the numbers dropped. Out of fifty-seven families who returned the questionnaire, thirty-five families definitely wanted to participate once the details of the program became known. Another seven families were on the fence.

The idea of getting together with classmates for a "club" meeting each month was a social engagement that sounded very attractive to both boys and girls. Both poor readers and avid readers responded in the affirmative. Some parents thought it would be a terrific way to encourage their child to read more; others seized the chance to spend some one-on-one quality time with their blossoming teenager. And some were attracted to the opportunity for meeting and networking with other parents.

The next level of logistics then had to be faced. Who would help organize each monthly meeting? Who would volunteer to be small group discussion leaders each month? Where and when would these meetings take place? Who would develop the plan for each evening's activities? The energetic and dedicated university librarians volunteered to lead the discussion groups each month, and they all agreed to attend a planning meeting the week before the club met.

Organizational Details

After receiving feedback from the enthusiastic sixth-graders and their parents, the numerous logistical details fell into place easily. The most convenient meeting place was in the school library, which the school administration was more than happy to make available. Parents were given a choice of meeting days and times, and they requested a weeknight between the hours of 7 and 9 p.m. The majority of parents—especially those who commuted a considerable distance—did not want to come back to the school on the weekend. The monthly meeting schedule was set up in advance, with meetings purposely scheduled for different days of the week to accommodate everyone who wanted to participate.

The monthly book selection consisted of only Newbery award–winning titles that were available in paperback. The books were chosen from that acclaimed awards list since "it has long been recognized that imaginative literature plays an important role in the acquisition of reading skills."[4] For those wishing to replicate this program, consider using the Printz Award or titles from YALSA's awards and selected booklists at www.ala.org/yalsa/booklists.

A librarian, acting as coordinator, collected money from the parents and students ahead of time to purchase copies of the selected book using her educator's discount in a local bookstore. She also collected numerous copies of the Newbery award–winning titles from a variety of branch libraries in Gainesville's excellent public library system. Not one of the borrowed books was ever lost. The free copies were loaned to some of the volunteer academic librarians and students because it was necessary for each student and parent to have his or her own copy.

Each month a reminder confirming the meeting place, date, time, and book title was distributed to the sixth-graders by their language arts teachers. The students were asked to take the reminder home, have the participating parent sign the confirmation of attendance, and return it to their teacher, who would collect and forward them to the librarian coordinator.

Planning Meetings

Gathering for breakfast or lunch approximately one week before the club meeting, the discussion leaders and academic librarians always enjoyed the time spent talking together about the characters and themes found in that month's selection in a book club atmosphere of their own. Wishing never to go unprepared into the book club meetings with the students, each librarian not only read the book, but also came up with a variety of unusual ways to lead the discussions. It was clear that the university librarians enjoyed the program and believed in what they were trying to accomplish through it.

They all considered this a personally rewarding activity rather than a burdensome task. Although very few of the academic librarians had children of their own and most had no experience working with young adults, they were committed to the program's success and were pleasantly surprised by how enjoyable it was to spend evenings with sixth-graders discussing literature. In reality, some of the discussion topics and questions were never presented because the passionate sixth-graders frequently knew what they wanted to discuss. "Students grow in several ways. . . . They become more aware of the strategies they use as readers, and more responsible for monitoring and 'fixing up' their own comprehension. . . . They learn to clarify their ideas, develop speed and fluency, and become more effective listeners."[5]

Although most of the book club meeting time was spent in lively discussions about themes and characters, the academic librarians planned a few other activities. They played excerpts from the audiobook copy of *Bud, Not Buddy,* and they played some of the music of the era depicted in that book. During the month when everyone was reading *Maniac Magee,* they made a display of the works of Jerry Spinelli and put the display in the school library. Because Louis Sachar had visited the school a few years earlier, they were able to put together a photo display of his visit the same month they read his acclaimed novel *Holes.* Biographical sketches of the authors were often provided, and it was decided that one of the sixth-graders would present the information about the author's life to the entire group. Each participating sixth-grader was able to repeatedly enhance his or her own public-speaking skills in this supportive environment.

Reading Club Meetings

At the first meeting, some simple ground rules were agreed upon by all involved. They were quite basic: Try not to interrupt when someone else is speaking; everyone's opinion matters; parents and kids can agree or disagree; always have respect for one another. Everyone was encouraged to offer his or her viewpoint or interpretation. Despite the different socioeconomic groups represented—many students were on free breakfast and lunch programs—and the mixture of males and females, everyone remained flexible throughout the months of interaction.

Although it was stipulated that a parent was to attend with the sixth-grader, a few times an older sibling would fill in for a parent; another time the parent could not come, but they made transportation arrangements so the sixth-grader could participate anyway. A couple of mothers had to bring another child to some of the meetings and that, too, was allowed. Infrequently, when a parent was missing, one of the university librarians filled in for the parent during the parent-child interaction, which was held at the beginning of each session. Upon signing in and attaching their name tags, each parent and child would be given a list of the discussion topics for the evening. Those topics resulted from the academic librarians' discussions during the prior week's organizational meeting.

All parents and students would sit next to each other so that they could see and speak directly to one another. The book club meetings always began with each parent and child taking the first ten or fifteen minutes for private discussion of the questions just handed to them. Then each sixth-grader would offer to the group the joint family viewpoint and interpretation unless the parent and child disagreed. In that case, each would speak separately. As you would expect, much laughter and friendly arguments would ensue during the initial opening discussions.

After everyone had an opportunity to express their viewpoints, they would divide into smaller discussion groups and move away from one another, into various rooms and corners of the library, where each of the volunteers would be prepared to initiate the lengthier discussion of already agreed-upon themes or the meaning of a specific quotation or two from the book. Most of the chosen novels had themes that touch the hearts of this age group: loneliness, dysfunctional families, racism, bullying, failure, sibling rivalries, and a variety of fears that many sixth-graders need to confront and discuss with concerned adults. With their parents listening and learning, the youths would reveal their concerns, always in reference to the book's characters or themes, and sometimes for the very first time.

The university librarians frequently discovered that there was no need to do anything but allow the sixth-graders to take the topic and run with it. Often the passionate response of these young, creative, and probing minds would be enough to consume the next two hours without any input from the volunteer discussion leaders. "Research has shown that students from diverse backgrounds are more likely to participate in smaller groups than larger ones, and that they are more comfortable talking in a peer-controlled group than in a teacher controlled one."[6]

Two Necessities: Refreshments and a Time to Socialize

Any program involving kids and parents must include refreshments. The supportive school administration paid for the cookies, donuts, fresh fruit, juice, and soft drinks that were arranged on a tablecloth with fresh flowers at every meeting. The refreshments were not, however, made available at the beginning of each program. The final thirty minutes of meeting time consisted of an informal gathering around the refreshment table, creating a time for relaxed discussions and reminders about the next meeting and the next book selection. Sometimes, of course, a couple of sixth-graders had already started the next selection and would make positive comments about what everyone had to look forward to at next month's meeting. The sixth-graders' enthusiastic response to the Newbery titles became infectious, and the adults found themselves looking forward to reading the next book and participating in the next discussion. Inevitably, the participants would linger, eating and chatting well beyond the meeting's end.

Comments of the Participants

A few comments from the sixth-graders reveal why they kept coming back to the monthly programs:

- "This book [*Bud, Not Buddy*] just makes me want to read!"
- "I think I like reading more. I am a better reader, but I like reading more!"
- "[The book club] helped me get more interested in books."
- "My mom [and I] . . . we are closer."
- "The best part is that you get to read a fun book,

and you get to communicate with people while eating."

- "The best part has been the discussions."
- "My vocabulary was getting better and it made it easier to understand the book."
- "I got to get together with some of my friends and discuss the book and see their point of view, not just my mom and dad['s]."
- "I like reading a lot because you can learn more things about life. I have been getting better [at reading]."

The stressed parents grew to learn that they can communicate with their child and foster closeness and trust through literature. They can discuss issues of importance to their child by talking about characters in a story. Loneliness, dysfunctional families, sexuality, and bullying are all issues that some parents have a difficult time knowing about if their hurting child won't discuss these problems with them.

Discussing novels with a child helps bring critical issues into the open. And dealing with opposing viewpoints in a nonthreatening atmosphere can lead to resolving family conflicts. Parents responded positively by saying:

- "It was fun to be reading something together."
- "He reads quite a lot anyway, but I think he's learned he can discuss what he reads and really think about it."
- "Every night we would spend half an hour in a quiet spot reading together. That was nice."
- "My husband even read to us a couple nights so it was a real nice time as a family. . . . Thank you!"
- "It has actually brought all members in on the relationship. My other son and daughter began reading the same books so they could discuss them with us also."
- "We reminded each other to read daily. As we came to a part that was interesting or sad, we would discuss it. Sometimes he came to me to discuss, and sometimes the reverse was true."
- "[I had] more motivation to read by the time we got to books three and four."
- "[It has] given me insight on her interpretations and reactions. . . . [It] impressed me as to how much she did understand and process."

The comments of the university librarians who volunteered to work with kids for the very first time and on a monthly basis were just as positive:

- "Thank you for giving me the opportunity to do this. I had so much fun and think that it's a great program for all involved. . . . I can't wait for next time!"
- "That was a blast last night! What a great group of kids! . . . I'm just amazed at the insight some of those kids have at that age . . . and even the little sisters . . . how old were they anyway? They were so into it! It's nice to see the family interacting as a unit like that."
- "Beautiful. Just beautiful! Thanks for letting me be a part. Looking forward to next month's selection!"
- "I thought it was a lot of fun and the kids obviously enjoyed themselves and had great insights about the book. Great idea. . . . I'm glad to be part of it."
- "[I] didn't have to lead anything. . . . [I] had two passionate sixth-graders who just had one topic/question after the other to bring up, and everyone else just sort of joined in the nonstop discussion."
- "We then relocated around the library into smaller discussion groups, which is when the kids really blossomed into passionate, thinking, articulate critics. They were amazing. The quiet and soft-spoken [kids] . . . readily added their thoughts and held their own with the more verbal [ones]. . . . We had two younger siblings and a mentally handicapped brother in attendance because that was the only way the parent and sixth-grader could make it, and that was just fine, no problem."

Variations on the Program

Determine where the greatest need for a literacy program is in your community. It could be in one of your local schools or a local detention center, homeless shelter, hospital, after-school program, daycare center, preschool program, or in one of the local "failing" schools. Children in need of adult attention and support are everywhere if you look beyond the university gate. As research has shown, "Reading ability turned out to be one of the best predictors of later success both at work, [and] in marital and parental relationships."[7]

More than ever, children are suffering from problems never before seen in such large numbers among our young people: health issues including obesity, childhood diabetes, and high blood pressure, in addition to having low reading scores, below-grade reading comprehension levels, and behavioral problems, often linked to too much violence in the media or in their communities. Caring adults need to pay attention and extend themselves to help solve these problems. Clearly, there are enjoyable and long-lasting benefits for all involved. Merit is not inevitably followed by recognition, and school administrators are among those who sometimes "regard as expendable those things about which they are indifferent."[8] Therefore, strongly consider partnering with a school librarian, which is mutually beneficial in terms of visibility and advocacy for libraries. Remember that school library media specialists are sometimes isolated and outnumbered by teachers, who tend to look first and foremost at their own departmental needs.

Be sure to include your participation in the service component of your tenure packet. You can organize a group of tenure-track librarians to develop a program similar to the successful one tried by the University of Florida librarians. For an outreach program like this, flexibility and a willingness to revamp organizational details along the way are keys to success.

Above all else, have fun, relax, and lend a hand to the local effort to increase a child's literacy level. It is "imperative that academic librarians be associated with their colleagues' efforts to help kids become successful readers and successful students."[9] Because every community is in need of volunteers to work with children and young adults, give some of your time, energy, and professional expertise to a group you haven't reached out to: the young adults just outside the college gates. You might end up providing the crucial experience resulting in that young person making it to the other side of those gates.

NOTES

1. Laurie Dias-Mitchell, "Multicultural Mosaic: A Family Book Club," *Knowledge Quest* 29 (March/April 2001): 17–21.
2. Gayner Eyre, "Back to Basics: The Role of Reading in Preparing Young People for the Information Society," *Reference Services Review* 31 (2003): 219–26.
3. Richard Dougherty, "Kids Who Read Succeed; and the Academic Librarian," *College & Research Libraries News* 3 (March 1991): 155–56.
4. Eyre, "Back to Basics," 222.
5. Cynthia Calderone, "Book Clubs: Interacting with Text in a Social Context," *Florida Reading Quarterly* 39 (2003): 28–33.
6. Ibid., 29.
7. Virginia Mathews, "Kids Can't Wait . . . Library Advocacy Now!" *School Library Journal* 43 (March 1997): 97–101.
8. Diane Gallagher-Hayashi, "Moving the Fence: Engaging Your Principal in Your School Library Program," *Teacher Librarian* 28 (January 2001): 13–17.
9. Dougherty, "Kids Who Read Succeed," 156.

CRAFTING CHEAP AND SUCCESSFUL TEEN PROGRAMS

Charli Osborne

The reasons for programming on the cheap are not new to this economic downturn; they have existed in libraries for years. Small libraries with little or no budget for programming as well as fledgling teen and YA librarians just starting out have been doing this dance for years. There's no need to reinvent the wheel. Use what you have readily available or can get for free or low cost. Read on for ten easy tips for low- and no-cost programs for teens.

1. **Keep your projects simple.** You can find lots of great craft ideas created for younger kids that you can adapt for older participants. Teens can always improve on something easy; but if it's too hard, they tend to get frustrated and give

This article originally appeared in the Fall 2009 issue of YALS.

up. Just keep your age group in mind as you choose your projects.

Example: Pet Rocks

Needed supplies: clean rocks, all shapes and sizes (collect on walks or have teens bring in their own), acrylic paint and paintbrushes, or permanent markers.

Optional supplies: wiggle eyes, pipe cleaners, fabric scraps, tacky glue. Let the teens create fantastical pets by painting or using markers to add details to their rocks.

Ta-da—Pet Rock!

2. **Have the proper supplies on hand.** Nothing sinks a fun time faster than finding out you don't have the right kind of glue or have run out of green tissue paper. Choose projects only if you have all the needed supplies on hand. Make a checklist and use it—check off each item as you collect it. Recycle, reuse, and repurpose all materials that you can.

Example: Sock or Glove Creatures

Needed supplies: socks (finally an opportunity to use all those single socks that are orphaned by dryers everywhere) or gloves, thread, needles, scissors

Optional supplies: wiggle eyes, fabric scraps, fabric glue, pipe cleaners, bits of old jewelry, polyester batting, or cotton balls. Let the teens create traditional sock puppets or let them stuff their creatures with batting or cotton balls.

3. **Try registration.** If you register your teens, you'll know how many people to expect and prepare for. This is especially helpful if you have multiple components to your program that need to be gathered, bought, and set up in advance. It also gives you the opportunity to contact participants, either by phone or e-mail, the day before the program to remind them that they signed up. This reminder can keep you from having a disappointingly low turnout at a program.

4. **Limit the number of teens per program.** Believe it or not, this can create more interest in your programs! If registration is required and limited for a program, it sounds exclusive and special—something teens love. It's important to make sure everyone gets some one-on-one attention, and this is one way to do it. You can always add another session if the program fills up.

5. **Consider asking for a deposit.** Although it may seem counterintuitive, this works wonderfully to get teens through the door. Many people consider free programming to be "worthless" programming. Asking for a dollar or two to hold a place instantly adds value. It also teaches and encourages financial responsibility. When the teens attend the program, return the deposits. If they don't attend, keep the money to use for more programming. Make sure to keep the deposit money in a safe place.

6. **Hire an expert!** If you don't have the know-how in your chosen craft, find someone who does. This doesn't have to be expensive—you may know someone who is willing to barter time or expertise with you. Don't forget to approach local businesspeople.

Example: Scrapbooking

If you have a scrapbooking store in town, ask the owner if they would be willing to run a program and donate supplies. This collaboration is a win-win scenario and can result in a well-attended program for you, since you have built-in advertisement and good word-of-mouth for the store.

7. **Promote widely.** You probably have a few teens who come to all your programs. Encourage them to talk to their friends. Send flyers with your teens to the schools. Put information in the local papers. Put up posters in the local teen hangout, whether it is Starbucks or the bowling alley. (Make sure you get permission first!) Talk up your programs at school visits, booktalks, and during other programs. Let parents know about your programs—they may sign up their teens.

8. **Don't hover.** Be available to help if asked, but let the kids make mistakes, ask for help from one another, and socialize. Consider every program a process program and not a results program. This isn't school—it should be fun!

Example: Multimedia Art

Needed supplies: paper or poster board to use as background, fabric scraps, wallpaper samples, tissue paper, ribbon, cording, scissors, and white or tacky glue. Give the teens a thematic suggestion to get them going and watch the fun.

9. **Make it a contest.** The best contests are anonymous, decreasing pressure on teens to be perfect while still allowing them to be creative. Recruit judges from your schools, local businesses, and library staff. Or ask the teens to vote. Anonymous contests avoid the whole "I'm only voting for my friends" faction if you have a teen vote. Prizes don't have to be expensive—certificates you print yourself can be quite impressive, especially if you call in the local newspaper to take photos of contest winners with the certificates.

Example: Design and Fly a Paper Airplane

Needed supplies: paper, measuring tape, books about paper airplanes. Give the teens about twenty minutes to design and create their paper airplanes. Have contests for flight distance, stunt capability, and design creativity.

10. **Evaluate and keep statistics.** Know what programs could have included twenty more kids and which ones flopped. Make a note if the teens ask you to do the program again and then do it again after a few months.

Cheap and Easy Passive Programming

Coloring Sheets

Everyone loves to color, whether they are young or old, male or female. Sign up for Dover Publications sampler e-mails to get free coloring sheets and puzzles delivered right to your e-mail box. All you have to do is download and print! Provide colored pencils, crayons, or fine-tip markers, and let the teens take over

from there. Display the completed coloring pages and follow tip number 9 to make it a coloring contest judged by local art teachers or the teens themselves. Free coloring page and puzzle samples can be found at www.doverpublications.com/sampler4. Dover also has great "grown-up" coloring books.

Magnetic Poetry

Buy adhesive strip magnets. Create and print sheets of words. Have teens assemble the magnets and display the completed magnetic poetry set with a cookie sheet. Old cookie sheets or other tins make great storage for your magnetic words. Expand on this idea and have the teens create poems for a particular theme. Don't forget tip number 9: print up the teens' poems and have a poetry contest judged by local teachers or let the teens vote on their favorite poems. Instructions on how to make a magnetic poetry set are at http://www.readwritethink.org/parent-afterschool-resources/activities-projects/make-magnetic-poetry-30150.html.

Where to Get Supplies

Ask library staff and patrons for donations of items such as yogurt cups (good for paint cups), toilet paper or paper towel rolls (many uses), cookie and pie tins (great to hold supplies), and other items that you can recycle, reuse, and repurpose.

Explore dollar and thrift stores. Don't forget your local grocery store—you can sometimes find great deals on ingredients for crafts there. Ask your local home decorating store if they have wallpaper samples that they want to get rid of.

Find More Inspiration

Looking for even more ideas? Check out YALSA's book *Cool Teen Programs for under $100*, edited by Jenine Lillian for YALSA. This essential, affordable guide offers helpful chapters on budgeting and marketing, plus more than twenty-five inexpensive, creative programs implemented by YALSA members across the United States and Canada. The book is available at the ALA Store, www.alastore.ala.org.

THE BOOK VS. THE MOVIE

Jesse Vieau

Challenge your community of teenagers to a fun and engaging October by celebrating great stories and the different formats that have been used to tell them. Most libraries circulate feature films, which are comparable to the stories recorded on paper, and programming around this form of media may be a sensible approach to teen appeal. It's also a great way to rebrand the act of reading and allow teens to make the connection between the Hollywood movies they enjoy and the books that inspire those adaptations, even for those who consider themselves nonreaders. The teen population has always had a great foothold in what defines pop culture along with deciding which books are popular enough to turn into a movie. Take full advantage of both film and print by celebrating books that have been made into feature films with a "The Book vs. the Movie" marathon this Teen Read Week.

Showing the movie with a projector on the wall and serving popcorn and drinks are nice incentives for participation. If you do not have sufficient space or electronic equipment to accommodate viewing a movie, you might be inclined to bring discussions and viewings on the road to a lunchtime or after-school group or other facilities serving youths like the closest YMCA, Boys and Girls Club, or community center. People are often looking for collaboration, but if nothing else they may at least appreciate the library's gesture.

You might also consider including teens in correctional and rehabilitation facilities like your local jail or juvenile detention center into the discussion. There are many great books that were turned into movies with the ability to teach and inspire this population. Some of these institutions employ teachers or librarians who are might be able to partner with you. Something of this nature should be explored well before Teen Read Week as it is not often a simple or expedient process to gain access to these populations if you do not already have that relationship. A partnership with these institutions is a great way to make sure you are exploring and considering all the possible avenues to reach teenagers who might enjoy another perspective on reading.

Choosing a structure that will allow your teenagers to participate is of great importance. As always, you'll need to take into consideration the schedules of likely participants at home, school, work, and play, along with the time it takes to read. If you'd like to stick within the seven-day celebration, you should aim to get advertisement and buy-in completed in September so teens will have time to read the book before the event takes place during Teen Read Week. Four hours should suffice to hold a book discussion before watching the movie and then having another discussion comparing the two versions after viewing the movie.

If you have enough money to purchase or subsidize theater tickets, you could consider choosing a title that will be playing in theaters and take a field trip. Fitting the discussions into this kind of outing is tricky but definitely doable. Some options include holding a discussion at your library before going to the theater as a group (check the legalities with your supervisor); waiting until after the movie to lead a group discussion at the theater or back at the library; using online technologies to support the majority of your discussions; or any combination of the above.

If your library has a blog, you might consider asking teens to respond online as well. If you do not already have a way for teens to participate online, there are many easy ways to offer its convenience and to promote participation in this media club. You can create free accounts on Web communities already listed in the book or at a movie realm like Goodreads or Flixster. You can bring the discussions to one or more of the larger online social networking communities where your target population already have accounts and spend time such as Facebook and MySpace. Creating a page or group on these sites may ensure or increase participation since teens will be more likely to be reminded about them while logged in and exploring. Or you can create a stand-alone blog or forum using sites like Blogspot, WordPress, or Ning.

Take some time to survey current members or likely participants for what they find appealing and appropriate. Remember that age-appropriateness is not

This article originally appeared in the Fall 2010 issue of *YALS*.

always mirrored between the two formats. Directors and screenwriters offer their own interpretations and personal touches, sometimes resulting in a version intended for audiences of a different maturity level than that of the book. Just because you've already watched the PG-13 movie doesn't mean the book couldn't have been the equivalent of a G or R rating. The same goes for having already read the book. Do your research beforehand. Creating a list with room for suggestions will help focus the decision when surveying the participants.

Some stories have many movie versions from throughout the years, and it can be fun to incorporate the interpretations of directors from different time periods into the conversation. Lewis Carroll's classics *Alice in Wonderland*, *Through the Looking Glass*, and *What Alice Found There* offer all kinds of possibilities, especially considering the newest cinematic reinvention is available on DVD. You could show a different version of the movie each night of the week throughout Teen Read Week, with the newest rendition on the final night as the main event.

You can find many lists of stories with book and movie versions by doing a quick Internet search, but here are some titles I've used or plan to use in the future:

- *The Lovely Bones* by Alice Sebold
- *Coraline* by Neil Gaiman
- *V for Vendetta* by Alan Moore
- *Public Enemies: America's Greatest Crime Wave and the Birth of the FBI, 1933–1934* by Bryan Burrough
- *Speak* by Laurie Halse Anderson
- *Youth in Revolt* by C. D. Payne
- *Beastly* by Alex Flinn
- *The Blind Side: Evolution of a Game* by Michael Lewis
- *The Hitchhiker's Guide to the Galaxy* by Douglas Adams
- *Angus, Thongs and Full-Frontal Snogging: Confessions of Georgia Nicolson* by Louise Rennison
- *Whip It* by Shauna Cross
- *Push/Precious* by Sapphire

Movie License Information

Showing movies without possessing a Public Performance License violates copyright law. If your institution does not have a Public Performance Site License, check into possible money sources to purchase one from places like Movie Licensing USA (available from http:// www.movlic.com/library).

WRITE HERE, WRITE NOW: HOLDING A CREATIVE WRITING WORKSHOP SERIES AT YOUR LIBRARY

Heather Prichard

On a Thursday afternoon in early June 2006, I stood in our branch library's windowless large conference room before a very diverse group of young people ages eleven to fifteen. They sat at tables arranged in a large U shape. They studied me, looking a little like an unconvinced jury. This didn't worry me too much. I had led library instruction sessions for college freshmen in a previous job and had seen these looks many times before, both the self-conscious, quick eye-averting glances and the deliberately nonchalant slightly raised eyebrows coupled with peeks at the ceiling and room corners. I knew nothing about these particular young people other than that they were interested enough in writing stories and poems to show up at a library on a nice summer day. That's quite enough. Over the next eight weeks, I would be struck at how creative and thoughtful they each were. I would be amazed when they wrote very poignant stories about such topics as the current war, hopes, relationships, losses, and family dynamics. Interacting with them stripped away some of my own preconceived notions about their age group. Their seriousness amazed me. Hopefully, their

This article originally appeared in the Fall 2008 issue of *YALS*.

notions of thirtysomething reference librarians were also positively altered.

On that first day, after briefly introducing myself and getting them to introduce themselves so I could begin to learn their names, I got down to business. "Let's come up with some ground rules," I said to the group. I kept a flip chart and marker ready. Collectively, the group watched me, quietly waiting. No one wanted to be the first to speak.

"Okay, I have the first one," I said. "Don't interrupt when someone is talking or reading." Then, after a few moments, I gestured to a girl of about twelve with long dark hair who was sitting in the middle of the U-shaped arrangement. She was thoughtful for a moment before saying quietly, "Don't laugh." I wrote it down. The group began to stir, and then they were all raising their hands with other rules. They made more rules about showing respect and being nice to one another. I wrote down all of their rules because I wanted them to know their opinions would be respected and valued. Sharing one's personal writing and creativity with a group who may be waiting to mock you is a scary proposition for any age group. I wanted them to feel as though they were part of a community of like-minded individuals.

One of the pluses of voluntary extracurricular programs such as this is that, as a leader, you probably won't see many behavioral problems. The biggest challenge will be just getting the participants to open up. Most young adults possess incredible imaginations, but accessing those imaginations may be difficult because they are constantly being drilled to conform in school and at home. "This is not going to be like school," I told them. "Here, we're just interested in having fun and being creative."

Over the next two months, we met for a couple of hours every other week. They wrote stories and poems, read them aloud, and, at my coaxing, gave each other feedback. Trust began to develop between the group members in a very organic way. In his May 2005 article, writing teacher Chris Street addressed this phenomenon:

> If students see themselves as contributing members of a writing community, then the motivation to sustain and enhance that community may well cause students to value and contribute to their newfound identity. Students will likely begin to identify with other writers, thus adding to the classroom community in productive ways.[1]

Long-term adult writing groups are built this way, but none of my workshop participants had driver's licenses, much less expectations of creating a group that would meet without me past the eight weeks of our workshop. This workshop would be a success as long as the participants felt that it was a success.

In that summer of 2006, I had been a reference librarian for just six months. Arranging programming was one aspect of my job description where I felt the least prepared by my recent library school training. Apart from offering the same kinds of general craft and guest-speaker programs as my predecessor, I hoped to develop a program that I could personally facilitate. I was inspired to develop a writing workshop for tweens and teens by a positive personal experience: when I was in fourth grade, I was fortunate enough to be involved in an annual young authors conference while living in Michigan. My positive memories of that experience led me to believe that some of the young people in my current community might also be interested in a program for writers. What better place to learn and share creative writing than a public library?

While in college I had taken every undergraduate creative writing class my university offered. I felt comfortable that my undergraduate classroom experiences in a workshop setting where writers share and critique one another's work would help facilitate a similar group for young writers. The workshop format would be the model for the program series. But I want to encourage my fellow librarians who have not done this before: Even if you have no writing workshop experience and are only looking for a low-cost program series for an underserved population at your library, you can lead a successful writing group. A onetime program may be better suited to your needs than an ongoing series such as the one I designed.

Planning

In preparation for the first "Write Here, Write Now" workshop series, I did the following: After conferring with my colleagues (especially the children's librarians at the Tates Creek Branch), we decided which age group to target. The twelve-to-fifteen-year-old age range seemed to be underserved by current youth programming. Young people in this group were too old for storytime but too young to be part of the teen advisory board. Like Goldilocks, they may just be looking for a comfortable fit at the library.

I decided how many participants to allow to register for the program. It would be wonderful if ten to twelve participants from our area of the city joined the group. I had found in other workshops that more than twelve would be too large of a group for everyone to get equal attention, so I put a cap on registrations. In subsequent workshop series, I had not limited the initial registration because I had found many participants do not complete the entire workshop. Expect about a third of the initial group to drop out. This is especially true if a parent signs up a youth who is really not interested in creative writing.

I contacted the language arts instructors and school librarians at the middle schools and high schools located nearest my library. I e-mailed them a summary of the workshop objectives and sent them flyers to post in their classrooms advertising the summer workshop. I used the instructors' school e-mail accounts, which were available on school websites. This was especially helpful for me because, as a new librarian, I had not yet developed relationships with the schools or instructors. It was easy to craft one e-mail with an attachment and send it to each appropriate teacher and school librarian.

I created flyers about the program and posted them in all of our system's branch libraries. I also put information in the printed calendar that is mailed out each month.

Next, I arranged for a local award-winning children's and young adult author to lead the group's final session. This was to be the greatest cost of the program—$100.

Running a Writing Workshop

As the workshop drew closer, I developed an objective and agenda for each meeting. I quickly found during my first workshop series that the participants will expect to write during the sessions. For the sessions to be effective, they need to be planned out. Using prompts such as photographs, individual writing exercises, and group exercises such as those found in the resource list at the end of this article make this manageable for anyone.

It's important to lay out the parameters of the workshop so the participants understand that they are free to create. In doing these workshops, it's become evident that young people today are far more comfortable when they know what is expected of them. To an older student, you may be able to say,

"Write whatever comes to your mind." But this can be very daunting to a young writer who really wants to be shown what's considered acceptable. The rest of the world is usually telling them that they must conform and memorize facts. In school they may be encouraged to read classic books that don't seem to have much contextual relevance to their lives. Despite their own rich experiences, young people often feel stifled. In a workshop, if things go well, the participants will move past the sense of needing to constantly conform. Through the creative process, they will come to appreciate their own ability to communicate as well as create.

It seemed really important that participants be able to walk away with a finished product at the end of the workshop. Near the end of the workshop, I began asking each participant to submit a favorite piece. Most of the time we agreed on which story or poem was their best.

Many writing groups create collections of their work called chapbooks. I priced printing services and found that creating a chapbook collection of participants' writings would cost less if created in-house using Microsoft Publisher software and our own color computer printers. Desktop-publishing software and fancy color copiers have made booklet creation a breeze. I was able to find free stock photographs on the Internet, providing a great inexpensive way to illustrate the collection.

Our Final Meeting

Over the course of two months, the windowless conference room had become a comfortable space. The workshop participants bunched together to compare stories and laugh before each session started and during breaks. They were no longer strangers to one another.

On the Saturday afternoon of our group's last meeting, they milled about a bit more nervously. Their parents had been invited to attend the finale party, so the group in the room was double its normal size. Chapbooks would be distributed and a public reading would follow a thirty-minute presentation by local children's book author George Ella Lyon. There was a table of cookies and drinks to one side of the room and chairs in rows for everyone to sit. The young writers stood around eating cookies while their parents looked on proudly, if not a little suspiciously.

Lyon gave a rousing presentation about how to keep a journal. Then she showed galley proofs of a book on which she was currently working. She described the publication process and told of book projects she had worked on that had not gotten published. The workshop participants were in visible awe of her, and she was extremely warm and open with them.

The time came for the public readings. Despite visible signs of nervousness, the young writers obviously enjoyed the attention, especially when Lyon made comments after each reading. The parents attending were all smiles and gave thanks after the program. This was the highlight of the workshop series. The participants were amazed by the experience of meeting a real published author and having her give them feedback on their writing. Her honorarium was very reasonable and the only real expense of the program. If you have authors in your area who are willing, it is a wonderful experience to have them come in and lead a session.

When it was all, over the expenses to the library proved to be very minimal and the cost of my time was paid back handsomely in the development of relationships with an interesting group of young adults.

Challenges

Over the course of the first workshop series, these are the challenges we faced:

- Creating an interesting curriculum
- Keeping young adults interested
- Having parents sign young adults up for the series when the child had little interest in writing
- Navigating the emotional differences between twelve- and fifteen-year-olds
- Working in-depth in such a short time with young adults. Instead I found that I should keep things light and fun so kids would be more interested and feel less self-conscious about their writing.

I had initially wanted to have the chapbooks cataloged in our system so the participants could look themselves up, but it was not possible for this to be done at my library—however, you might want to look into this for your own library's system.

Subsequently, I have arranged two other writing workshops on the same model, tweaking what didn't work and strengthening what did. For example, I have found that participants do best when writing during the meeting rather than when given a homework assignment. Their schedules are very busy, even in the summer, and they may not take time to write at home. Second, although they are in a very creative period in their lives, young people may have a hard time coming up with ideas for writing. By incorporating prompts such as photographs and first sentences to invent stories around, I was able to get the participants to write freely. One great resource I have used each time is *Jump Write In!: Creative Writing Exercises for Diverse Communities, Grades 6–12* by WritersCorps, Judith Tannenbaum, and Valerie Chow Bush. It is filled with wonderful writing exercises and examples of writing by teens and tweens. There are many books and websites available on the subject of creative writing. Any of them can give you ideas for writing exercises.

Conclusion

When I began the initial planning of the creative writing workshop series "Write Here, Write Now" for tweens and teens, my main objective was just to create a safe place to work with young adults interested in writing. As Bonnie J. Robinson points out, "Among the many functions of creative writing workshops is creating a community of learners to support the writing activities of student writers."[2] Creating a chapbook collection of the participants' work that they could keep gave them a sense of accomplishment, and they were inspired and motivated by the local published author who led the last meeting. The program itself was very inexpensive other than the $100 honorarium for the author. All the participants needed for the program was a notebook and a pen or pencil.

There has been a great deal of recent research in adolescent behavior, such as that done by the Minneapolis-based Search Institute. This research—important to teachers and librarians—has shown, among other things, that extracurricular programs can have a lifelong positive impact on the success of young people.[3] As librarians dealing day-to-day with tweens and teens, we are in a position to provide a positive influence and help them build developmental assets. One way we can help provide asset-building situations is through implementation of programs such as a creative writing workshop. Such a program gives young people a safe environment where they can be creative and create relationships with peers and adults, as well as build on the following external assets from the Search Institute's list: receiving support through adult relationships, feeling empowerment through personal and psychological safety, learning boundaries and expectations through positive peer influence, and using time constructively through creative activities and youth programs.[4]

NOTES

1. Chris Street, "A Reluctant Writer's Entry into a Community of Writers," *Journal of Adolescent & Adult Literacy* 48, no. 8 (May 2005): 640.

2. Bonnie J. Robinson, "The Creative Writing Learning Community Webpage," *Academic Exchange Quarterly* 9, no. 1 (Spring 2005): 180–81.

3. Search Institute, www.search-institute.org/about (accessed May 18, 2008).

4. "What Are Developmental Assets?," http://www.search-institute.org/content/what-are-developmental-assets (accessed May 18, 2008).

LESSONS ILLUSTRATED BY TEEN READ WEEK: FOSTER, FACILITATE, CONNECT, FOLLOW

Jennifer Velásquez, 2008 Best Teen Read Week contest winner

There is one thing every librarian working with teens needs to remember: Teens come up with better ideas than you do. Just go with that.

I'm not saying your ideas aren't good. I'm just saying that they are your ideas. When it comes to teen programming, don't let your ego and expectations get in the way.

Our goal at the San Antonio Public Library is to foster the involvement of teens in the development of quarterly programming "themes," so working with preselected themes (such as Teen Read Week) is often humbling. When introducing what is perceived to be a "created by a committee of well-meaning adults" theme, I have been greeted with looks of sympathy from teens.

In 2008 "Books with Bite" was the theme for Teen Read Week, and I thought it would be an easy sell. The graphics featured fangs/drippy blood or pink-frosted donuts for the less supernaturally inclined. What's not to love? It was this juxtaposition of images that said "zombies" to the teens at the San Antonio Central Library. From that it was a short stream-of-consciousness trip to our opening Teen Read Week celebration, "The Zombie Prom."

The library staff's role in the process was to facilitate the realization of the teens' vision and connect with resources/partners in the community. Teens in a local high school's art class made decorations for the event: paper zombies were put on the walls, because no prom is complete without wallflowers. The teens envisioned zombie makeup, so staff found a theatrical makeup artist. They required music, and a popular local club DJ was contacted and volunteered his time. There were snacks, prom pictures, a prom king and queen, putrefied flesh—everything you might expect at a prom, and all was accomplished at low cost. Library staff fostered, facilitated, connected, and essentially got out of the way. Zombie Prom was recognized by YALSA as the Outstanding Teen Read Week Celebration of 2008.

One more thing to remember: Let programs die once they have run their course. Will we have Zombie Prom again this fall? You bet. But once the trend fades, we won't try to keep it alive (no pun intended). The teens will move on to other interests; it is our job to follow them.

This article was written expressly for use in this book.

THREE

TEEN READ WEEK
COLLECTION DEVELOPMENT

REDEFINING READING, GETTING a little shallow, and a survey of the habits of urban middle school students all offer guidance on how to plan collection development for Teen Read Week at your library.

GO AHEAD: JUDGE A BOOK BY ITS COVER

Darcy Lohmiller

The bookstore clerk was perplexed. "You don't want me to try and get a different copy? You only want these?" I nodded. I only want those books. The exact ISBNs listed. No substitutions. She nodded back but seemed uncertain. What did it matter if it was hardback, library binding, or paperback? The content was the same. But the content doesn't matter if no one checks it out. It's not what's inside that counts. I select books by their covers.

My method of book selection may not follow the rules of librarianship, and I'm not even sure what those rules are. I took a class in resource selection in 1980, my sophomore year in college, but I was only dabbling in different subjects. All I remember was that books could receive very different reviews. Taste in books was subjective. Selecting books was a bit of a gamble.

Fifteen years later I was hired as a part-time librarian at the new middle school, joining the existing staff of a full-time librarian and part-time secretary who had worked together for more than ten years. I was in charge of magazines and audiovisuals, and the full-time librarian chose the books. She was methodical with book selection, taking home stacks of *Booklist* and *School Library Journal* and filling out mounds of consideration cards. On each card, she wrote the essentials of any book she considered purchasing: title, author, ISBN, hardback or paperback, recommended age, and subjects. The cards were rubber-banded and filed away until it was time to place the order with the book jobber, then each card was placed inside the received book for cataloging. Her desk was filled with bundles of those soft, smudgy cards.

When she retired, I assumed responsibility for the fiction collection but found those thick bundles of frayed consideration cards cumbersome and clumsy. I didn't like flipping through the cards, and I didn't like writing so much by hand. Instead, I typed my notes

This article originally appeared in the Spring 2008 issue of *YALS*.

onto a tidy spreadsheet that I printed out when I was ready to place my order. I called the jobber and read my numbers to them; they told me if it was available, came from a secondary warehouse, was on back order, or was out of print. It was simple, and they provided a 30 percent discount and MARC records. The box of books came in three days.

When a box of new books arrives, librarians are like giddy children on Christmas as we slice through the tape and peel open the top. We "ooh" over the neat stacks of crisp covers and clean pages, and groan over the occasional disappointments, such as a 1975 vintage cover with kids in striped T-shirts and dopey grins indicating a madcap farce, or a cover with a schmaltzy scene of a guy and girl embracing, gazing at a distant mountain with melancholy anguish on their faces. Other failures include covers that date themselves with trendy fashions and hairstyles, or covers that try to include as many aspects of the book as possible, and in doing so fail to intrigue or entice the reader. Illustrations that say too much will alienate readers. Let them discover the book themselves.

I learned the importance of book covers in my first year as a librarian when I began reading the young adult titles in our collection. I chose Chris Crutcher's *The Crazy Horse Electric Game* because on its cover were three kids celebrating an apparent victory on a baseball field, and I needed a sports book in my repertoire. One boy was hoisting another boy, whose arm was pumped in triumph, while a girl (with big hair and short shorts) gazed at him with pride and joy. Once I began reading the book, however, I realized that this was the scene from the first chapter. The hero then gets into a water-skiing accident and is partially paralyzed, his parents' marriage crumbles over their guilt and grief, and he is quickly alienated from his friends, family, and past life. He runs away to Oakland, California, to a world of gangs, drugs, and pimps (one whom he befriends), struggling to make a new life for himself. Gritty stuff. Hardly your typical sports story. But anyone who sees the cover will expect baseball action, a little romance, and a triumphant ending. Those who want rough edges will avoid this, and those seeking simplicity will be quite surprised. And most will reject the book because, frankly, the kids look a little dorky. In 2003 HarperCollins reissued the book with a different cover. A young man extends his mitt toward the camera, his face obscured by his arm. Action, intensity, and baseball. Now that's more like it.

Covers are important to library patrons, but no more so than with middle school students, who are acutely conscious of appearances and how they determine one's place in a delicate social hierarchy. Library books are not just read; they are seen. Bad covers stand out like a student at an empty table in the cafeteria, like the girl with the wrong shoes or the boy with the high-waisted pants.

Adults may wait for a book, but students will not. If a girl loves a book, five of her friends will want to check it out too. Today. This is an ephemeral moment that I must grab before they have discarded books for boys, so I want them to read as much as possible before that happens. Therefore I buy five paperback copies of the book rather than one that is hardback or library bound, and circulate them until their pages fall out. Sales representatives try to sell me on the merits of one good library-bound book over three cheap paperbacks, but I am not convinced. Like bookstore clerks, I think they see my selection process as haphazard and unprofessional.

It may be unprofessional, but it is not haphazard. I read every issue of *Booklist* and *School Library Journal*, marking the books that sound interesting and adding them to my spreadsheet, noting whether they should be purchased in hardback or if I should wait until they are released in paperback. Paperbacks stretch my budget. Taking a chance on a $6 paperback is easier than investing in a $17 hardback that may turn out to be a dud. But hardbacks are also important. My "new books" display needs them for added pop, so I purchase a few starred-reviewed books, new books by popular authors, and the newest book in a series. But kids like paperbacks just as well, especially if they are quality paperbacks with great covers. Whenever I find an old book with a new, updated cover, I grab it and the makeover works. The book is new and fresh again, and becomes rediscovered.

It's sad when a good book with a bad cover goes out of print, leaving little hope that it will ever be read. Patricia McKillip's *The Night Gift*, with its ill-conceived 1970s line drawings, is a tough sell. No matter how many times I booktalk it, I can't seem to entice a student to check it out. While I don't claim to be a brilliant book-talker, whenever I put a lot of effort and belief behind a book, students will buy it. But not *The Night Gift*, which I refuse to weed from my collection until it's back in print and I can replace it with one that has a better cover.

The Internet is not only a helpful resource for checking if a book is back in print, but also for judging a book's cover. A search on a bookseller's website gives me the book's ISBN, editorial reviews, customer reviews, recommended ages, and a color photo of the book. But I also need to physically handle the book to trust my first response as typical of a student's response. I flip open the book, not only to check the quality of the binding, but also how the book feels in my hand. Does it open easily, wielding softly and welcoming the reader in? Or does it want to slam shut, its stiff binding threatening to crack under too much pressure?

The world is increasingly visual, and the youngest generations have little patience with anything that is not as clear and sharp as high-definition television. The pages should be white, the margins wide, and the font large and bold. No italicized scripts, no extra serifs. Old books languish on my shelf, their yellowed pages filled with tiny black print. I open them up and close them again. My forty-six-year-old eyes have trouble reading this, but thirteen-year-old eyes refuse to even try. They are accustomed to Harry Potter, the Lord of the Rings, the Chronicles of Narnia, and Eragon shown on large screens with high-tech special effects. Movies can create interest in the books on which they are based, but the printed versions need to have some dazzle as well.

When Anthony Horowitz's *Stormbreaker* was being made into a movie, I needed a few more copies to meet increased demand. At the bookstore, I found two new covers: a Penguin imprint with a royal blue cover and a thick silver slash emblazoned across the front and a movie tie-in edition with the movie's young blond star on the cover and movie photographs inside. The photographs of the movie's star were appealing and would be even more so to girls attracted to the pretty boy they chose to portray Alex Rider: tousled blond hair, angelic features, full lips—every thirteen-year-old girl's dream guy. But my target demographic is not teenage girls. It is Jake, the jock who doesn't usually read but who came to the library one day asking for the fifth book in the series. I heard him tell another boy that "these are the best books"; his friend was convinced and checked one out. The series is the second most popular in my library, just trailing behind Darren Shan's Cirque du Freak series. Would Jake and his friend be drawn to the pretty-boy cover? I decided that they would not.

With this audience, a blue cover emblazoned with a silver slash had a much higher cool factor than a cute movie star. I could not risk alienating the audience that is drawn to this book because they are the very same patrons to whom it is usually most difficult to plug books. They want a thriller—all adventure with little character development—that moves quickly and decisively through an exciting plot. And the cover needs to say that. In fact, the *Stormbreaker* movie went from a British release straight to DVD without creating much buzz.

Movie covers may create interest, but they become dated as quickly as a bad movie. A good book cover is like a good book. It accurately represents its genre, it has wide appeal, and it stands the test of time. It never alienates the reader with dated cultural references, nor underestimates the reader's intelligence by hammering home the book's theme. It should be as artistic a representation of the author's creative vision as the book itself. When done well, the book will be checked out until the date-due slip is full and the pages are falling out. And then the student will still insist on waiting until I glue it back together. I get my money's worth from a good book cover.

Here are some covers that have stood the test of time: Alvin Schwartz's Scary Stories to Tell in the Dark series, fifty-four checkouts in ten years. Stephen Gammell's 1986 illustrations continue to be as creepy and chilling as Schwartz's stories. The cover for Harry Mazer's *The Last Mission* has not changed since its original publication in 1979, but you cannot go wrong with a picture of a fighter jet's engine in flames. Bantam Books had the foresight to use illustrations of the dogs portrayed in Jim Kjelgaard's books—Irish setters and Siberian huskies thankfully never need updating, as many of his books are out of print. Robb White's *Deathwatch* still has John Mantha's 1972 cover, but its scene of the southwest desert, a man in the distance with a gun, and the clawing hands of his human prey still intrigues readers thirty-five years later. And although Aladdin Paperbacks recently published an updated cover of Gary Paulsen's *Hatchet*, the old one managed to maintain interest for more than twenty years. Long after I have thrown out the novelization of *Buffy the Vampire Slayer*, I will be checking these books out to readers who know timeless, quality stories when they see them.

EMERGENCE OF SPOKEN WORD RECORDINGS FOR YA AUDIENCES

Francisca Goldsmith

Spoken word recordings for young adults offer an alternative to print reading, a means to experience dramatic performance, and a resource for multitaskers. Audiobook producers now recognize the niche market of the young adult audience that magazine publishers identified a half century ago and that book editors have been striving to address across three decades. Just as with their print material tastes, young adults seek and enjoy recorded titles that include a mix of those intended more primarily for juvenile and adult audiences as well as those specifically targeted to people of junior high and high school age. Young adults are not homogenous as listeners any more than they are homogenous as readers. The young adult audiobook audience includes teens who can't decode print versions of the texts they need or want to read, teens who enjoy the embodiment of text in voice (or voices), teens who want to enjoy the art of literature while they pursue a secondary activity, and teens who hold an only partially misguided belief that listening to an assigned text will be a quicker route to achieving completion of a school assignment.

With several major production companies using sophisticated studio equipment and the skills of accomplished actors, teen listeners have a variety of publisher narrative production styles, as well as individual titles and genres, from which to choose. Some audiobook production companies select particularly youthful-sounding actors to read young adult novels, while others match readers to texts with attention only to gender, and still others broaden demographic classification details to include matching ethnicity of reader and character. Some audio productions provide listeners with audible bridges between recording sections, such as at the ends of discs or MP3 chapters, usually in the form of mood-appropriate musical bars. Yet other recordings allow the audience to hear the silences between chapters and simply let the silence of the playback device inform listeners that they need to move on to the next chapter. Compact disc recordings generally allow teen users to select from among two- or four-minute-long tracks, while MP3 players retain the track number at which a recording was turned off, making it easy to restart the book at the last-heard point.

Availability and Style

Material now being recorded for young adult listeners is a particularly interesting assortment. Audiobook and other spoken word recordings offer young adult listeners a gamut of literary and performance types: narratives read aloud by a single skilled reader, recorded plays and full-cast readings of narratives, and the opportunity to hear authors deliver their own works orally. Newly published books sometimes appear in recorded format at the same time, or within a few months, of the release of the print format. This gives avid teen readers, as well as those who cannot access print, a supply of brand-new material for listening. On the other hand, audiobook producers also look to older material for recording prospects. In some cases, hearing a work first published 10 or even 110 years ago can truly breathe new life into it, even for listeners familiar with the print version of the same work.

Another arena from which spoken word recordings may be gathered successfully for teen listeners is from among archival recordings by poets and other writers. Hearing the author deliver his or her own words can inspire a level of human understanding as well as the meaning of the text at hand. Recordings give teen listeners a more accessible experience with drama than that offered by most silent print readings. Recorded theatrical productions can engage the teen listener by giving a text the auditory aspect of the life its author intended.

A professional reader's capacity to "voice" characters in a differentiated manner appeals to teen audiobook listeners. "Voicing" refers to the combination of accent, pacing, pitch, or any of the other qualities that distinguish natural voices from person to person. It is the means by which a single reader can present individual characters, including the tone of the narrator, as distinct from the others within the book. Another method of presenting individuals within a text is supplied by full-cast readings in which

This article originally appeared in the Spring 2003 issue of YALS.

different actors share the reading, through role or character assignments, of the single work.

Audiobooks for adults may run to twelve or more parts, lasting through twenty or more hours of listening. Teens are less likely candidates for such marathon sessions with a single work that must be heard in consecutive order, although some fantasy listeners, as with fantasy readers, willingly stay with a recording of a 400- or 500-page book if it is done exceedingly well. The capacity for attending to a tale unfolding across its performance time can be an issue for some teens. Beyond half-hour television shows, teens generally are most accustomed to hearing and watching films and often have experience with being an audience to staged plays; such narratives require that the audience pay attention for a couple of hours at most. With recordings of books, most teen listeners seem able to stretch the time necessary for the full work to be heard to about six or eight hours, and they are ready to offer four or five hours at least. While these running times are almost always broken up into several sessions by the listener, he or she still must carry what was last heard on into the next installment of listening.

The two situations in which teen audiobook listeners are most likely to consume their aural experiences are both intimate, just as most book reading in our society now is an intimate activity. One is through personalized equipment, with headphones making the listener as alone with the material as is the silent visual reader. The other is within the confines of the family car, frequently in situations that are cross-generational. Here, the intimacy between text and reader is joined by the intimacy experienced when a very small group—often one with familial relations and thus interwoven personal histories—shares a literary work together. This kind of intimacy offers families with teens an opportunity for communication that otherwise may be problematic in their current daily relationships. Sharing the enjoyment of a recording's humor, pathos, or wonder offers an ideal invitation to share feelings about the performance and the story.

Quality Counts

What qualities should be embodied in text that is brought into recorded format with young adult audience appeal? The choice of text is important: books that require the reader to retrace his or her way back through paragraphs of argument each time a new point is established don't make for enjoyable listening; while those where the narrative flows along, carrying the reader-listener on the tide of the plot or character, allow a listener to move through the recording without rewinding or resetting the tracks in order to continue the journey. Writers who use creative orthography to communicate characters' accents are more readily consumed aurally than visually. The choice of reader or readers is also of utmost importance. There are books that really can stand up to a stolid oral delivery that is without differentiated voicing or compatibility between author and reader's gender or cultural accent. Other texts become minimized when heard aloud unless they are read with drama, or become off-putting when there is an unlikely schism between the sound of the reader and the tone of the author's narrative voice. The reading should, therefore, enhance the written work on which it is based.

The quality of the recording must, of course, be technically competent too. The major production companies all attend to the necessary details of having even pacing and sound levels, checking the product reliability of performance on standard equipment, and providing packaging that has necessary information for the listener. Production companies offer varying levels of information on their packaging. Some packaging provides clear descriptions of the correlations between sides or tracks and chapters, while other containers simply offer the complete running time for the full work. The more information available about how the recording matches the printed text, the easier it is for those who listen and follow the print together to match up starting and stopping places. Information about running time also allows listeners to plan a listening session, whether or not it is one that is shared with another activity (lap running, a bus ride, and so on). Cover art may be the same as the print book jacket or be a reimagining of images from the book.

Extra Value for the Money

Audiobooks often include added value contents. Some end with an author interview. Others, being read by the author, inform the listener as to the very specific pacing the writer intended his or her story to have, information that is transferable to future silent reading experiences with that author's works. References to characters singing or playing musical instruments may be actualized within the audiobook format.

Some productions even include a variety of sound effects, such as barking dogs or chugging trains, which are consonant with the book's text. Some production companies also utilize a trailer at the end of the audiobook recording to suggest three or four titles that the listener might also enjoy, generally crossing over authors but not genres or specific plot types in these recommendations.

Because of the price, most teens don't purchase their own audiobooks. Instead, adults tend to do the first level of selection for teen listeners, whether the adults are librarians, rental shop owners, or parents. Several professional selection tools are available to the first two groups.[1] Parents tend to select from library or store shelves without reading recording reviews, even though these same parents may be inveterate consumers of editorial opinion about printed books. This funnel effect means that teen audiobook listeners today have a relatively small range of options within most of their local browsing situations.

It takes a listener some time and effort to accrue the necessary experience with audiobooks to be able to understand his or her own taste in the style of delivery. Just as some readers have genre preferences, which they have learned by reading both in and beyond that genre, audiobook listeners develop an understanding of personal preference in terms of narrator characteristics, pacing, and types of written material that can be enjoyed, or even enjoyed more thoroughly, when heard rather than seen in print. Balancing this need for wide-ranging experience with relatively small venues for sampling presents a dilemma. Libraries and schools are attempting numerous projects to respond to that dilemma: by shelving print and audio side by side, creating audiobook discussion clubs, marketing audiobook collections on standard reading lists, and so on.

A Variety of Uses

The hope by some reluctant readers that an assigned text can be consumed both more readily and more quickly (the night before the due date!) in recorded format tends to bring knowing smirks from library staff. However, it may be that students who expose themselves to hearing even the opening cassette or compact disc of a lengthy work are more likely, in fact, to absorb some authentic understanding of at least the beginning of the book they have neglected to read visually. In the case of those with less than

adequate decoding skills, certainly their absorption of the aural passages has a better chance of providing them with the means to think critically about that part of the text. On the other hand, listeners unfamiliar with a particular audiobook seem to need at least half an hour to become accustomed to the pacing of the reader. Also, many secondary classroom-assigned texts are slow to unfold in their opening chapters so that the first part of the recording may contain only the passages that set the situation or describe the characters, leaving the partial listener-reader with no information about the ensuing conflict that makes the story a critical success.

Picture book and early chapter book kits with accompanying recordings have been on the market for some time, attracting children on the cusp of becoming independent readers, as well as the adults who work to foster this reading skill in them. Should the older child, the teenager, have to pair an audiobook with the text format in order to have the experience "count" as reading? My own experience with high school students who are learning English has pointed up some notable observations. It seems that, just as some of us are visual learners, others are aural learners, and still others are kinetic learners, so that the process of tying the audiobook to the print book may differ at a biological level among individuals. Without regard to how competently these English-language students read in their native languages, or what those native languages are, some find tracking print while hearing a book to be beneficial to building print-recognition skills in English, while others feel a real need to approach the print and the audio format serially, and not all of these do so in the same order.[2]

This would seem to indicate that a major benefit of using audiobooks in a high school classroom setting is their provision of content to discussion group members seeking to engage critical thinking and aesthetic skills. Literary devices are not lost in the recording process (except in the unlikely circumstance of offering listeners a recording of shaped poetry). It is just as possible to discuss these based on a listening experience as on a print experience. Furthermore, a discussion of the enactment of the author's work gives listeners the opportunity to recognize and build their aesthetic understanding of how performance "works" on its audience.

While most young adult books are so brief that abridgment would be unnecessary as well as inconsiderate, some producers offer teen listeners recordings of selections from longer texts. Clearly taking this tack with poetry can enhance the listener's experience, as it may focus more on specific aspects of the poet's work. Providing short stories as stand-alone recordings or bundling only a few together also enriches the types of literary experiences available to teens, even those with attention spans too slight to attend to a collection of a dozen tales ranging through 200-plus pages. The issue of accepting or disallowing abridged audiobooks is a lively one in both libraries and classrooms. However, some abridgments are so "gentle" that to discount the inclusion of these works because of the "a" word is tantamount to stripping the print collection of traditional published texts once the newly surfaced unedited version reaches print.[3]

The United States is not the only place where audiobooks for teen listeners are becoming popular. At least two Australian audiobook producers distribute their products here and warrant attention because of the high caliber of selections made for recording. Both Belinda Audio and the Louis Braille Institute of Australia select Australian young adult literature for recording that has appeal here as well as abroad. The readers generally have light Australian accents that are readily understood in the States, even by English-language-learning students. In most cases, the print editions of these Australian audiobooks are available here, so that those who eschew offering spoken word recordings without parallel print can expand both collections.

For libraries, the issues of packaging and parts replacement are crucial. Both Recorded Books and Listening Library offer replacement plans. Both of these companies, as well as all those mentioned above, supply library purchasers with heavy plastic casings that tolerate moderate to heavy circulation and make shelving on standard bookshelves easy. Listening Library provides excellent descriptions on both exterior packaging and individual tape sides about chapter contents, pagination, and playing time. The other companies mentioned above offer sufficient information to make finding a particular place within the text, or judging the length of a particular listening session, possible.

In recognition of the mounting interest in offering young adults a range of spoken word recording options, YALSA's former Media Selection and Usage Committee has undergone several changes, now known as the Amazing Audiobooks for Young Adults committee. The committee reviews nearly 200 new audiobooks targeting teen listeners each year and publishes a list of notable recordings at each ALA Midwinter Meeting. Previous annotated lists of the committee's selections are available on the YALSA website at www.ala.org/yalsa/audiobooks.

NOTES

1. *AudioFile* is published bimonthly, with each issue providing critical reviews of about 100 new audiobooks; *School Library Journal*, published monthly, also includes reviews of new audiobooks in each issue.

2. Francisca Goldsmith, "Earphone English," *School Library Journal* (May 2002): 50–53.

3. NAXOS Audio regularly produces classic texts, such as *Walden* by Henry David Thoreau (2001), that provide the listener with access to every meaningful passage of the print text while omitting some superfluous ones; the result is more in keeping with what should be termed an alternative editing rather than an abridgment.

READING: IT'S NOT JUST ABOUT THE BOOKS

Linda Braun

In the YA literature class I teach for Simmons College Graduate School of Library and Information Science in Boston, I ask students to find out what thirteen- to eighteen-year-olds say about their reading interests and preferences. As a part of the process, the library school students ask each teen to fill out a reading log. The log is used to chart reading during a twenty-four-hour period and is meant to include anything and everything that a teen reads. In the most recent set of logs, the following reading was listed:

- text messages
- e-mail
- MySpace/Facebook

This article originally appeared in the Summer 2007 issue of YALS.

- orchestra music
- *Seventeen* magazine
- iTunes
- IM
- specific websites

While traditional forms of reading did appear in the logs, book reading was almost always related to school assignments. The reading assignments listed included textbook reading as well as fiction reading assigned for a particular class.

Sometimes I ask teens with whom I'm working to fill out the same kind of reading log. Whenever I ask teens to fill out a log and then talk to them about what they recorded, it's quickly apparent to me how surprised many of the teens are about how much and how often they read on a regular basis. Many of the teens say they don't like to read, but then they realize, "Oh, it's not that I don't like to read; I read a lot. It's that I don't like to read certain types of things."

More adults realize that teens read constantly. What is less often realized is the need for librarians and teachers to accept and promote nontraditional forms of reading—blogs, wikis, text messages, and the like—as readily as they accept and promote traditional forms of reading: books, magazines, and so on. If adults do accept and promote the nontraditional (or new), they will realize that reluctant readers and nonreaders are few and far between. They'll notice that every teen is indeed a reader.

The previously mentioned reading logs are a real demonstration of the frequent reading that teens do. They read via technology in order to find information, communicate with others, improve skills, and so on. Consider these examples of what teens read using technology-based tools.

- **Blogs:** Teens read blogs to keep up on topics of interest, including technology, world news, and gossip. They read blogs written by friends and favorite authors. This reading is a way to collect information, find out about the world, and learn about how people think and live. Teens read fiction to be carried away by a good story and to live vicariously through others. That's some of what they get from blog reading. Similarly, teens read magazine articles to learn about something in which they are interested or to find out what's hot and what's not. They do the same with blogs.

- **Games:** To succeed in game play, teens often have to read about characters in the game, the history of the game, ways to improve play, and so on. In many ways this reading is very similar to the nonfiction reading that teens are frequently required to complete as a part of a school assignment. For school, they read history about places, directions on how to complete a task, and biographies of famous people. In the game-related reading of teens, there is an investment in the content that perhaps is different from the investment they might have for school assignment reading. Because of the high interest in learning how to succeed in a game, teens are more likely to remember, understand, and value what they read about game play. That's quality reading, even if it's not school related.

- **Podcasts:** Most podcasts include a website for show notes. This site provides information on topics discussed and includes links to resources mentioned in each episode. These show notes web pages are not much different from annotated resource lists and bibliographies that teens read as a part of research they might need to do for a school assignment. After listening to a podcast, teens like to go to the show notes site to find out more about topics discussed in the audio. They want to find out more. Again, they are invested in the reading. This is exactly the kind of investment we would like teens to have when they look through the resource lists and bibliographies associated with school assignments.

- **MySpace/Facebook:** Reading biographies is often a requirement for teen English or history classes. Aren't MySpace and Facebook forms of biography? Teens read about the interests of others via MySpace and Facebook pages. They learn about the lives of authors and the lives of entertainers. Is it possible to suggest that MySpace and Facebook are the early twenty-first-century version of a profile or interview in a magazine?

- **iTunes:** Finding and downloading music requires research skills similar to those librarians strive to teach. Using iTunes also gives teens the chance to read about the music and musicians in which they are interested—more biography and history reading.

- **Text messaging and IM:** Texting and IMing are all about dialogue, and dialogue is something that's a key part of many high school English classes. When teens communicate via text messaging or IM, they continue to process, learn about, and participate in dialogue. It's a different form of dialogue. Imagine if teens compared the dialogue in a text-message conversation with their friends to the dialogue in a favorite book or class assigned book. What would they discover? What would they learn?

Librarians regularly encourage teens to read fiction, history, biography, and so forth. As the above list demonstrates, this reading doesn't have to take place within the traditional book and magazine format. If you think about the technology-based reading in which teens are currently involved, in most cases you'll be able to see connections between that reading and the more traditional forms of reading that librarians and teachers promote on a regular basis.

What can librarians do to recognize and promote nontraditional forms of reading that teens do? Consider these ideas:

- Initiate conversations with teens about what they spend time reading that isn't a book or magazine. Ask if they consider text messaging, IMing, and looking at blogs as reading. Find out why or why not. Ask what kinds of reading they would like to be able to do for school assignments. What forms and formats should school-related reading take? Find out what type of reading teens would like to see promoted in the library.

- Talk to teachers about the technology-based reading that teens are involved in and help them to see how these newer forms and formats connect to the more traditional reading promoted on a regular basis. Consider working with teens or teachers on a chart, diagram, or other graphic organizer that shows the connections between the traditional and the new.

- Rethink your use and publication of materials and booklists. Move away from calling lists "booklists" and begin to use a more encompassing term. Maybe you can simply call all materials lists "favorites" (to connect with what teens save in their Internet browser). Whatever you call the lists you create to let teens know what's available to read, make sure to include blogs, wikis, websites, MySpace pages, Facebook pages, and game sites and resources on the lists.

Don't make negative judgments on the quality of what teens read simply because the reading is taking place through nontraditional means. As of today, whenever you find yourself questioning or judging what a teen likes to read using technology, ask yourself, "Why is this different or less valid than reading a book?" Is your answer one related to format? If so, then remember that writing on the Internet—for example, a blog post—doesn't equal bad or poor writing. There are numerous blogs by teens, adults, and journalists that are excellent examples of high-quality writing. Of course not all blog posts are high-quality writing, but not every magazine article or book is either.

Most important, don't make judgments based on what you don't know. Start text messaging and IMing so you know firsthand what that dialogue is like and entails. Remember that to encode and decode messages in these real-time instantaneous formats takes great skill. Read blogs, wikis, and social networking sites to find out what's available and to learn about the writing that's taking place online. Visit music and gossip sites to learn what teens are reading about their favorite entertainers and entertainments.

The more willing that adults are to recognize the important role that technology-based reading has in teen lives, the more likely it is that teens will start to think of themselves as readers (and the adults will think of them as readers too). After all, that's what we want, isn't it? We want a world of readers, not just a world of those who read books.

WHAT DO YOU WANT TO TELL US ABOUT READING? A SURVEY OF THE HABITS AND ATTITUDES OF URBAN MIDDLE SCHOOL STUDENTS TOWARD LEISURE READING

Sandra Hughes-Hassell and Christina Lutz

In today's world librarians seem to be overwhelmed with "information-seeking" rather than "readers." Under those conditions it is easy to forget that a major goal of a good librarian is to help the young move up the ladder to become lifelong adult learners.—Dorothy M. Broderick

Helping teenagers develop and nourish a love of reading for pleasure is high on the list of priorities for most school and young adult librarians. Leisure reading is defined as the reading teenagers do by choice as opposed to the reading teenagers are assigned by teachers.[1] As students move into middle and high schools, the amount of reading they are assigned usually increases dramatically, but what about the reading they do on their own? How many teenagers like to read? How many actually do so, and how often? What do they like to read and where do they get their reading materials? Surveys answering these questions are only sporadically conducted. A review of the literature showed that there are often gaps of several years, even decades, between similar studies. Even more of a challenge is uncovering information specifically about urban young adults, particularly low-income students and minorities.

In fall 2002 the librarians at two middle schools located in a large city in the northeastern United States wanted to gain a better understanding of the leisure reading habits of their students. They modified the Teen Read Week (TRW) survey, which asked questions about teens' reading habits, distributed the surveys to their students, and then asked us to analyze the data. The following article reports on the research and discusses the results from one of the schools, a small urban middle school that serves a primarily low-income, African American population.

Design of the Study

The librarians who initiated this study wanted to better understand the leisure reading habits of their students. They not only wanted to know how their students felt about leisure reading, but also about specific reading habits and preferences. The librarians felt that the TRW survey, administered since 1999 by Smart Girl and YALSA, addresses just these concerns and, therefore, chose to use it as a basis for their survey, modifying the original survey to meet their needs. The five-page, twenty-item questionnaire that they developed focused on factors related to reading by choice: whether teenagers read in their leisure time; if they do, what, when, and why they read; the topics and types of characters or people they like to read about; how they obtain their reading material; and who encourages them to read. If they don't read, why not? The questionnaire included four open-ended questions: What was your favorite book when you were in elementary school? What was your favorite book in middle school? What is the best book you've read this year? Is there anything else you'd like to tell us about reading?

Two hundred forty-five students attend the school that is the focus of this article. The school serves grades six through eight as an alternative middle school and is a member of the Coalition of Essential Schools. The school day includes a twenty-minute sustained silent reading, in which every member of the school community—adults as well as students—participates. Twenty-one percent of the students are Caucasian, 72.8 percent African American, 2.9 percent Hispanic, and 2.5 percent Asian American. Sixty-one percent of the students qualify for free or reduced lunch. Results on the 2002 State Assessment indicate that while 32 percent of the students are performing at or above the proficient level in reading, the majority (67 percent) are still scoring at basic or below-basic levels.[2]

This article originally appeared in the Winter 2006 issue of YALS.

A total of 214 students completed the survey. Of these, 44.4 percent of the respondents were male and 53.7 percent were female (there were four respondents who did not specify their gender). The students ranged in age from ten to fifteen, with the average age being twelve.

Data was analyzed using the Statistical Package for the Social Sciences to determine what percentage of respondents, both overall and by gender, claimed they did or did not read in their spare time. For nonreaders, reasons they gave for not reading were examined. For readers, factors relating to types of reading material chosen for leisure reading were analyzed: what, when, and why they read; the topics and types of characters or people they like to read about; how they obtain their reading material; and who encourages them to read.

What the Students Said about Leisure Reading

Reading as a Leisure Activity

Seventy-three percent of the students said they engage in leisure reading: 23 percent of the students said they read "constantly," while 49 percent indicated they "read when they get a chance." Twenty-two percent said they read only what they were assigned for school, while 6 percent said they did not read at all.

The majority of the students read more than two books per month outside of their schoolwork, with 22 percent saying they read two to three books a month and 17 percent reading three to five books a month. Eleven percent indicated that they read five to ten books per month, 8 percent said that they read ten to twenty books per month, and 10 percent of respondents were especially avid readers, stating that they read more than twenty books per month. Seventeen percent of the students said they read less than one book per month. Fifteen percent of the teens reported doing no reading outside of their schoowork.

Girls tended to read both more often than boys (32 percent of girls versus only 12 percent of the boys said they read "constantly") and a greater amount per month. The largest percentage of girls, 20 percent, read three to five books per month, while the largest percentage of boys, 26 percent, read two to three books per month. Additionally, 28 percent of boys did not read at all except for school assignments, while only 17 percent of the girls reported similar behavior.

About half of each gender said they liked to read, but often did not have the time.

The most frequently cited time for students to engage in leisure reading was at night, with 40 percent indicating that they did so. Two students wrote that they liked to read at night because it helped them "to fall asleep," while another reported that "reading calms me." Nighttime reading was followed by "when the teacher tells me I should," cited by 25 percent of respondents. Twenty-two percent reported that they read after school, and 20 percent read during school vacations and over the summer. Only 16 percent said they read on weekends.

Students' Attitudes toward Leisure Reading

When asked if they enjoyed reading, 37 percent responded yes, 58 percent responded sometimes, and 4 percent stated no. Females were split between stating they definitely enjoyed reading (48 percent) and stating that they sometimes enjoyed reading (50 percent). Only one female respondent stated that she did not like to read, while 8 percent of male respondents said they did not enjoy reading. Sixty-seven percent of boys sometimes enjoyed reading, while 24 percent of boys stated that they definitely liked to read.

As table 1 shows, the majority (57 percent) of students responded that they liked to read "for fun." Half found reading "relaxing," while 55 percent said they "get attached to the characters," and 42 percent felt reading was exciting. Many of the students expressed positive feelings about reading, including such comments as "Reading is the best," "Reading is excellent," and "It is very fun." One respondent enthused: "Reading is enjoyable. I love to read when it rains or snows. I love romance books, especially one where the setting is winter, and you're bundled up with the one you really love." One student said, "I just really enjoy it! As a matter of fact I want to be in journalism!" Another said that she liked to read "because I like to write, and so I can have an idea on what to write."

Forty-two percent of the students said they read for educational or learning purposes. Several mentioned their belief that reading will help them academically, with one student commenting that "reading is good for getting a job, and good for becoming a writer." One student told us that "reading . . . helped me get to average. I was below," while another agreed that "it's helpful in your education." Another student wrote, "You can learn a lot just from reading about other people's lives."

Those who did not enjoy reading seemed to prefer other activities rather than to reject the act of reading. (see table 2). When asked why they don't read, forty-one percent said they liked "other activities better." The preferred activities included playing video games, surfing the web, watching television, and spending time with friends.. Thirty-three percent said they had "too much schoolwork." Some students showed a grudging tendency toward reading. "I would say that reading is a little fun," allowed one student, while another felt that "reading is ok when you are bored. But sometimes I get into it." Another mused, "I don't like reading but I'm good at it."

A few who did not enjoy reading indicated that they had difficulty with it or had trouble concentrating. Twenty-five percent reported that reading made them "tired" or gave them "a headache," although one student wrote that "I love reading but it makes my head hurt. I still read." Twenty-five percent also agreed that they had trouble concentrating. Only 9 percent of the students reported that they did not read because they simply were not good at reading. Twenty-eight percent of boys responded that they did not read because it was boring, while only 12 percent of girls agreed. It is interesting to note that only four students reported that their friends made fun of them if they read.

TABLE 1. If you read, why do you like to read? Check all that apply.

Reason	Males (%)	Females (%)	Total (%)
For escape	19.5	25.6	22.6
For fun	47.0	67.0	57.0
To learn something/it's educational	40.0	45.0	42.0
For brain stimulation	19.0	19.0	19.0
It's relaxing	43.0	56.0	50.0
For a time filler	24.0	26.0	25.0
For motivation	16.0	21.0	18.0
I get attached to the characters I'm reading about	44.0	64.0	55.0
It's exciting	31.0	53.0	42.0

TABLE 2. If you don't read, why not? Check all that apply.

Reason	Males (%)	Females (%)	Total (%)
Too busy/no time	23	39	30
Boring/not fun	28	12	20
Can't get into stories	18	30	26
Boys are more interesting	1	35	18
Girls are more interesting	42	2	23
I like other activities better	43	39	41
I have too much school work	30	35	33
Reading makes me tired or gives me a headache	20	30	25
I have trouble concentrating	18	33	25
I'm not good at reading	5	12	9
I'd rather play video games	55	32	44
I'd rather surf the Internet	34	36	35
I'd rather watch TV	50	60	56
I'd rather spend time with my friends	47	56	52
I can't find a good book	20	40	30
Books are too long	21	18	19
My friends make fun of me	2	1	2

Specific Influences on Reading

The top three adults who teens say encourage them to read are their parents, teachers, and school librarians. Eighty percent said that their parents encouraged them to read; this was equally true for boys and girls. Sixty-six percent said their teachers encouraged them to read, followed by the school librarian at 29 percent. A surprisingly large number, 25 percent, said their siblings encouraged them to read, while 23 percent cited the encouragement of their friends. Seventeen percent said the public librarian influenced them to read.

Leisure Reading Materials

Many students expressed interest in reading periodicals, specifically magazines and newspapers. Seventy-seven percent of the girls liked fashion and beauty magazines, while 71 percent of boys were fond of sports, car, and wrestling magazines. The majority of students preferred music and entertainment magazines (63 percent of music and 55 percent of entertainment), and nearly half enjoyed video magazines. News magazines such as *Time* and *Newsweek* garnered only 7 percent of the response. While many in the newspaper publishing industry fear that young people are not joining their audience, 17 percent of the students indicated that newspapers are among their favorite reading material. In fact, 24 percent of boys listed newspapers as a favorite reading item.

As table 3 shows, celebrities, "people or characters like me," and "people my age who have done some cool or amazing things" are among the most popular topics for urban teens' leisure reading. Sixty-three percent were interested in celebrities, with especially heavy interest from girls (76 percent). Sixty-eight percent of boys liked reading about sports figures. Fifty-eight percent liked reading about people or characters like themselves—particularly girls, at 73 percent. Fifty-seven percent of girls liked to read about "characters my age wrestling with tough issues, like drug abuse or crime." More boys than girls preferred reading about "fantasy characters," with 49 percent of boys enjoying these characters.

Three of the open-ended questions asked stu-dents

to list their favorite book—in elementary school, middle school, and this school year. Favorite books in elementary school included the Goosebumps series (Stine), *The Cat in the Hat* (Seuss), *Green Eggs and Ham* (Seuss), the Baby-Sitters Club series (Martin), *Wayside School Is Falling Down* (Sachar), *There Is a Boy in the Girl's Bathroom* (Sachar), and the Harry Potter series (Rowling). Only five multicultural titles were mentioned by the 149 students who answered this question: *Roll of Thunder, Hear My Cry* (Taylor), *Maniac Magee* (Spinelli), *Justin and the Best Biscuits in the World* (Walter), *Happy Birthday, Addy* (Porter), and *A Picture of Freedom: The Diary of Clotee, a Slave Girl* (McKissack).

There was a great deal of overlap between the titles the teens listed most frequently as their favorite book in middle school and the best book they have read this school year. Unlike the elementary list, this list was dominated by multicultural subjects and included both young adult and adult titles. Prominent on the list were biographies of African American celebrities and sports figures, such as Aaliyah and Allen Iverson, and urban, or hip-hop, literature, such as *The Coldest Winter Ever* (Souljah), *Flyy Girl* (Tyree), and *True to the Game* (Woods). Several award-winning multicultural young adult novels were also mentioned, including *Bud, Not Buddy* (Curtis), *Monster* (Myers), and *The Watsons Go to Birmingham—1963* (Curtis). Also popular were problem novels and horror, mystery, and inspirational genres. Titles mentioned

TABLE 3. What do you like to read about? Check all that apply.

Topic	Males (%)	Females (%)	Total (%)
Celebrities	50	76	63
Animals	36	26	31
Musicians	35	37	36
Sports Figures	68	22	44
Historical Figures	18	23	21
People or characters like me	41	73	58
People or characters a lot different than me	23	55	41
Fantasy characters	49	38	43
People or characters my age wrestling with tough issues, like drug abuse or crime	31	57	44
People my age who have done some cool or amazing things	40	53	47

included *Go Ask Alice* (Anonymous), *It Happened to Nancy: By an Anonymous Teenager, a True Story from Her Diary* (Sparks), *Annie's Baby: The Diary of Anonymous, a Pregnant Teenager* (Sparks), *Flowers in the Attic* (Andrews), *Devil in a Blue Dress* (Mosley), and *Chicken Soup for the Teenage Soul* (Canfield).

Sources of Leisure Reading Material

. When asked to indicate all of the places where they get books to read, the most commonly cited source of books was a bookstore (61 percent), followed by the school library (59 percent), the public library (54 percent), the classroom (42 percent), and friends (39 percent). A significant number also reported that they get books at home and through their families. About 10 percent specifically wrote in the names of family members, including parents, grandparents, siblings, aunts and uncles, and cousins; and approximately another 6 percent mentioned that they read books from their home libraries. One student wrote, "In my home I have more than six hundred books." Book clubs, including Scholastic and Black Expressions, were also mentioned, as was the Internet and such specialty stores as comic stores and thrift shops. Interestingly, an overwhelming majority of girls, 75 percent, find their books at bookstores, while the largest number of boys relied on the school library (53 percent).

What We Learned from the Teenagers about How to Support Their Leisure Reading

This study provides a preliminary understanding of the leisure reading habits of inner-city teenagers. One of the most compelling findings is that urban teenagers are reading. In general, 73 percent of them indicated that they read in their leisure time, albeit for some readers it might be only an occasional pursuit. Another significant finding is that urban students engage in leisure reading almost as frequently as their rural and suburban counterparts. Constance Mellon reports that 82 percent of the rural teens she surveyed said they read in their spare time. Mary Anne Moffitt and Ellen Wartella found that 78 percent of the rural and suburban students they studied claimed to read for pleasure.[3] Despite stereotypical notions that urban or minority teenagers may find themselves the objects of scorn or ridicule for reading, our survey found only

four students who reported that their friends made fun of them if they read. Instead, a large number cited their friends both as sources of encouragement to read (23 percent) and as sources of reading material (39 percent).

These two findings have important implications for the publishing industry. Since urban teenagers are reading, the publishing industry needs to view them as a viable market and provide more of the types of materials these teens request, especially young adult novels that accurately reflect urban life. In a recent study of young adult novels, Sandy Guild and Sandra Hughes-Hassell found that from 1990 to 1999 only twenty young adult novels depicting the lives of urban minority youths were published and reviewed positively in standard selection tools, such as *School Library Journal* and *Voice of Youth Advocates*.[4]

The survey also revealed some overwhelmingly favorite books that seemed to relate specifically to an urban, African American experience. Recognizing these and similar titles can guide future collection development and reader advisory services. It can also help school librarians collaborate with teachers and public librarians in developing reading lists and programs that feature these and other titles. While not endorsing the outmoded view that librarians should necessarily steer readers to high-brow literature, it is a possibility that the middle school student who enjoys Sister Souljah's *The Coldest Winter Ever*, as a dozen or so of our respondents stated, may also enjoy the work of such authors as Walter Dean Myers and, later, Toni Morrison.

It is important to note that the students' exposure to multicultural topics and genres seemed to begin in middle school, rather than elementary school. The favorite books mentioned from the elementary years were fairly traditional, with few multicultural titles cited. In this school system, many schools do not have libraries, particularly on the elementary level. Of the 177 elementary schools in the district, only 35 employ a librarian. This underscores the role of the school librarian in promoting new and appropriate materials, both to students and as a collaborating member of the faculty.

This study also supports the research that shows a need to actively promote reading with boys.[5] While the boys in this survey were only marginally less inclined to read than girls, more of the boys expressed a negative attitude toward reading, and more cited direction from teachers as a motivation to read. There are also some significant gender differences in what the teens choose to read. For example, more boys read newspapers than girls (24 percent to 12 percent), and they also prefer material such as comics and sports, car, and wrestling magazines by large margins (71 percent to 19 percent for the magazines). This could reflect boys' greater interest in sports, which 84 percent cited as a passion, versus 39 percent of girls. One boy even specifically wrote the word "sports" next to the word "newspapers" on his survey. Sixty-eight percent of boys also indicated they like to read about sports figures, while only 22 percent of the girls shared that interest.

Periodicals, including magazines and newspapers, were without question the favorite leisure reading material of these teenagers. This finding has several implications for teachers and librarians who work with urban teenagers. First, we need to recognize reading magazines as legitimate reading. As Mellon points out, adults often send the message that the only reading that counts is reading books.[6] Since magazines are the type of reading material that urban teenagers most enjoy, we must encourage, even promote, them by providing and circulating popular magazines in both library collections and classroom collections. Second, school libraries in particular should note boys' preferences for periodicals when making collection development decisions. Not all schools make daily newspapers accessible to students, particularly at the elementary and middle school levels, and some librarians and teachers are reluctant to purchase magazines. However, school libraries were the most frequently cited place for the boys in our survey to obtain reading materials. Third, we need to understand the characteristics of magazines that make them appealing to urban teens and to use these characteristics to expand their reading repertoire. According to Patrick Jones, Michelle Gorman, and Tricia Suellentrop, teens are drawn to magazines for several reasons, including (1) the quantity and quality of pictures; (2) the speed with which information can be gathered from magazines; (3) the availability of magazines; (4) the "coolness" factor; and (5) the reading level.[7] Taking these factors into consideration, librarians and teachers might pair magazines with nonfiction books that contain quality pictures, lots of captions and sidebars, and a focus on the topics most appealing to these teens—celebrities, sports, video games, music, and television and movies. Comic books and graphic novels, which also share

similar characteristics, should be shelved next to the magazine collection and circulated as well.

The important role played by parents and teachers in encouraging urban teenagers to read was underscored by this study. Twenty-five percent of respondents to our survey said that they read "when the teacher tells me I should," which was the second most popular time students said that they read and was particularly cited by boys. It is important to remember that this was a school that had an established sustained silent reading program as an integral part of each school day. The adults in the school participated in the program along with the students. Thus, while teachers were instructing students when to read, the choice of materials was left to them. However, students still seemed to view this as reading for school, as the timing was not self-directed. A question that educators and librarians now need to consider is how to make the connection between sustained silent reading and leisure reading for pleasure.

While librarians may be disappointed that the teens did not mention them more frequently as influencers, they should be heartened by the finding that the school library and public library are among the teens' primary sources for reading materials. The school library in particular was the most popular source for the male respondents, with 53 percent listing the school library as their source for reading material.

The significance of bookstores as a source of reading material is worth exploring. There may be several factors influencing this choice. The city in which the students live has recently undergone major cutbacks in both school and public libraries. In fact, the school our respondents attended no longer employs a school librarian. In addition to removing one of the top three advocates for reading cited by the teens themselves, a major source and promoter of multicultural and urban-based titles has now been lost.

Another reason why so many of the students buy books rather than borrow from their school libraries may be because they are reading books published for adults, many of which may not be owned by the school due to age-appropriateness issues. One twelve-year-old student told us, "I enjoy reading books meant for older readers, like teenagers sixteen and up and adults." There is evidence that the young teens in our survey are also trading the books they buy among their circles of friends.

The fact that few of the students engage in leisure reading in the summer needs to investigated. Research has shown that students who do not read in their free time often lose academic ground even if they are not initially remedial readers.[8] The students in this study, like many urban teenagers, cannot afford to lose academic ground in the summer, as most already score below the proficient level in reading. Whether measured by the number of books read, the time spent reading, or regularity of library usage, summer reading is critical to summer learning.[9] Teachers, school librarians, public librarians, and parents need to collaborate to foster and encourage involvement in summer reading. Most public library systems, including the one serving this middle school, provide summer reading incentive programs aimed at teenagers. It is imperative that these programs be designed to take advantage of the personal interests of urban teenagers. As Richard Allington points out, personal interest "remains the most potent factor in the development of reading processes."[10] Areas that could be explored include multicultural literature, urban young adult literature, magazines and e-zines for teens, celebrity biographies, comic books, the Internet, and graphic novels. A program that has proven to be extremely popular with urban teenagers is the Free Library of Philadelphia's Teen Author Series.[11] The program connects teenagers with a Who's Who list of American writers, including such minority authors as Ilyasah Shabazz and Julia Alvarez. The teens receive free copies of the authors' books and get to interact with the authors as they speak about their books, their lives, and the process of writing. Libraries might also consider collaborating with local hip-hop radio stations and such radio personalities as Wendy Williams, also known as the "Queen of Urban Radio," to promote participation in summer reading programs.

Conclusion

Connecting urban teens to appropriate books is of utmost importance. Those who did not read often cited a general lack of interest—that books were "corny" or just not interesting. Matching readers to the correct reading level is important as well. One student reported that "books are too long (sometimes)," while another said he or she could not "find a good book" and another wrote that "sometimes I like reading, but only if I'm interested in [the book]."

Obviously, subject matter is of utmost importance

to these readers. Librarians and teachers at all levels need to make an effort to provide materials that reflect students' interests, such as celebrities, sports, and popular culture, as well as items that address multicultural and urban topics.

A key hook for all students is to make periodicals more available to readers. Rather than resisting subscribing to or circulating newspapers and magazines, these should serve as a legitimate and nurtured part of the library's collection. Students also need time to read. Many reported that they would read more if they had more available time. Although they were given time to read during the school day, many still viewed this as teacher-directed rather than self-directed. Working with public libraries and parents to institute summer reading programs could help make the most of free time in the summer and help keep students from backsliding during vacation.

Finally, gender differences need to be recognized. Our results showed that the school setting had a greater influence on the leisure reading habits of boys. School librarians and teachers need to be particularly cognizant of this fact, and develop programs and services that are specifically geared toward boys and include the types of materials boys seem to prefer, such as periodicals and sports-related items.

NOTES

1. Constance A. Mellon, "Teenagers Do Read: What Rural Youth Say about Leisure Reading," *School Library Journal* 33 (February 1987): 27–30.

2. Pennsylvania Department of Education, "2002–2003 PSSA Results," March 8, 2005, www.pde.state.pa.us (accessed October 1, 2005).

3. Mellon, "Teenagers Do Read"; Mary Anne S. Moffitt and Ellen Wartella, "Youth and Reading: A Survey of Leisure Reading Pursuits of Female and Male Adolescents," *Reading Research and Instruction* 31, no. 2 (1992): 1–17.

4. Sandy Guild and Sandra Hughes-Hassell, "The Urban Minority Young Adult Audience: Does Young Adult Literature Pass the Reality Test?" *New Advocate* 14, no. 4 (2001): 361–77.

5. See, for example, Jami Jones, "Priority Male," *School Library Journal* 51, no. 3 (2005): 37; Allison Haupt, "Where the Boys Are," *Teacher Librarian* 30, no. 3 (February 2003): 19–24; Michael Sullivan, "Why Johnny Won't Read," *School Library Journal* 50, no. 8 (2004): 36–39.

6. Constance A. Mellon, "Leisure Reading Choices of Rural Teens," *School Library Media Quarterly* 18 (1990): 223–28.

7. Patrick Jones, Michelle Gorman, and Tricia Suellentrop, *Connecting Young Adults and Libraries*, 3rd ed. (New York: Neal Schuman, 2004).

8. Richard C. Anderson, Linda G. Fielding, and Paul T. Wilson, "Growth in Reading and How Children Spend Their Time Outside of School," *Reading Research Quarterly* 23, no. 3 (July 1998): 285–304; Larry J. Mikulecky, "Stopping Summer Learning Loss among At-Risk Youth," *Journal of Reading* 33, no. 98 (1990): 516–21; Barbara M. Taylor, Barbara J. Frye, and Geoffrey Maruyama, "Time Spent Reading and Reading Growth," *American Educational Research Journal* 27, no. 2 (1990): 351–62.

9. Barbara Heyns, *Summer Learning and the Effects of Schooling* (New York: Academic Press, 1978).

10. Richard Allington, "What's Special about Special Programs for Children Who Find Learning to Read Difficult?" *Journal of Reading Behavior* 26, no. 1 (1994).

11. Meg McCaffrey, "Star Power," *School Library Journal* 51, no. 1 (January 2005): 48–49.

CHILDREN'S AND YOUNG ADULT TITLES CITED

Andrews, V. C. *Flowers in the Attic.* New York: Pocket Books, 1979.

Anonymous. *Go Ask Alice.* New York: Simon & Schuster Books for Young Readers, 1971.

Canfield, Jack. *Chicken Soup for the Teenage Soul.* Deerfield Beach, FL: Health Communications, 1997.

Curtis, Christopher Paul. *Bud, Not Buddy.* New York: Delacorte, 1999.

———. *The Watsons Go to Birmingham—1963: A Novel.* New York: Delacorte, 1995.

Martin, Ann M. The Baby-Sitter's Club series. New York: Scholastic.

McKissack, Patricia. *A Picture of Freedom: The Diary of Clotee, a Slave Girl.* New York: Scholastic, 1997.

Mosley, Walter. *Devil in a Blue Dress.* New York: Norton, 1990.

Myers, Walter Dean. *Monster.* New York: HarperCollins, 1999.

Porter, Connie Rose. *Happy Birthday, Addy.* Middleton, WI: Pleasant Co., 1994.

Rowling, J. K. Harry Potter series. New York: Scholastic.

Sachar, Louis. *There Is a Boy in the Girl's Bathroom.* New York: Knopf, 1987.

———. *Wayside School Is Falling Down.* New York: Avon, 1989.

Seuss, Dr. *The Cat in the Hat.* New York: Random House, 1957.

———. *Green Eggs and Ham.* New York: Random House, 1960.

Sparks, Beatrice, ed. *Annie's Baby: The Diary of Anonymous, a Pregnant Teenager.* New York: Avon, 1998.

———, ed. *It Happened to Nancy: By an Anonymous Teenager, a True Story from Her Diary.* New York: Avon, 1994.

Spinelli, Jerry. *Maniac Magee.* Boston: Little Brown, 1990.

Souljah, Sister. *The Coldest Winter Ever.* New York: Pocket Books, 1999.

Stine, R. L. Goosebumps series. New York: Scholastic.

Taylor, Mildred. *Roll of Thunder, Hear My Cry.* New York: Dial, 1976.

Tyree, Omar. *Flyy Girl.* New York: Simon & Schuster, 1996.

Walter, Mildred Pitts. *Justin and the Best Biscuits in the World.* New York: Lothrop, Lee, and Shepard, 1986.

Woods, Teri. *True to the Game.* Havertown, PA: Meow Meow Productions, 1994.

I GOT GRAPHIC! USING VISUAL LITERATURE WORKS!

Jodi Leckbee

In mere moments my students are transported to Poland in the 1930s, and they, like the main character Vladek, are witnessing the horror of the Holocaust. They watch helplessly as German soldiers hang a group of men on the street; they experience the fear these family members felt because they are there with

them and can see it on the expressions of their faces. I repeat they can see it themselves. This is the power of the graphic novel, compelling visuals that move literature beyond just a simple collection of words into a form of visual literature. My students are reading a graphic novel called *Maus: A Survivor's Tale* by Art

This article originally appeared in the Summer 2005 issue of YALS.

Spiegelman. The image and the text work together on the page, bringing the complicated story of a man and his father to life, one comic strip frame at a time.

I discovered the power of using graphic novels in my classroom, not to replace, but rather to enhance the learning of literary analysis for my students. Some educators assume that the art of great writing is diminished by using visual images to convey what authors so successfully accomplish with words. Thematic structure, the use of metaphor, simile, exaggeration, and other literary tools are not abandoned within a graphic novel, but rather enhanced by the ethical underpinning and multicultural perspective that the artist brings to the table. In many of these novels, students connect visually and can relate personally to the archetypes found within the pages.

Graphic novels, already popular with teen readers, act as a bridge, allowing them to transcend the apathy usually felt toward reading assignments. Because many students are not excited by reading, and peer pressure punishes many of those who are, graphic novels have a "cool" factor, and a teen is rarely embarrassed to be seen reading one. In fact, many teens possess expertise in the area of graphic novels, especially manga, and are willing to share their own personal library and knowledge. Letting students teach me about the reading they love has helped me transfer that same enthusiasm to reading response assignments and class discussions. I have also found great success by pairing a graphic novel with other forms of literature to support a thematic unit.

When I teach *Maus*, I am incorporating the novel into a larger unit on the Holocaust. I like using literature and film to connect with my students. Most students feel that this subject matter is far removed from them. Using *Maus* brings them closer to understanding the idea that this kind of crime toward humanity could happen again. After interacting with the graphic novel, the students will present what they have learned in the form of a brochure. The brochure assignment on *Maus* requests that the students write about their own lives, thereby bringing the experience of Holocaust participants directly to them. My intention is to have my students interact with the experiences that the characters in the novel survive in an emotionally powerful way. The art of the graphic novel makes this experience visceral and far more intense. The brochure assignment asks them to follow one character as they move throughout the novel as well as compare and contrast themselves to the character. Students will create diary entries for their character based on events that occur in the novel. This task requires them to put themselves in the story and give a voice to the pictures they are seeing. The combination of the images in *Maus* and the video I use in class, *Night and Fog*, force my students to visually face the horror of the Holocaust. I stand by the old adage "Seeing is believing."

When I teach my unit on compassion, I use the graphic novel *A Family Matter* written by Will Eisner. I like to partner this reading with the novel *Of Mice and Men* by John Steinbeck. Eisner—who is considered the father of the graphic novel and coined the term— writes and illustrates honest human stories that can easily win over skeptics who believe that all graphic novels are based on fantasy and superhero formulas. I don't want to diminish the use of superhero comics in an English class, however: what better way to teach the Hero Cycle than by using actually superheroes? Using superheroes also gives me the opportunity to discuss genre and subgenre with my students. Anyone who believes that all superhero comics are alike just has not read enough comics. There are traditional superheroes, modern superheroes, teen superheroes, teams of superheroes, parodies of superheroes, anti- hero superheroes, and even feminist superheroes. The world of the graphic novel is just as varied as other forms of literature. As English teachers, we should read as much of this genre as possible before we can make educated decisions about what is appropriate for our students and our classrooms.

I started down the road of graphic novels by teaching an entire unit using comic books. I set up a gallery of comic book and graphic novel covers around the room. The number of distinct genres found today surprised my students. Just like fiction, graphic novels have many different categories: superhero, fantasy, horror/supernatural, science fiction, humor, crime, real life, historical fiction, myth/legends, nonfiction, educational, and manga. Some of these genres are further divided up into subgenres, illustrating the range of material available. But there is more. I haven't even fully opened the door to the world of manga. The manga form of the graphic novel is a phenom- enon in well-educated Japanese society, outselling any other form of literature. They have become quite popular in the United States as well and allow a unique opportunity for students to gain a multicultural perspective. Manga requires students to read from the bottom right side of the page to upper left, creating opportunities for them to experience reading in a new way. After asking my students to spend time reading several different graphic novel titles, they were given a Multiple Intelligences project to complete on the novel of their choice. With this assignment, I was able to have students think about how graphic novels are written, the art involved in the process, and the thought behind the author's intent.

With many standardized tests introducing a visual component to assessment and the overload of visual mediums in their everyday lives, the graphic novel is uniquely poised to tap student's enthusiasm and further their learning. Why shouldn't educators use the power of the graphic novel to help students become better readers and writers? The multidimensional nature of comics and graphic novels allows teachers to think about literature in a new creative way. Exploring the visual world of graphic novels will heighten your students' interest in reading and expand intellectual possibilities rather than contract them. A literary piece, like a graphic novel, is calling on students to use both their analyzing and synthesizing skills, actually requiring more involvement and focus in their reading. Therefore, teaching graphic novels provides educators another way to engage the minds of our students. Not unlike the use of film and music in English classrooms, graphic novels should be acknowledged as a valuable learning tool. Sometimes you just have to see it to believe it.

TEEN READ WEEK MARKETING, PROMOTION, AND OUTREACH

THESE ARTICLES WILL give inspiration for how to use Teen Read Week to promote reading at your library, highlight special collections, reach out to unique populations, and more.

GET REAL! BOOKTALKING NONFICTION FOR TEEN READ WEEK

Jane V. Charles

Booktalking is a surefire way to increase your visibility in the young adult community, spark an interest in YA literature, and generally reach out to teens. Visiting schools to booktalk also offers an opportunity to promote YA programs and events at your library—and Teen Read Week provides a good reason to make an appointment at your area schools.

Veteran booktalkers know that the best way to win over a young adult audience is to begin their booktalks with works of nonfiction. The more shocking, bizarre, absurd, silly, spooky, frightening, gross, and alarming, the better. People of all ages love learning about and sharing astonishing stories about things that have actually happened. Young adults, especially the younger set, enjoy checking out illustrations and photographs of the disgusting, spine-tingling, and unimaginable. They like stories that cause them to respond emotionally and physically, making them feel scared, exhilarated, and curious, and giving them

goose bumps, chills, and sweaty palms. They want to feel involved and connected to the stories that you share with them. Since spinning true tales is an effective means of captivating a young adult, why not booktalk only nonfiction during your next school visit? Booktalking nonfiction allows you to connect teens with informative, yet intriguingly fun, meaningful, and sometimes even outrageous nonfiction.

To successfully booktalk true tales, select books from a wide range of topics to reach as many young adults as possible. Sports, poetry, history, music, entertainment, crafts, folklore, crime, psychology, UFOs—it's all fair game. Select books from all major collections—adult, young adult, and children's—that will pique their interest. Look for titles from YALSA's Nonfiction Award at www.ala.org/yalsa/nonfiction. Start with the lighter nonfiction reads, such as urban legends, ghost stories, and fun science, and then introduce more serious works about topics like the

This article originally appeared in the Fall 2005 issue of *YALS*.

civil rights movement or true crime. Your goal is to show that works of nonfiction aren't dry, educational reads; they are truly intriguing, exciting, alive, and often inspiring!

Nonfiction booktalks are especially amenable to audience participation. Ask questions throughout your booktalk—for example, "Who's ever heard of a _____?" "Have you ever seen a _____?" or "Who knows what a _____ is?" Be flexible. If one particular title or subject is not resonating with your audience, quickly wrap up the talk and try another book about a different subject. Don't be afraid to read an excerpt from a title if a certain passage is particularly well written, enlightening, and engrossing. Place sticky notes on pages featuring quotable text or captivating images that you want to share during your talk. Walk around the room with the book open to a compelling image. If after you've displayed the book's eye-catching visuals, one of your audience members shouts, "I didn't see it!" or "Show me!," you know you've succeeded.

Booktalking nonfiction is particularly conducive to using a broad range of booktalking techniques. Here are a few ways to transform yourself into a raconteur:

- Write a booktalk of vignettes about someone or something amazing from a particular work.

- Create a talk solely consisting of notable facts and astounding statistics.

- Take on the identity of a person who inhabits the book. Without breaking from character, begin and end the booktalk in that person's voice.

- Read one or two short poems before, during, or after your talks.

- Pretend your booktalk is about a work of fiction, and then surprise your audience with a "Sound fantastical, preposterous, unreal? This really happened. You can read about it in _____."

No matter what style you choose or what technique you prefer (don't worry, the hook and approach will come to you), always leave them hanging at the end. Make them run, not walk, to the closest library to check out the books depicting the true tales you've shared.

Samples of Successful Nonfiction Booktalks

Below are two booktalks for works of nonfiction that resulted in positive reactions from a wide range of young adults. I also have included an outline of the talks. When creating a booktalk, I write it out to get a handle on how I want to approach the booktalk, what questions I want to ask the audience, how I should build suspense and leave them hanging. After writing and reviewing my written booktalk, I create a brief outline that covers the main points of my talk. I review the outline in my car before going into the school. Creating and reviewing outlines of my booktalks helps me remember the main points of each talk and keeps them natural. It is especially useful when booktalking multiple titles for several classes all in one day.

John Fleischman, *Phineas Gage: A Gruesome but True Story about Brain Science* (Houghton Mifflin, 2002)

In 1848 a man named Phineas Gage suffered a horrible, gruesome accident in Vermont. The accident involved a tamping iron. What is a tamping iron? Anyone know? A tamping iron is a round tool that is two inches in diameter, three feet long, weighs about thirteen pounds, and ends in a sharp, narrow point. Well over one hundred years ago during the nineteenth century, men who worked on the railroad used tamping irons to set explosives. Why did they set explosives? To blast through rock, mountains, and anything else in the way of setting down railroad tracks. Phineas Gage used his tamping iron to set explosives on a regular basis. No big deal. But then, one day, something went terribly wrong. With the iron resting between his legs and the sharp end pointing directly toward his head as Phineas prepared to set an explosive, the iron suddenly shot off—exploded!—tearing through his left cheek, whizzing behind his left eye, and exiting through the front part of his brain. The iron left Phineas's head just as quickly as it had entered, taking a bit of his brain along with it. Believe it or not, Phineas was alive. The iron went completely through his skull, yet he did not lose consciousness. Right after the accident, Phineas was able to talk and move around just like everyone else. He even walked himself into town to get "stitched up" by the local doctor. But there wasn't much the doctor could do. The doctor said to himself, "Phineas surely will die!" Yet amazingly, Phineas lived for several years after the accident. But he wasn't the same Phineas. He was different—very different. And here the real story begins. (Good for younger YAs.)

Outline
1848
Phineas Gage
Gruesome accident
Tamping iron
Set explosives for RR
Something went wrong
Iron shot through head
Phineas OK
But not really

Marc Aronson, *Witch-Hunt: Mysteries of the Salem Witch Trials* (Atheneum, 2003)

What is a witch? Are witches real? In the late seventeenth century, the people who lived in Salem, the first town established in the Massachusetts Bay Colony in modern-day Massachusetts, thought that witches were indeed real. The colonists—called Puritans for their deeply religious, strict way of life—believed that witches were diabolical creatures who used magic to carry out the devil's evil work. Witches could curdle milk, hobble animals, and cause children to sicken and die. The Puritans wanted to purge all witches from society. More than three hundred years ago, the colonists of Salem discovered that witches were living among them, doing great evil. No one knows for certain how it all began. But in early 1692, nine-year-old Elizabeth Parris and her twelve-year-old cousin Abigail Williams started acting very strangely. Without warning and for no apparent reason, they suffered pinches and bites, their bodies twisted in unnatural ways, their throats choked, and they talked gibberish. Their invisible tormenters were a mystery to all. Soon other girls in Salem showed similar signs of affliction. Hysteria soon gripped the town, and the law had to step in. The girls began pointing fingers and assigning blame. They claimed that witchcraft was the cause of their anguish and that witches were living among the residents of Salem, masquerading as good Puritans. They could see and identify their tormentors, even though they remained invisible to the unaffected. When the girls named names, the good Puritans of Salem believed them. What followed was unimaginable, horrible. Hideous monsters, pacts with the devil, spirits, trials, condemnation, hangings, and death plagued this New England colony for an entire year. Was witchcraft really to blame for the girls' trouble? How did town leaders test the accused for signs of witchcraft? What happened to the accusers? (Good for older YAs.)

Outline
What is a witch?
Seventeenth-century Salem
Puritans
Witches evil and real
Elizabeth and Abigail attacked
Cause: witchcraft
Hysteria in town
Law stepped in
Girls accused some as being witches
Town believed
Witch trials
Why?

Finding Nonfiction Titles to Booktalk

Below is a bibliographic compilation of YA nonfiction titles. These works address topics and ideas that resonate with young adults and are pulled from YALSA's 2010 Award for Excellence in Nonfiction for Young Adults nomination list, the 2010 Best Books for Young Adults booklist, and the 2010 Quick Picks for Reluctant Young Adult Readers list.

Abrams, Dennis. *Rachael Ray: Food Entrepreneur.* Chelsea House, 2009.

Agard, John. *The Young Inferno.* Frances Lincoln Children's Books, 2009.

Allen, Thomas B., and Roger MacBride Allen. *Mr. Lincoln's High-Tech War.* National Geographic, 2008.

Alsenas, Linas. *Gay America: Struggle for Equality.* Abrams/Amulet, 2008.

Batten, Jack. *The War to End All Wars: The Story of World War I.* Tundra, 2009.

Bausum, Ann. *Denied, Detained, Deported: Stories from the Dark Side of American Immigration.* National Geographic, 2009.

Beckwith, Lois. *The Dictionary of High School B.S.: From Acne to Varsity, All the Funny, Lame, and Annoying Aspects of High School Life.* Orange Avenue, 2009.

Benson, Michael. *Beyond: A Solar System Voyage.* Abrams, 2009.

Bernier-Grand, Carmen T. *Diego: Bigger than Life.* Marshall Cavendish, 2009.

Blackshaw, Ric, and Liz Farrelly. *Street Art Book: 60 Artists in Their Own Words.* Collins, 2009.

Borgenicht, David. *The Worst-Case Scenario Survival Handbook: Middle School.* Chronicle, 2009.

Bright, J. E. *America's Next Top Model: Fierce Guide to Life: The Ultimate Source of Beauty, Fashion, and Model Behavior.* Universe, 2009.

Butzer, C. M. *Gettysburg: The Graphic Novel.* HarperCollins/Bowen, 2009.

Calcines, Eduardo F. *Leaving Glorytown: One Boy's Struggle under Castro.* Farrar, 2009.

Carlson, Laurie. *Harry Houdini for Kids: His Life and Adventures with 21 Magic Tricks and Illusions.* Chicago Review, 2009.

Chaikin, Andrew, and Victoria Kohl. *Mission Control, This Is Apollo: The Story of the First Voyages to the Moon.* Viking, 2009.

Cliver, Sean. *The Disposable Skateboard Bible.* Gingko, 2009.

Conley, Erin Elisabeth, Karen Macklin, and Jake Miller. *Crap: How to Deal with Annoying Teachers, Bosses, Backstabbers, and Other Stuff that Stinks.* Orange Avenue, 2009.

Cooper, Martha, and Henry Chalfant. *Subway Art: 25th Anniversary Edition.* Chronicle, 2009.

Davidson, Tony. *One-Track Mind: A Revealing Insight into the Obsessed Minds of Men.* Random House/Virgin, 2009.

Dubosarsky, Ursula. *The Word Snoop.* Dial, 2009.

Fagerstrom, Derek, and Lauren Smith. *Show Me How: 500 Things You Should Know; Instructions for Life from the Everyday to the Exotic.* Collins, 2008.

Fleming, Candace. *The Great and Only Barnum: The Tremendous, Stupendous Life of Showman P. T. Barnum.* Random/Schwartz & Wade, 2009.

Garza, Mario. *Stuff on My Mutt.* Chronicle, 2009.

Gavin, Francesca. *Hell Bound: New Goth Art.* Laurence King, 2008.

Girdler, Chris. *The Travel Book: A Journey through Every Country in the World.* Lonely Planet, 2008.

Gorrell, Gena K. *Say What?: The Weird and Mysterious Journey of the English Language.* Tundra, 2009.

Gray, Theodore. *The Elements: A Visual Exploration of Every Known Atom in the Universe.* Black Dog & Leventhal, 2009.

Hampton, Wilborn. *Babe Ruth.* Viking, 2009.

Happycat, Professor, and icanhascheezburger.com. *How to Take over teh Wurld: A LOLcat Guide 2 Winning.* Gotham, 2009.

———. *I Can Has Cheezburger?: A LOLcat Colleckshun.* Gotham, 2008.

Hart, Carey, and Chris Palmer. *Inked.* Artisan/Workman, 2008.

Heiligman, Deborah. *Charles and Emma: The Darwins' Leap of Faith.* Holt, 2009.

Heimber, Justin, and David Gomberg. *Would You Rather . . . ? Gross Out: Over 300 Disgusting Dilemmas Plus Extra Pages to Make Up Your Own!* Falls Media, 2008.

Hoose, Phillip. *Claudette Colvin: Twice toward Justice.* Farrar/Melanie Kroupa, 2009.

Hopper, Jessica. *The Girls' Guide to Rocking: How to Start a Band, Books Gigs, and Get Rolling to Rock Stardom.* Workman, 2009.

Horvath, David. *Ugly Guide to Being Alive and Staying that Way: Hi! It's the Uglydoll.* Random House, 2009.

Jacoby, Annice. *Street Art San Francisco: Mission Muralismo.* Abrams, 2009.

Jenisch, Josh. *Art of the Video Game.* Quirk, 2008.

Jurmain, Suzanne. *The Secret of the Yellow Death: A True Story of Medical Sleuthing.* Houghton, 2009.

Kaufman, Michael T. *1968*. Roaring Brook Press/Flash Point, 2009.

Komanoya, Rico. *Gothic Lolita Punk*. Collins, 2009.

Madden, Kerry. *Harper Lee*. Viking, 2009.

Mann, Charles C. *Before Columbus: The Americas of 1491*. Simon & Schuster/Atheneum, 2009.

Marrin, Albert. *Years of Dust: The Story of the Dust Bowl*. Dutton, 2009.

Martin, Russell, and Lydia Nibley. *The Mysteries of Beethoven's Hair*. Charlesbridge, 2009.

Mawji, Nasim, Chris Doherty, and Burt Jensen. *Hollywoof!: Celebrity Dogs Bite Back*. DK, 2009.

Metselaar, Menno, and Ruud Van der Rol. *Anne Frank: Her Life in Words and Pictures from the Archives of the Anne Frank House*. Roaring Brook, 2009.

Miller, Kerry. *Passive Aggressive Notes: Painfully Polite and Hilariously Hostile Writings from Shared Spaces the World Over*. HarperCollins, 2008.

Minguet, Eva. *Tattoo Delirium*. Collins, 2009.

Murphy, Jim. *Truce: The Day the Soldiers Stopped Fighting*. Scholastic, 2009.

Nardone, Tom. *Extreme Pumpkins II: Take Back Halloween and Freak out a Few More Neighbors*. Penguin Group/Home Book, 2008.

Nelson, Marilyn. *Sweethearts of Rhythm: The Story of the Greatest All-Girl Swing Band in the World*. Dial, 2009.

Noyes, Deborah. *Encyclopedia of the End: Mysterious Death in Fact, Fancy, Folklore, and More*. Houghton, 2008.

O'Brien, Anne Sibley, and Perry Edmond O'Brien. *After Gandhi: One Hundred Years of Nonviolent Resistance*. Charlesbridge, 2009.

O'Meara, Stephen James. *Are You Afraid Yet?: The Science behind Scary Stuff*. Kids Can Press, 2009.

Osborne, Linda Barrett. *Traveling the Freedom Road: From Slavery and the Civil War through Reconstruction*. Abrams, 2009.

Oser, Bodhi. *Fuck the World*. Chronicle Books, 2009.

Pahlow, Mark. *Who Would Buy This?: The Archie McPhee Story*. Accoutrements, 2008.

Palladini, Doug. *Vans: Off the Wall: Stories of Sole from Vans Originals*. Abrams, 2009.

Partridge, Elizabeth. *Marching for Freedom: Walk Together, Children, and Don't You Grow Weary*. Viking, 2009.

Pollan, Michael, and Richie Chevat. *The Omnivore's Dilemma: The Secrets behind What You Eat*. Dial, 2009.

Raczka, Bob. *The Vermeer Interviews: Conversations with Seven Works of Art*. Millbrook, 2009.

Reef, Catherine. *Ernest Hemingway: A Writer's Life*. Clarion, 2009.

Regan, Sally. *The Vampire Book*. DK, 2009.

Renn, Crystal. *Hungry: A Young Model's Story of Appetite, Ambition, and the Ultimate Embrace of Curves*. Simon & Schuster, 2009.

Rubin, Susan. *The Anne Frank Case: Simon Wiesenthal's Search for the Truth*. Holiday, 2009.

Sandler, Martin W. *The Secret Subway: The Fascinating Tale of an Amazing Feat of Engineering*. National Geographic, 2009.

Smithson, Ryan. *Ghosts of War: The True Story of a 19-Year-Old GI*. Collins, 2009.

Seventeen Magazine. *Mega Traumarama!: Real Girls and Guys Confess More of Their Most Mortifying Moments!* Hearst, 2009.

Shields, Brian, and Kevin Sullivan. *WWE Encyclopedia: The Definitive Guide to World Wrestling Entertainment*. Brady Games/DK, 2009.

Small, David. *Stitches: A Memoir*. Norton, 2009.

Smith, John. *Inked: Clever, Odd and Outrageous Tattoos*. teNeues, 2008.

Smith, Larry, and Rachel Fershleiser. *I Can't Keep My Own Secrets: Six-Word Memoirs by Teens Famous and Obscure*. HarperTeen, 2009.

St. George, Judith. *The Duel: The Parallel Lives of Alexander Hamilton and Aaron Burr*. Viking, 2009.

Stenning, Paul. *The Robert Pattinson Album*. Plexus, 2009.

Stone, Tanya Lee. *Almost Astronauts: 13 Women Who Dared to Dream*. Candlewick, 2009.

Stutts, Ryan. *The Skateboarding Field Manual.* Firefly, 2009.

Su, Lac. *I Love Yous Are for White People: A Memoir.* Harper Perennial, 2009.

Swanson, James L. *Chasing Lincoln's Killer.* Scholastic, 2009.

Turner, Pamela S. *The Frog Scientist.* Houghton, 2009.

———. *A Life in the Wild: George Schaller's Struggle to Save the Last Great Beasts.* Farrar/Melanie Kroupa, 2008.

Turner, Tracey. *Deadly Perils: And How to Avoid Them.* Walker, 2009.

Von D, Kat. *High Voltage Tattoo.* HarperCollins, 2009.

Walker, Sally M. *Written in Bone: Buried Lives of Jamestown and Colonial Maryland.* Carolrhoda, 2009.

Warren, Andrea. *Under Siege!: Three Children at the Civil War Battle for Vicksburg.* Farrar/Melanie Kroupa, 2009.

Willin, Melvyn. *Paranormal Caught on Film.* David and Charles, 2008.

Booktalking Tips

Getting Started

- Pinpoint which schools fall under your purview.
- Gather contact information for those schools.
- Write a letter of introduction to send to school librarians.
- Follow up your correspondence with phone calls.
- Schedule a time to meet with school librarians to discuss YA services.

- Discuss booktalking in classrooms, at class assemblies, or via school news.
- Schedule booktalking visits.
- Start booktalking!

Preparing the Booktalk

- Approach your booktalk as an advertisement.
- Introduce the characters and plot in a creative, suspenseful way.
- Build up to the most compelling part of the story, then leave a cliffhanger.
- Do not reveal major plot points or resolutions.
- Prepare an attention-grabbing opening and closing.
- Write out your talk and create an outline.
- Don't memorize your talk.
- Incorporate visuals: images from books, props, and so on.
- Booktalk a variety of genres.

Delivering the Booktalk

- Limit your booktalk to three to five minutes.
- Review your outline before the talk.
- Open your talk with a few questions.
- Make eye contact.
- Walk around the room, gesture, and change your facial expressions.
- Ad lib: keep it natural and free-flowing.
- Bring a variety of materials to display: magazines, CDs, audiobooks, DVDs, and so on.
- Before you start, tell your audience that if they listen closely, they will earn prizes—for example, candy, bookmarks, temporary tattoos, mood pencils—for correctly answering questions about your booktalk.

FIFTY WAYS TO PROMOTE TEEN READING IN YOUR SCHOOL LIBRARY

C. D. McLean

When I want to know how to promote reading to teens, I go to the fount of school library knowledge: independent school librarians! In recognition of YALSA's fiftieth anniversary, these fifty tips, hints, ideas, and techniques from independent school librarians across the United States and Canada will give many young adult librarians a successful start in promoting reading to their teen patrons for the next fifty years.

First Step: Be Adventurous!

1. Step out of your comfort zone and promote something other than fiction. Many teens (boys especially) are not fiction readers; they may be more interested in your magazine collection. Let your teens know which magazines are available in their library.

2. Remember those reluctant readers. Promote Quick Picks for Reluctant YA Readers as "Fast Reads," which is less pejorative. Have a spinner filled with Fast Reads and label it as such. One librarian uses neon-green labels for easy identification of Fast Reads.

3. Get graphic. Graphic novels are appropriate for boys and girls, tweens and teens. Many times they appeal to students who wouldn't ordinarily pick up a book. If you have concerns about age appropriateness and have a collection that serves both middle and high school students, you can always break out the collection by division or grade level.

4. Think outside the book club box. An anime club can lead to a manga or graphic novel club; strategic games or MMORPGs (massively multiplayer online role-playing games) can lead to a fantasy book club; and a writing or an author club can lead to reading about writing or reading a particular writer's work.

5. Create some library leaders. Make the library in your school a place for young leaders to develop their skills. They can run your circulation desk,

shelve books, and more.

6. Spotlight poetry. Sponsor a poetry slam contest or partner with your school's literary magazine to host an event.

7. Have a "Book Love" session once a month. Serve cookies and ask teachers and students to talk about a book they have recently read and liked.

8. Write about books. Consider reviewing for a young adult magazine and have your students review as well. Sometimes the lure of seeing their name in print may push them to read more books.

9. Appeal to boys and competitive students. Have a word reading club and stand back and watch the numbers grow! Some librarians have reported that they have several students who read more than a million words in one school year.

Second Step: Be Bold!

10. Put your cool stuff up front. I have my graphic novel collection near the front entrance of the library. Other librarians use that high-traffic area to promote their magazine collection.

11. Books don't have to stay on the shelves. One librarian puts high-interest books next to her computers, and those books circulate.

12. Use the lure of the forbidden. Tell them a book is banned or controversial, or just give them some of the crazy details (for example, boyfriend is on crack and parents are abusive) and a questioning "Are you up to the challenge?" look.

13. Tie the book to a movie. If a movie is based on a book, you have an automatic tie-in; but don't be afraid to go beyond the specific book and, for example, tie in the Dragonriders of Pern series with *Eragon*.

14. Make mine a contest. Have a book-related contest featuring a work such as Harry Potter or the last book (*The End*) of Lemony Snicket's A Series of Unfortunate Events.

This article originally appeared in the Fall 2007 issue of *YALS*.

15. Pimp your contest prizes. Book gift certificates are great, but go with whatever will draw your kids into the library, such as gift cards for coffee, iTunes, or local eateries.

16. Make your prize match your audience. One librarian at a school for girls has a special bracelet for her seventh-grade *Gone with the Wind* (GWTW) readers. If they read all one thousand pages, they get a GWTW bracelet, which has been very well received!

17. Mix it up. Instead of holding separate book clubs for students and faculty, have them both at one meeting. You'll be rewarded with amazing discussions.

Step Three: Marketing Is Key!

18. Take advantage of schoolwide meetings. Berkeley Preparatory School has a convocation every morning with twenty minutes of announcements. There is always at least one slide on a new book in the slide show of announcements. YALSA offers scripts on the Teen Read Week website (www. ala.org/teenread) for public service announcements, which you can adapt.

19. Make your booktalks a blast. Several librarians dress in character when giving booktalks. So indulge your inner actor!

20. Use props. Props can bring your booktalks to life.

21. Use student actors to do your booktalks. Teens are more likely to listen to their peers.

22. Podcast or tape your booktalks. Don't just present to a class; make a video and keep it on your library's website. Better yet, ask your teens to create podcasts of themselves talking up their favorite books.

23. Move 'em out. Prepare a book truck with brightly colored graphics indicating the genre and filled with popular books; take it out to the cafeteria, study halls, or anywhere students gather.

24. Create short films. Promote the library using faculty and student actors in a video you can post on your library's website.

25. Celebrate Teen Read Week in whatever manner works for you. For example, because Teen Read Week falls in October, have teens read Halloween stories to primary school students.

Fourth Step: Be Organized!

26. Make it a point to promote your new books. Make sure a significant percentage of books get a book blurb and are on display to generate interest.

27. Print out posters. Use posters of newly acquired books and post them throughout the campus (including the restroom stalls!).

28. Change your bulletin boards frequently and make them interesting. It's easy for bulletin boards to become stagnant and easy to ignore.

29. Create bookmarks. Have your students and faculty contribute reviews and make those reviews into bookmarks. The bookmarks could have their photo, the book's cover, and a snippet of their opinion on the book.

30. Make your e-mail signature line an advertisement. Update your signature file on your e-mail account with a "What I'm Reading Now" tag and encourage your faculty and teens to do it as well.

31. Use promotional materials. If you go to ALA Midwinter Meetings or Annual Conferences, bring back the advanced reader copies and give them out to your students. They love free books, and you can get advanced reviews of books.

32. Give out books. If your budget permits, be willing to buy books for your book club members. Free books are a great draw.

33. Create perks for book club members. Let your book club kids get first crack at the new books. Knowing they are getting special treatment is a big plus for teens.

Fifth Step: Be Welcoming!

34. Throw book parties. Make the library a welcoming place by hosting parties designed to attract readers. One library had an *Eclipse* Read-In on August 7, 2007, when Stephenie Meyer's new book was released. They had games, prizes, readings, vampire movies, and even a vampire potluck lunch. (For more information on this program, visit http://hhlibrarytwilight.blogspot.com.)

35. Try non-book-related events. Remember that teens gravitate to online social activities, so by hosting a *Dance Dance Revolution* (DDR) night, gaming night, or *Guitar Hero* night, you may attract kids who might not normally come to the library.

36. Appeal to teen writers. What's that they say about writers being readers? Host an Eat 'n' Speak or a poetry slam. Teens are always writing; what better way to get them into the library than to have them read their own works?

37. Bring in authors. An author visit may spark interest in reading more of that author's work or inspire a teen to read or write.

38. Celebrate Banned Books Week. Feature banned books and appeal to the lure of the forbidden.

39. Celebrate National Poetry Month. Bring in a poet to speak during National Poetry Month. Many English teachers are more open to using a particular poet's work than they are to using an entire book in their curriculum.

40. Offer snacks. If you provide food, they will come. You don't need to have a full meal; try providing just dessert or pizza. For example, if you are reading a book that has a wedding, consider getting a faux (meaning less expensive) wedding cake for dessert.

41. Kick-start your summer. Host a summer book fair before school ends to encourage reading over the summer.

42. Waive fines. If you charge late fines, be willing to take money off if they come into the library and read. (For example, give fifty cents off the fine for every half hour of reading in the library.)

Sixth Step: Be Willing to Ask for Help!

43. Let teens lead. Have your students lead the book club discussion or pick the book.

44. Use blogs. Have your students run your book discussion blog.

45. Highlight readers' favorite books. Have a faculty or student Pick of the Week or Month. Display it all over campus, not just in the library.

46. Use social networking sites. Ask your students or tech department for help in creating a Facebook or MySpace page (or do it yourself), and list what you are reading or what books you recommend.

47. Get teen input. Ask your students what titles they think are missing from the library, then buy them if appropriate.

48. Have a bookstore field trip. Take your students to the bookstore with you. Several librarians take students with them to help pick or review materials for the library.

49. Involve teachers. Ask your faculty to sponsor a book for summer reading. Many students will want to read what their favorite teacher is reading.

50. Harness teens' creativity. Get your students to create the displays and bulletin boards. They know what's hot and may have a more interesting way of presenting information.

TEEN READ WEEK COLLABORATION

Megan Fink

Laughter can boost your endorphins, lower your blood pressure and heart rate, and improve your immune system, not to mention lighten your mood.[1] With that in mind, create an environment where teens can enter their school and public libraries for a visit that will produce a smile and improve their health! Communication, collaboration, and implementation are the three most important components of a successful Teen Read Week celebration at a school or public library.

Communication and Collaboration

The most important aspect of Teen Read Week is to talk to your students and your teen patrons about what they like. It sounds simple, but successful YA programming consists of activities that teens enjoy—and who is a better expert than your target audience? If you don't have a teen advisory board or teen book club, ask your frequent patrons and students what they would like for a Teen Read Week party. Explain the ideas behind Teen Read Week, offer them some examples, and

This article originally appeared in the Summer 2007 issue of *YALS*.

let them suggest activities. One of my eighth-grade students suggested this teen-friendly activity: Host a movie trivia contest where you use quotations from famous comedies (such as *Napoleon Dynamite*) and teens have to guess which movie they're from, à la *Jeopardy!* rules. Buy prizes with the money from the copy machine.

For events, try backward planning: in other words, know where you want to end up on Teen Read Week with teen events and then start planning in August. If you're a public librarian, ask the principal or the school media specialist at your local middle or high school if you can visit during a workday and discuss Teen Read Week events coming up in October. Then meet with the school media specialist and coordinate events. School librarians should contact their local public libraries and ask for the YA librarian or teen services director. According to Michele Gorman, teen services/library supervisor at ImaginOn in Charlotte, North Carolina, a "communicative partnership" is the first step for successful collaboration and involves sharing information about Teen Read Week for the benefit of both school and public libraries.

Likewise, school librarians can promote literacy with Teen Read Week and highlight new genres with their students. Teen Read Week can even serve to enhance the school library's mission of supporting the school curriculum. Standard 5 from Information Power states that "the student who is an independent learner is information literate and appreciates literature and other creative expressions of information."[2] The tenets of Teen Read Week from YALSA highlight the same goal of promoting teen literacy, which intersects with many middle and high school English classes and their collaborations with the school library. From the simple to the superb, these activities are suggestions to celebrate Teen Read Week in a school or public library.

Implementation and Activities

These activities can be used with virtually any Teen Read Week theme.

- **Soundtracks:** Ask students to select their favorite books. Their assignment is to make up soundtracks for the books. They can compile any type of music or songs. Have them bring in CDs and iPods with their books' soundtracks. Then ask the group to compare them. While this activity can be used on a variety of books or on the same book, students should be able to explain why certain songs belong with certain chapters, plots, and characters of the book.[3]
- **Films:** Host a themed movie festival with snacks.
- **Cartooning:** Invite local artists and amateur cartoonists to submit their creations and hang them in the library. Host an open house and display their cartoons. Teach teens how to use animation software like Flash to create a short animated cartoon. Then have a cartoon marathon, projecting them on a big screen. Include old cartoons as well as new favorites.
- **Improv night:** Invite a local improv group to teach kids how to act, or ask the drama teacher from the local school to help instruct.
- **Can you judge a book by its cover?** Copy twenty book covers and the blurbs on the back and inside flap. Then create false blurbs for those same twenty books. Let the students decide which is the true blurb and which is false and why.[4]
- **Game night:** Use board games such as Catch Phrase, Balderdash, or Guesstures.
- **Wacky Olympics:** Make up a series of Wacky Olympic challenges. Go through an obstacle course with "X-ray glasses" on and try to beat the other teams. Use other gag games where you have to perform with your opposite arm or leg, such as the Flingshot Flying Chicken.[5]
- **Video contest:** Invite teens to make a funny short video like *Whose Line Is It Anyway?* where a group acts out a scene, incorporating audience-suggested lines on pieces of paper given to them. Show the winning video during Teen Read Week celebrations.
- **Carnival:** Have a dunk tank, pie-throwing contest, sumo wrestling, gladiator joust, bungee run, or other carnival-type event. Most of these activities require a rental, but parent-teacher associations are a possible source, or propose that the public library partner with the school.

Libraries are known as sources of information, but doing something fun and out of the ordinary during Teen Read Week may improve teenagers' health. According to *Psychology Today*, "Laughter may also improve our mood through social means. Telling a joke, particularly one that illuminates a shared experience or problem, increases our sense of 'belonging and social cohesion,'" thus improving the mood of your everyday stressed-out teen.[6]

NOTES

1. Peter Doskoch, "Happily Ever Laughter," *Psychology Today*, July/August 1996, http://psychologytoday.com/articles/pto-19960701-000032.html (accessed February 27, 2007).

2. American Association of School Librarians, *Information Power: Building Partnerships for Learning* (Chicago: ALA Editions, 1998), 26.

3. British Council, "Teenage Reading Group Ideas," http://www.encompassculture.com/readinggroups/readinggroupideas/teenagergideas/ (accessed October 8, 2010).

4. Ibid.

5. Flingshot Flying Chicken available from Gag Works, www.gagworks.com (accessed October 8, 2010).

6. Doskoch, "Happily Ever Laughter."

POPULAR CULTURE AND TEENS

Kimberlee Ried and Kaite Mediatore Stover

In 2002 the television show 8 *Simple Rules for Dating My Teenage Daughter* brought up the idea that being a teenager is similar to being a member of the Mafia. Bridget, the sixteen-year-old daughter, says, "[Teen life] is a highly structured secret society with its own set of rules and consequences." Go against the norm in the world of adolescents and you may not have a run-in with Tony Soprano, but to some teens that may be preferable to going to school each morning.

It's a secret world these teens live in, one that adults will never penetrate, and we're not welcome anyway. Incredibly enough, we were all once inhabitants of the same secret society. However, one of the requirements of being a member of the tribe is that you don't recognize anyone outside of it, even former members. It's a society with current membership only, no matter how recently you've left the club. And yet when we work at it, we can all remember what it was like to be the smartest flunking student in a class or the most uncoordinated member of the seventh-period volleyball team. We all have a defining teenage moment we reach for when recalling "the best years of our lives." It's the one that makes us cringe and feel grateful we're grown-ups.

There are universal concerns among teens that exist from culture to culture and generation to generation: acceptance (both peer and self-), love, friendship, school, and the future, to name a few. Only the cultural regalia that help teens come to terms with these issues change, and these are the items that are teen-specific: slang, clothes, idols, books, television, movies, and that catchall known as "stuff." These trappings are the only clues that some of us are likely to get to tell us who today's teens are and what is important to them.

Keeping Up with the Teenses

Serving this special population is difficult for anyone who works with teens, but more so for librarians. Library staff are already working against a built-in "uncool" stereotype. Pop culture is one of the ways that librarians communicate with teens to get them into the library. We'll never be "cool," but we don't have to be "dorky" and "lame."

Every generation has its defining moments—some are historical; some are political. But generally these moments are of a more ephemeral nature and usually superficial. The vast majority of the current teen references to pop culture expire quickly. There seems to always be an entirely new vocabulary in vogue among adolescents.

To reach teens, the adults who work with them must constantly stay on top of their world. But do keep in mind that no matter how deeply the teen culture is studied, the "anthropologists" will never become members of the tribe.

Keeping up with the latest in teens' social lives is an industry unto itself. The term "teenager" didn't become popular in the media until the 1940s and was coined by Madison Avenue advertising executives looking to pitch products to an emerging market. Teens have been a commercial business ever since. In 1982 Peter

This article originally appeared in the Fall 2003 issue of YALS.

Zollo cofounded Teenage Research Unlimited, the first market research firm to specialize exclusively in teenagers. In the second edition of *Wise Up to Teens*, Zollo writes that teenagers have more buying power than any other group in the nation and combined can spend almost half of the defense budget for the United States. The economy may rise and fall, but teens will always have money to spend on clothes, music, cosmetics, cars, fast food, movies, video games, cell phones, computer equipment—and the list goes on. These are the items that most readily come to mind when listing the most advertised products.

As long as teenagers have enough money to drive the segments of the economy that contribute to popular culture icons and trends, they will always get to call the shots.

How to Stay Current When Nobody's Watching

Staying current is the easiest and most entertaining work-related activity for YA librarians. Imagine telling your coworkers that watching MTV or reading teen magazines or websites is necessary to your job. But you'll never know what the teens are listening to, watching, or reading if you don't listen, watch, and read the same things. Perusing YA reading material will also help in collection development and reading recommendations.

Publishers will always put out a paperback biography of the latest hot young television, movie, and music stars. You'll never know who those folks are if you don't watch (or at least surf) the same shows, read the reviews of the movies (don't go if you think you won't like them), or listen to Top Forty stations. Most of the information that YA librarians and specialists need about teen preferences is already out there.

Librarians can help teens by recognizing their particular culture. Collection development, programs, teen spaces, and perceived attitudes toward adolescents are all areas that youth service personnel should address. There are numerous ways to stay on top of the teen lifestyle. Make the effort to read young adult books and magazines, many of which are of excellent quality as literature. An easier way to be "in the know" is to observe the teens who frequent your library or community. Pay attention to how they dress, what they check out—or better yet, ask their opinions!

In the Stacks

Teens may not want to talk to adults, but they like it when we ask for their opinions. Use the same techniques with teens as you would with adults, just tone it down. We are usually so thrilled to be approached by a teen for a leisure reading recommendation that we may tend to let our enthusiasm control the transaction. Think like a teen and be cool.

Offer assistance whenever you see a teenager in the stacks. Teens don't like to admit to a stranger that they may need help. Be sensitive to their feelings and listen carefully to what the teen tells you. Don't suggest a book that doesn't come close to what the student describes. Teens do know what they want, and most don't like to deviate from their preferred authors and genres. If you do want to suggest something different, be certain to make connections between the asked-for material and the suggested title. This technique can be very handy for making a connection between what's hot and trendy in the pop culture world and what your library actually has on its shelves. Sometimes passive readers' advisory with young adults is the least offensive method and gets the best results.

Have booklists on interesting topics, particularly those relating to any pop culture reference, ready for teens to take with them or use for browsing the collection. Sometimes just having a list makes choosing materials easier for teens. Narrowing the choices down still gives the teen control over what he or she is reading without being intimidated by a large collection.

Bookmarks are handy little readers' advisory devices. Teens probably won't use them for their intended purpose, but with a short list of suggested titles coupled with the library's hours and phone number, it's a nice reminder of a place where teens are welcome. As an incentive to encourage teen input, make a contest out of the bookmarks. Design some with pop culture questions that test their knowledge. Then offer a prize (movie tickets are always enticing) as the incentive for participating.

Have lots of displays on topics interesting to teens and be sure to change them regularly. Design eye-catching, colorful displays that relate to a hot topic in the news or in their world. Cover art is the first thing any reader notices, teen or adult. Try to separate genres within the YA collection. Put the series novels together. This is to your benefit as well as the readers'.

Lastly, if you have the space, make a teen-friendly

area in your library with comfy chairs, low shelving, and lots of magazines and paperbacks. This is a prime opportunity to showcase the latest in pop culture for teens. Display those posters of famous stars; order them from ALA Graphics or tear them out of the magazines before they get ripped out by a patron. If you can't put aside a specific space, then designate some shelving for YAs only. Keep it as neat as possible. Although teens tend to be messy, there's no bigger turnoff than a sloppy bookshelf. And finally, if you have the funds, make sure you have a collection of CDs as well as comic books, graphic novels, and magazines for teens to check out.

You Can't Go Home Again

Does this mean you need to vegetate every Saturday night for three hours in front of MTV? No. Being aware of the popular teen culture touchstones doesn't require total immersion. But don't touch that radio dial when some pop star starts singing about words for body parts that you've never heard before. You'll need to know what it is when a youthful patron comes in asking about it.

EASY ON THE EYES: LARGE PRINT BOOKS FOR TEENS
Elizabeth Burns

Large print books—those are for when you get older! Teenagers are lucky—they don't have to worry about small newspaper print or hard-to-read menus. Except some do! Teenagers with low vision or reading disabilities and those who are reluctant readers need large print books. Statistics for teenagers with low vision can be hard to find. Lighthouse International says that "3 percent of individuals age six and older, representing 7.9 million people, have difficulty seeing words and letters in ordinary newspaper print even when wearing glasses or contact lenses."[1]

Teenagers with dyslexia and reading disabilities also benefit from books with a larger type size.[2] Wesley Yandell Jr. reported on the success of using large print in *School Library Journal*:

> Larger print is easier on students' eyes, something that may be a factor with kids who have undiagnosed vision problems. There may be a psychological factor as well. When kids first learn to read, they use large print. As their reading acuity grows, the type size shrinks, and some students may perceive the smaller print as harder to read. The use of large print may unconsciously help them return to their earlier learning experiences, when they perceived reading as easier and more enjoyable.[3]

As explained by the National Library Service for the Blind and Physically Handicapped (NLS), the minimum type size for large print is 14 point, but most large print books are in 16- or 18-point type. Novels are in 10- to 12-point type, and newspapers are often printed in 8-point type.[4] Isabel Warren-Lynch, executive art director for Random House Children's Books, says that picture books are printed in 16- to 24-point type—and up! Middle grade books are in 14-point type.[5] As teenagers leave behind children's books, they find that print, literally, gets smaller. Reading can turn from fun to being a chore.

Commercial large print publishers don't always carry young adult titles. Thorndike Press publishes at least two young adult books each month.[6] The Library Reproduction Service Large Print School Books and InfoCon publish a large number of books for teens and also provide "large print on demand" for titles that cannot be found elsewhere. Prices can vary widely, with on-demand services costing more. Resources listed in the sidebar have more information about some of the numerous sources for large print books, newspapers, and magazines.

The Amazon Kindle and Sony Reader eBooks allow users to increase the type size of any book to 20 points, turning a regular book into large print at no additional cost.

You don't need to have everything in your collection—you just need to help your teens find sources for large print. Some NLS regional libraries—

This article originally appeared in the Fall 2009 issue of YALS.

including the New Jersey State Library's Talking Books & Braille Center and the Wolfner Library for the Blind and Physically Handicapped—have large print books available. A teen who is eligible for NLS services may be able to borrow large print titles from their NLS regional library.

Large print isn't something teenagers want—it's something they need. Libraries can meet that need by helping teenagers find those books. Large print is not just for seniors!

Large Print Resources

For more information about large print reading materials, visit some of these websites:

- National Library Service for the Blind and Physically Handicapped, Library of Congress, *Reading Materials in Large Print: A Resource Guide*, www.loc.gov/nls/reference/circulars/largeprint.html
- Texas School for the Blind and Visually Impaired, Large Print Suppliers and Publishers, www.tsbvi.edu/Education/lpsuppliers.htm

Large Print Young Adult Publishers

- American Printing House for the Blind, http://shop.aph.org
- InfoCon Large Print Books, www.infocon-inc.com
- Library Reproduction Service, large print schoolbooks, https://largeprintschoolbooks.com
- Thorndike Press, thorndike.gale.com

NOTES

1. Lighthouse International, "Prevalence of Vision Impairment," www.lighthouse.org/research/statistics-on-visionimpairment/prevalence (accessed July 1, 2009).
2. Learning Disabilities Association of America, "Dyslexia," www.ldanatl.org/aboutld/parents/ld_basics/dyslexia.asp (accessed July 1, 2009).
3. Wesley Yandell Jr., "Big Is Beautiful: For Struggling Readers, Large-Print Books May Make a Huge Difference," *School Library Journal*, April 1, 2007, www.schoollibraryjournal.com/article/CA6430170.html (accessed July 1, 2009).
4. National Library Service for the Blind and Physically Handicapped, Library of Congress, "Reading Materials in Large Print: A Resource Guide," NLS Reference Circular, 2005, www.loc.gov/nls/reference/circulars/largeprint.html (accessed July 1, 2009).
5. Isabel Warren-Lynch (executive art director for Random House Children's Books), personal communication with author, June 5, 2009.
6. Thorndike Press, Large Print and Reading Independence, thorndike.gale.com (accessed July 1, 2009).

GET CONNECTED WITH TEEN TECH WEEK

Linda Braun

When Teen Tech Week (TTW) launched in 2007, the library world was still learning about the role that the collaborative web and social media played in teen access to and creation of information. In June 2006, less than a year before YALSA launched TTW, MySpace became the most popular social networking site in the United States.[1] Since then, the world has seen Facebook take off as the primary social networking space for many teens and adults. And in that time librarians, parents, and educators have learned a lot more about why social networking, social media, and the collaborative web are of interest to young people.

Research continues to shed light on teen use of technology and the role that adults play in that use. For example:

- In April 2010 the Pew Internet & American Life Project published a report on teens and mobile phones. The project's research found that "daily text messaging among American teens has shot up in the past 18 months, from 38 percent of teens texting friends daily in February of 2008 to 54 percent of teens texting daily in September 2009."[2]

- In June 2010 a report from the Online Technology Working Group, which presented their findings to Congress, found "that the best way to assure youth safety on the Internet 'points to the growing importance of online citizenship and media-literacy education, in addition to what has come to be seen as online safety education, as solutions to youth risk online.'"[3]

- Another report from the Pew Internet & American Life Project, published in May 2010, looked at how people manage their reputations online and found that younger people—eighteen- to twenty-four-year-olds—were more likely than older people who used social networking spaces to spend time making sure that the information posted online about them was accurate and what should be available in an online social network setting.[4]

What's clear from all of the recent reports is that adults do play a part in helping young people, children and teens, understand how to be safe and smart when using technology. This research also demonstrates that adults need to understand how teens use technology to be able to provide the best support and education possible. For example, if teens already know that they need to manage their online profiles, librarians don't need to spend time talking to them about the importance of that action, Instead librarians need to provide information on how to use the tools available for managing privacy and profile content.

TTW launched as an initiative to assist librarians in highlighting the need to help teens use technology successfully. One key aspect of that is demonstrating to other adults in the community that for teens to be smart about technology, they need to have opportunities to use technology. While we do know a lot more about teen technology use now, there is still a need for this aspect of TTW as schools and libraries continue to limit teens' access to technology tools. As a result, teens don't always have the training and education they need to be effective users of technology when outside of the school setting.

TTW also provides a perfect opportunity for informing adults in the community about teen use of technology and to show off new tools that teens are using successfully for creation, collaboration, and information gathering. Consider the rise of interest in book trailers. When TTW launched in 2007, book trailers were perhaps only a glimmer in most technology user's eyes. However, with the rise of easy-to-use and inexpensive digital video cameras, and the availability of easy-to-use, web-based film-editing tools, producing movies as a way to get the word out about books in the library collection became not just a possibility, but a reality. Librarians who sponsor book trailer contests as a part of TTW activities give teens, librarians, and communities the opportunity to learn about the technology and see it in action.

Using technology to create book trailers is probably fun for a lot of teens, but the technology and creation of these trailers also provides librarians with opportunities to talk with teens about using published materials—music, images, and text—legally and in ways that don't infringe on an author's or artist's copyright. By talking with teens about copyright as a part of the book trailer production cycle, librarians get to make the connection to copyright with teens in a context that is meaningful at the moment.

Making technology meaningful when the moment is right is something that librarians have learned is critical in helping teens to become skilled users of technology. TTW helps with this by providing ideas to librarians on how best to integrate technology into their programs and services, and by providing best practices, resources, program ideas, and more to those supporting teen technology interests and needs.

Over the past several years, *YALS* articles on TTW and technology have provided inspiration to a lot of librarians looking for ways to support teen technology use. Inspiration is what you'll find in this section of this book. Use the ideas here to launch or expand the programs you provide in the library that incorporate technology, and by doing so you will help provide teens with what they need to be adept technology users.

NOTES

1. *Wikipedia*, "MySpace," http://en.wikipedia.org/wiki/Myspace (accessed November 12, 2010).

2. Amanda Lenhart et al. "Teens and Mobile Phones," *Pew Internet and American Life Project*, www.pewinternet.org/Reports/2010/Teens-and-Mobile-Phones.aspx (accessed October 9, 2010).

3. Online Safety and Technology Working Group, "Youth Safety on a Living Internet," www.ntia.doc.gov/reports/2010/OSTWG_Final_Report_070610.pdf (accessed November 12, 2010).

4. Mary Madden and Aaron Smith, "Reputation Management and Social Media" http://www.pewinternet.org/Reports/2010/Reputation-Management.aspx (accessed November 12, 2010).

BEST PRACTICES FOR
TEEN TECH WEEK

IN THIS CHAPTER, find ideas to create tech-focused volunteer programs for teens at your library, rev up your online homework help, and more. From a teen tech squad that utilizes teens as technology experts to booktalking research in a high school library, these ideas are adaptable to utilize in many different libraries.

HENNEPIN COUNTY LIBRARY'S TEEN TECH SQUAD: YOUTH LEADERSHIP AND TECHNOLOGY FREE-FOR-ALL

Cynthia Matthias and Christy Mulligan

In the library meeting room, an air of controlled chaos reigns. In one corner, teens are hunched around a computer arguing heatedly about where exactly an audio track should end. In another corner, two teens are discussing the merits of different supernatural powers as they draw the main player character in the game they are designing. Next to them, a boy enhances a photograph he is going to import into a comic that he is creating. The door opens and an elementary school–aged boy pokes his head in: "What y'all doin' in here?" A teen employee hurries forward to invite the boy in and get him started drawing with a drawing tablet. This is what a typical Teen Tech Squad workshop looks like at Hennepin County Library.

Tech Squad a Model for Youth Leadership

In 2006 the former Minneapolis Public Library (now

merged with Hennepin County Library) hired its first Teen Tech Squad—a group of four paid teen employees who led technology workshops aimed at teens and school-aged children. Three years later, the program has evolved into a model opportunity for youth leadership and twenty-first-century skill building that can be adapted and used by libraries large and small. This opportunity is a perfect fit with Hennepin County Library's priority of helping youths succeed and preparing them to be vital contributors to our community. Many workshops are informal, allowing kids to drop in and spend as little or as much time as they wish on a wide range of technology projects from game and animation creation to sound recording and editing, stop-motion animation, and more.

Although teen interns hosting these programs have received training in many of the software programs used, they never claim to be experts. This creates a perfect environment for building literacy skills like

This article originally appeared in the Winter 2010 issue of *YALS*.

collaboration, communication, problem solving, and technological fluency.

Workshops focus on using free open-source software programs—welcome news to libraries as well as participants, who can build on and share projects outside of the library program. Finally, thanks to funding from the Best Buy Children's Foundation, Hennepin County Library is able to offer a much-needed employment opportunity to teens in the community. Teen Tech Squad interns will frequently say they would do it for free, but we know this job is creating an important and impressive first step on that career ladder.

The Teen Tech Squad has now expanded to three libraries—two within the city of Minneapolis and one in suburban Hennepin County. Each squad consists of four teen employees who are supervised by the teen or youth services librarian in their library. Although supervision is critical in helping these youths develop both leadership and job skills, much of the program's success can be attributed to the fact that interns work as a team to determine and evaluate the content and structure of the workshops they host.

Preparing for a Workshop

Team members meet before each workshop to create an outline and tip sheets for software programs, prepare examples, and pull together materials they will need. Each session is followed up with a briefing session, in which interns talk with their supervisor about successes, challenges, and ways that the program could be adapted in the future. These meeting sessions have been critical in shaping and adapting the program over the past three years. Team members may learn about a new software program from a workshop participant or receive feedback about activities that should be added to the program. Supervisors discuss these new ideas and help teams determine how new content can be integrated into open labs; they also tailor trainings to help them build the skills they need.

The workshops themselves take on a variety of formats. Most are informal, drop-in "Open Tech Labs," in which Teen Tech Squad members set up laptop computers loaded with a variety of software programs for participants to use. Tech Squad members work with participants to help them try out these programs or work through a project they have already started. Tech Squad members do, on occasion, schedule

more formal workshops that focus on teaching a specific program or activity (stop-motion animation, for example). These focused sessions are an effective way for Tech Squad members to introduce regular participants to new programs they have learned in training sessions with teachers from the Science Museum of Minnesota. Some workshops take place in library meeting rooms; others take place at tables in the public area of the library. Workshops are aimed at teens but open to interested participants of all ages. In all cases, Tech Squad members foster an environment where questions are encouraged, collaboration is key, and the goal is to experiment with new tools.

Continuing Education Strengthens the Squad

In addition to leading workshops, Tech Squad members have monthly continuing ed meetings. Continuing ed training may be with Learning Technologies Center staff from the Science Museum or simply a chance for the teens to brainstorm ideas. Training from the Learning Technologies Center staff allows Tech Squad members to learn about new technology tools, discuss instructional techniques, and share challenges they have faced in workshops with experienced teachers. In addition to these training sessions, supervisors schedule a monthly team meeting, in which interns spend three hours processing what they have learned, building example projects in new software programs, and setting practical steps for building learning into workshop sessions. Training with paid instructors requires a funding source and, as a result, may not be an option for all libraries. That does not mean that a Teen Tech Squad in your library must go without continuing education.

Teen Tech Squad interns at Hennepin County have often used monthly meeting time to go through online tutorials for programs and teach themselves and then create teaching outlines they can use with teen workshop participants. Setting aside time for learning and development is key.

Today's Tools of the Trade

Teen Tech Squad programs continue to adapt and evolve to provide new, challenging activities that meet the interests of youth participants. We are not sure what they will be using next week, but here is a current list of the Teen Tech Squad's tools of the trade:

Scratch (http://scratch.mit.edu)
Scratch is a graphically based programming language developed by the MIT Media Lab. Users can create animation, games, music, and interactive art using images and sounds they create in Scratch. Images and sounds can also be imported from external sources or from other programs such as Audacity and ArtRage. Users can share their projects with the world on the Scratch website and find answers to their programming questions in the sizable and active online user forum.

ArtRage (http://artrage.com)
ArtRage is a drawing platform that emulates physical drawing materials and implements. Media available include oil paint, pencil, crayon, and airbrush. Finished images can be exported to a variety of standard image formats. The full version of ArtRage is available for purchase, but the free trial version contains many of the full version's functions.

GIMP (http://gimp.org)
GIMP is an open-source image-editing platform. GIMP offers a wide range of options for manipulating photographs and other images as well as a simple paint program for drawing. GIMP supports most image file formats.

Comic Life (http://plasq.com/comiclife-win)
Comic Life allows users to format images in a comics-style layout. Users can import images and arrange and crop them to fit a variety of cartoon frames as well as add text using standard comic conventions such as speech and thought bubbles. The free thirty-day trial version of Comic Life gives users access to the entire suite of Comic Life functions.

Audacity (http://audacity.sourceforge.net)
Audacity is an open-source sound-editing platform. Users can record, cut, splice, and mix audio tracks as well as add simple audio effects. Audacity is also easy to use to convert sound files from one format to another.

Picasa (http://picasa.google.com)
Picasa is Google's digital photograph manipulation software. Picasa is primarily used to organize photographs online and on the computer, but it also has some basic photograph editing functions. The software has an online component for sharing images and a computer desktop application for uploading, organizing, and editing images.

SAM Animation (http://samanimation.com)
SAM animation is a software platform that allows users to create stop-motion animation with a computer and a video or still camera connected with a USB cable. The software allows the user to change the frame rate, to order and sort frames, to overlay text over the frames, and to sync a soundtrack with the frames. The completed movie can be exported in a variety of film formats.

PicoCrickets (http://picocricket.com)
PicoCrickets are not free, but they are versatile and appeal to a wide range of ages. Crickets are computers that are controlled by programs written with Pico Blocks, another graphically based computer language developed by MIT Media Labs. The programmer writes the program on the computer and beams it to the "brain" of the Cricket. Crickets come with motors and a variety of Lego pieces, which can be used to construct machines, structures, and creatures.

PicoBoards (http://www.picocricket.com/picoboard.html)
PicoBoards are not free, but they are a worthwhile investment. PicoBoards are connected to the computer with a USB cable and allow users to physically interact with their Scratch programs. PicoBoards have sound and light sensors, a slider bar, and serial ports that you can connect wires to with alligator clips.

Junk Boxes
One person's junk is another person's treasure—aluminum foil, toilet paper tubes, broken toys, wire, duct tape, paper cups, spools from rolls of receipt printer paper, paper clips—these are the building blocks for many of our programs. Workshop participants can use these materials to construct game controllers that can be used to interact with games designed in Scratch or creatures that are animated by Cricket motors.

Building Twenty-First-Century Literacy Skills

Teen Tech Squad workshops at Hennepin County Library provide a much-needed opportunity for youths in the community to create and explore new media and technology tools. Participants at Open Tech Labs probably would not describe what they are doing as "building twenty-first-century literacy skills," but that really is the beauty of these programs. What appears to teen participants to be a technology free-for-all is a golden opportunity for youths to learn, collaborate, experiment, and share mixed-media projects in an informal environment. That alone might motivate libraries to consider offering the programs. Sneak a peek into one of the Teen Tech Squad workshops, and behind that cloud of chaos, you will see that learning new technology is not the only outcome that this program achieves. Teen participants do not just want to attain proficiency in the software programs available. One of the most common questions they ask is, "How can I get that job?" Teen Tech Squad interns are role models, and each session brings another opportunity for them to grow as leaders, peer mentors, and to be a positive force in their community. What more could you ask for?

WHAT? NO BOOKS? THE OTHER SCHOOL VISIT

Julie Scordato

I love visiting high school classrooms. College prep juniors, world lit for sophomores, general English for the non-college-bound seniors. Yes, I love to teach them all.

Teach? Yes, you read that correctly. I can easily fill a whole class period without talking about one book and still promote library resources. While booktalking is an important facet of a young adult librarian's job, another great way to connect teens to the library is through the research class. Teaching research has several subtle yet far-reaching benefits. Teachers and school librarians are enthusiastic about getting support for their curriculum from an outside source. Sometimes a fresh face reiterating the same principles of searching can get the teens thinking beyond Google. The teens also tend to take me more seriously when I return to their class to do booktalks. Showing them practical, helpful, and convenient research sources builds my credibility for when I tell them about a good book they might want to read. Research classes also familiarize teens with the reference side of library service, something that goes beyond needing a book for a report or the school projects of their elementary school years. I've had the pleasure of receiving high school students at my desk after the class, asking for follow-up help or assistance on entirely new assignments. Whether in person or through e-mail, teens continue using library resources long after the research class.

We already know that teens are very comfortable with the ever-shifting possibilities of technology. Even if teens know that Google is one of the preferred search engines, their search for and analysis of information is often abysmal. One senior honors English teacher gave up halfway through grading her students' term papers because she was tired of seeing each one so poorly researched while her college-bound students insisted that whatever first hits they got were "all I could find." The difficulty goes deeper than dependence on search engines.

Teen Research Obstacles

A study published in the online *Journal of Medical Research* highlights the deficiencies of search skills in a sample of teens searching for medical information on the Internet. University of Michigan researchers concluded that for this group their main obstacles in finding quality information were vague search terms, misspelled words, and poor techniques for examining a website. Researchers also noted that teens had particular trouble in finding medical information on the local level, like finding a local chapter of Alcoholics Anonymous.

The most frequent issues impeding research for teens are lack of knowledge about how to analyze websites for quality, when to search other sources online, and how to choose and combine search terms. Inevitably, a portion of every research class I teach focuses on choosing and refining search topics.

This article originally appeared in the Winter 2005 issue of YALS.

Teaching Research for Everyone

Teens who are not obviously college-bound should not be overlooked when teaching online resources. I taught one class on library databases that I thought for sure would be tough to sell. The students were mostly eighteen-year-olds, obviously not college-bound, and definitely of the "killing time till graduation" attitude, but I managed to fire them up on EBSCOhost. The key to any research class is to find the interest and passion of the students. If they are junior honors English, yes, they are going to be passionate about getting a good grade on their big "worth half the semester's grade" research paper; if they are the aforementioned group of seniors, it's might be interviews with and pictures of favorite sports players or celebrities.

While English classes are the most obvious place to start, challenge yourself to connect your sources with other subject areas. Introduce teachers to some of the great medicine and health, science, and biography databases available. Making an appearance in a biology class to introduce, say, AccessScience is a fabulous way to broaden your contacts and partnership with the school and to impart to teens that the library can answer all kinds of information needs—not just for the humanities classes.

Another key to a successful research visit is to emphasize direct relevance early in the class. Whether it's for that big assignment or pulling up an interview with a popular celebrity, you have the burden of proof on why these resources are important to know. Generally, when I introduce myself as a librarian, I describe my job as the person who can "get you a recipe for vegetarian chili, a wiring diagram to a 1988 Camaro, and the history of the guillotine." This or a similar kind of mix can really get their attention. Be creative. I briefly talk about library policies and opportunities. Many teens don't have a library card or know what it takes to get one. The anxiety of losing items and paying overdue fines or past offenses still outstanding keeps teens away. I encourage you to work with your library and its policies in any way you can that helps teens get back into the library. Throw in something about volunteer or community service opportunities and dive in.

It's very important for teens to be working at their own or a shared terminal. You will have to figure out what works best for you physically. I like to work with a computer and projector combination so teens can follow my steps in the beginning of the class. Once we are deeply in the database, I abandon the projector to float around the room, guiding, troubleshooting, and making sure students are keeping on track and not playing online games.

To really drive home the point that search engines aren't the only tool, I like to compare a database search to a Google search using the exact same key terms. Four out of five times the Google results are not what the teens really want, and this leads right into a discussion about what to use a search engine for, when and how to analyze those hits to see if they are relevant and accurate, and, if not, what else should be tried.

Speaking of search engines, in every research class I teach, I inevitably discuss choosing and combining search terms and how to extrapolate terms from the broader research topic. Teens often need guidance in narrowing down their topics, and it is a sort of reference interview in itself. Common research topics, or at least common examples of broad topics, include things like "women in the military," "the 1960s," or "horror movies." Talking to them, asking what really interests them or what they really want to know, or showing them how broad their topic is will be the first step in getting them into actual research. Other teens will have a great topic but expect to plug in the title of their paper in natural language and get what they are looking for. Once again, part of my class is always dedicated to taking a topic like "America's Fascination with the Jeep" and explaining why that doesn't work in search engines or databases, then talking about breaking that topic down into what is really wanted, coming up with synonymous terms, and generally getting the teens thinking about translating their subject into terms that are specific, essential, and in various combinations.

Teens can really appreciate the different result-management options many databases offer. From e-mail, saving options, to HTML versus PDF formats, and charts, images, and other graphics available, you can use these features to add appeal to the databases and show off some basic tech-savvy. I usually focus on one database after I present a brief how-to on our online catalog. Ideally, a teacher gives me a list of tentatively chosen topics that students have submitted for their papers. This way I can prepare some dummy searches that will be directly relevant to my audience and get more mileage out of each class instruction.

Still not convinced a research instruction class is a productive use of time? Think of it as a way to

- introduce library services, such as electronic resources and professional, personal, reference
- make the library a valued resource of today and not an institute prompting nostalgia (storytimes and summer reading programs) and little else
- build partnerships with school librarians, teachers, and especially teachers outside of the English curriculum
- turn non-users into library users

Tips and Hints

- Have a list of tentatively chosen research topics submitted to you ahead of time.
- Be prepared for many students wanting to do pop culture–oriented papers: studies of fashion, music, or movies. Many teens will need help narrowing or broadening these kinds of topics to do successful research.
- Bring library cards and applications for both minors and adults, depending on which grades you are visiting. Eighteen-year-olds, for example, can sign up for a card on the spot. Make sure juvenile applications get to the minors, and give them all the details on how their parents can get them a library card.
- Sometimes a handful of students will have their library cards with them. Bring a small treat for anyone who can show their card, like candy or a fine amnesty card.
- Be prepared to have dummy card numbers or some other way to gain multiple-user remote access in the classroom.
- Have a backup plan in case the technology fails. Bring books to be prepared for booktalking instead, or have a prepared topic in mind for discussion, like censorship, intellectual freedom, or rights of privacy in the library.
- Create a short evaluation form for teachers to fill out regarding your school visit. Feedback is often helpful for refining visits and justifying them to administration.

ONLINE HOMEWORK HELP

Judy Michaelson

Not so long ago, the only option for providing homework help through the public library was organizing homework centers and using library staff, volunteers, or paid tutors. Students had to come to the library and in many cases needed to schedule an appointment in advance. The ability to access the service depended on geographic proximity to the library, transportation, hours of operation, and availability of a qualified tutor. With these limitations, many students could not take advantage of this library service.

With the advent of the Internet, libraries began to offer homework help through pathfinders on their websites. Although students could find useful information by following the links to highlighted websites, the information was static and there was no way to evaluate students' success in finding what they needed.

Throughout the past several years, a new model has been adopted by public libraries to complement the earlier models of homework centers and pathfinders—online tutoring services. By subscribing to an online tutoring service, libraries provide students with access to tutors through the Internet. This new model allows libraries to extend tutoring services to more students during more hours.

According to a new ALA study, online homework help is thriving in public libraries. "Libraries Connect Communities: Public Library Funding and Technology Access Study 2007–2008" reports that public libraries are using technology at record rates to help children succeed in school. More than 83 percent of public libraries offer online homework resources, including live tutors—up 15 percent in one year.[1] From these findings, it would seem that it's no longer a question of whether to offer online homework help but rather one of when and how.

Online homework help (also called online tutoring) leverages technology to provide the attention and

This article originally appeared in the Winter 2009 issue of *YALS*.

support of a live tutor skilled in the subject area where the student needs help. For the 73 percent of students who already turn to their computers at homework time, it is a natural fit and a welcome resource.

The greatest benefit for students is the on-demand nature of online homework help. Students can use their online tutoring time for help with an assignment or to build skills, study for a test, or brainstorm ideas for a science project.

How Online Tutoring Works in the Library Environment

Online tutoring services have been available through public libraries since 2000. The fundamental features of online tutoring or online homework help are

- the connection with a live tutor over the Internet
- immediate access to a tutor without an appointment
- the access to help on-demand in core subjects
- the availability of services outside of school and library hours
- the access to services through computers in the library or at home

Access to a tutor begins through the library's website, whether the student is in the library or at home. Some services are completely web-based while others require a software download. Students click on a link, authenticate with a library card number, and provide their grade level and the subject in which they need help. They are then connected to a tutor who has been screened and certified by the tutoring service. Tutors and students engage in an online chat; some services also permit voice communication.

Students and tutors share a whiteboard on which both can draw and write. On some services, websites can be shared and files can be uploaded and downloaded within the online classroom environment. Depending on the service you choose, more than one whiteboard might be available simultaneously and writing assistance might be on-demand in a secure tutoring classroom. Other services check writing assignments and provide assistance offline in several hours or the next day, sending an alert to the student's e-mail when his or her writing assignment has been reviewed by a tutor.

Factors to Consider When Selecting an Online Tutoring Service

Public libraries that have implemented online tutoring services find them to be an excellent tool for expanding service to teens and families. Online tutoring meets the needs of a hard-to-reach market segment and engenders high visibility and goodwill in communities.

Several companies now offer online tutoring programs for libraries. According to librarians who have evaluated various services, the five areas they generally highlight as most important to consider are

- tutor quality
- safety and the student experience
- customer support
- price
- reporting

Tutor Quality

Online tutoring is not the same as teaching. Students come to an online tutoring site with a specific need at a specific time—they have a homework problem they need help with or a test the next day to study for. Online tutors need to be trained to work effectively in the online environment. This means not only knowing their subject area, but having a good understanding of how to efficiently help students solve their specific problems and advance their learning.

Using online tools takes training. As you evaluate online tutoring services, be sure to ask specific questions about both initial training and ongoing mentoring. Some points to consider regarding tutors include

- the tutor certification process and background check
- the ongoing training and mentoring process
- the percentage of tutors based in North America
- the tutor support network
- the professional growth ladder to retain experienced tutors
- the tutor evaluation process
- the tutor's workflow (e.g., does the tutor help multiple students at one time)

Safety and the Student Experience

The goal in offering online tutoring is to provide a safe, positive learning experience for students. Online tutoring services approach the student experience differently, so it's important to assess the differences and determine which approach you are most comfortable with.

Some services cite a total number of tutors under contract, but it is possible that not all of them are serving public library clients. Because online tutoring services also offer their programs directly to consumers, some tutors may be reserved solely for private customers.

The essence of online tutoring is the one-to-one interaction. However, one-to-one doesn't always mean just one session at a time for the tutor. In some cases, a service might permit tutors to conduct several sessions simultaneously, toggling back and forth among them. Although allowing tutors to sign on to more than one session at a time might reduce initial wait time for the student, it can mean a student is kept waiting while the tutor is engaged in an additional session, slowing down the flow of the student-tutor interaction and possibly affecting the quality of the learning experience. Your library needs to evaluate which workflow is better for your students—waiting up front and then having undivided attention from the tutor or being admitted to the classroom without waiting but having a slower session while the tutor serves multiple students simultaneously.

Libraries implementing live online services want to be assured that students are operating in a safe and secure environment and that all interactions between tutors and students are in compliance with the Children's Online Privacy Protection Act (COPPA). Some services collect student e-mail addresses to return homework comments a day or so later. Some allow voice communication between students and tutors. Your library needs to decide how comfortable you are with less than total anonymity for students.

Some points to consider regarding safety and the student experience include

- the total number of tutors and percentage who work with public library clients
- the number of one-to-one sessions a single tutor can conduct simultaneously
- the method of file sharing and whether e-mail addresses are required

- the services provided during the live tutoring session versus those that require the student to wait for input
- the ability to review transcripts of all sessions for appropriate conduct, whether written or oral
- the ability to print whiteboard content, URLs of all websites shared, as well as the chat session
- the feedback mechanism to evaluate student satisfaction, including student comments

Customer Support

Libraries considering online tutoring services will want to look at several aspects of customer service. The first is the level of experience the vendor has working with public libraries and how well they understand library challenges such as funding, community outreach, management of computers in multiple locations, shortage of IT resources, and the like.

Although all services are accessible through the Internet, some require a software download to every computer where the service will be accessed. In that scenario, when there's a software upgrade, every computer needs to be upgraded—whether it's in the library or in a student's home.

Online tutoring services need to be marketed on an ongoing basis. Libraries will benefit from working with a vendor who understands library marketing and provides ready access to customizable tools to support library marketing programs. Assistance with your launch event, gaining press exposure, and the sharing of best practices from successful peer libraries can all help boost program usage.

Some points to consider regarding customer support include

- the software download required for each computer
- the availability of a dedicated client services representative for each client
- the variety of professionally designed and customizable marketing tools
- the track record of successful library programs and case studies for best practices

Price

To deliver online tutoring, a vendor needs to account for fixed as well as variable costs. This can be challenging when dealing with public libraries that offer the service free to anyone with a library card. Pricing models based solely on the size of the population served by the library or the number of library card holders don't account for differences in usage and may be unsustainable over the long term for the vendor. For example, take two libraries serving the same size population and paying the same amount for the service. Library A does two hundred sessions in a month and Library B does two thousand. Can a pricing model based solely on population be sustainable by the vendor who has to pay ten times more in tutor costs for Library B?

Some points to consider regarding pricing include

- the vendor's experience with the public library market
- the number of public libraries using the vendor's product
- the vendor's plans to account for usage variances in their pricing
- the vendor's understanding of funding alternatives for libraries

Reporting

Delivering a one-to-one online tutoring service represents a departure for libraries from standard services, making it hard to classify and measure. It's not a database of information; it's not a library program in the sense of an event. It's a unique service offering, and, as such, the ability to track usage down to the grade and subject level is important for evaluating the audience being reached.

Libraries considering an online tutoring service should request copies of reports and be sure they are comprehensive in their frequency and coverage. Some features that make sense in a school environment might not be well-used in the public library setting, so school-focused features should have their usage reported separately. Before investing in a service, talk to some of the vendor's clients and ask to see sample reports. Be sure that usage of all aspects of the service are tracked and reported on. Ask to see student comments if they are part of the feedback survey.

Some points to consider regarding reports include

- the frequency of the reports

- the completeness of the reports in covering all aspects of the service
- the distinct usage reporting on separate services such as learning modules
- the availability of user survey results, including comments from users
- the willingness of the vendor to share sample reports from other libraries

Side-by-Side Comparisons

Libraries evaluating online tutoring services have found the best way to compare the student experience is to request trial periods from the vendors you are considering. Setting up a trial period will give your library the opportunity to

- evaluate usability of classroom features
- evaluate the quality of the student's learning experience
- compare services that offer various modules with those that offer real-time online help exclusively
- feel confident in your purchasing decision

Once you log in to the service, keep your topics age appropriate. If you log in as a fourth-grade student, remember not to ask high school–level questions. For the most effective trials, ask the tutors of the services you are evaluating the exact questions in the exact same way. You probably have plenty of examples in your library from real homework assignments. Test a range of questions such as

- general math problems, like multiplying and dividing fractions, finding the area of a cylinder, or finding the angles of a triangle
- general writing examples with questions on punctuation or essay format to see how editing instruction is handled
- specific questions related to current events that will demonstrate how websites are used

During your trial period, evaluate all aspects of the services, from initial log-in to ending the session. Here are some questions to keep in mind as your evaluation team tests each service:

- Was the service easy to use the first time?

- Did the tutor take time to thoroughly clarify the student's question?
- Did the tutor use web pages effectively, when appropriate?
- Did the tutor engage you or the student in the learning?
- Did you feel the tutor simply gave you or the student the answer?
- Did there seem to be any unusually long pauses as you waited for the tutor to respond that might lead you to believe the tutor was working with more than one student at a time?
- Did the tutor provide positive reinforcement?
- Did you have to set up a personal account with your e-mail address to receive writing assistance?
- How long did it take to complete the session?
- If you uploaded a paper for assistance, did the tutor look at it in real time, or did you have to wait for an alert by e-mail?
- After the tutor logged off, how long could you stay on to review the session?
- Was there a print button? If not, how easy was it to print the chat portion of the session?

Finally, don't forget to ask for and contact ref-erences. Talking with each vendor's current customers is the best way to evaluate the intangibles of the services such as technical support and the overall responsiveness of the company. These intangibles can make all the difference in how satisfied you and your community are with your online tutoring service.

Conclusion

Online tutoring services offer your library an excellent opportunity to serve students and families, even when the library is closed. Libraries that have implemented these services receive praise from their communities and have the potential to generate great coverage in their local media. Students served by libraries with online tutoring return to the sites and tell their friends about the service.

There are differences among the vendors of online tutoring services, so as with all products and services you consider for your library, caveat emptor. In September 2008, the California State Library released an evaluation of online homework help services. If your library is considering adding online tutoring, take some time to review this report at www.library.ca.gov/lds/lds.html.

Good luck with your search!

NOTE

1. Larra Clark, ed., *Libraries Connect Communities: Public Library Funding and Technology Access Study 2007–2008* (Chicago: ALA, 2008).

CELEBRATING **TEEN TECH WEEK**
IN CHALLENGING SITUATIONS

TEEN TECH WEEK sets up a number of challenges for librarians, particularly in the areas of budget and in schools. In this chapter, you'll find creative yet economical options for your library, recommendations for celebrating Teen Tech Week in schools, and ways to make sure that all teens in your community—even those with disabilities—can participate.

TEEN TECH WEEK ON A BUDGET
Jami Schwarzwalder

Short on time and money this Teen Tech Week? Here are a few ideas on how your library can participate in Teen Tech Week, without giving you a nervous breakdown!

Idea 1: Hold a Contest

Last year for my Teen Tech Week, I held a "best of" contest. I let teens recommend and then vote for the best video game, movie, TV show, YouTube video, and website. My teens enjoyed the opportunity to share what they loved, but I used this information to evaluate our collection. I used both a paper and an online ballot, but the teens preferred to fill out the papers at my desk and then talk about their favorite media.

> *Pro:* Great for teen input.
> *Pro:* Reaches teens who do not come to regular programs.

> *Pro:* Can recommend books and other media teens might like on the basis of what they voted for.
> *Con:* Many teens complained that "best book" was left off the list.

Idea 2: Poster Tag Clouds and Comments

Similar to the contest idea, you could also put blank poster boards on the end panels of your stacks asking the teens a general question. I put up two posters last summer before *Harry Potter and the Deathly Hallows* was released that had at the top: "Snape Will Betray" and "Snape Is Loyal." I was surprised to see the responses and arguments that appeared on the posters. Over time I've created new posters and questions ranging from "What is your favorite manga?" to "If you could chose only two movies to ever watch again, what would they be?"

This article originally appeared in the Winter 2009 issue of *YALS*.

Pro: Great for teen input.

Pro: Reaches teens who do not come to regular programs.

Con: Provide pencils, not markers, to write on poster, in case you get anyone who wants to add "off-topic" pictures or phrases.

Con: This medium is anonymous. Teens who disagree often try to write bigger or cross out others, and teens who agree don't get a chance to correct.

Idea 3: After-Hours Alternative

Often you can't afford to have an after-hours program, but one of the draws to these programs is the ability to use all of the public Internet computers. Provide this by reserving computers at the library just for teens for a specified hour. If you want to have a focused program, consider printing a list of avatar-creation sites, ask the teens to post reviews on a blog or Teenreads.com, or compile of list of best online-game websites.

Pro: Uses equipment you already have.

Pro: Gives teens without the Internet at home more time to engage online.

Con: Do this during nonpeak hours so nonteen Internet users are not displaced.

Idea 4: Buy a Flip Video Camera

This idea does cost about $100 but shouldn't use much of your time. Like a digital camera, the Flip Video can be used to record impromptu actions of teens such as book and media reviews, *Dance Dance Revolution* skills, or something positive you can show staff or your board. Flip makes it easy to store and share videos. All of the software to view and edit is saved on the camera, where you can easily copy to your computer or e-mail to the teens. If you are daring, you can also purchase a digital photo frame for your teen area where you can display book covers and videos.

Pro: Gives teens a chance to comment and discuss their favorite mediums without being in one place.

Pro: Documents for staff what you do and the positive effect it has on teens.

Pro: Easy to use, even if you don't know a lot about technology or video.

Con: Encourage teens to not say their names when being recorded.

Con: Before you post on YouTube or another public website, get the teens' parents to sign a photo/video release form.

Con: If you don't have a digital photo frame, then there are not many ways to share videos with teens within the library.

Idea 5: Host a Handheld Gaming Meet-Up

Handheld gaming consoles are very popular (including the Nintendo DS) as is playing games using a phone or other handheld device. There are many games available for the Nintendo DS and the iPod Touch, for example, that allow players to play together if their friends have a similar device and a second copy of the game. Consider inviting teens and tweens who have these items to come to the library to play together.

Pro: Gives gamers a chance to socialize.

Pro: If you advertise at game stores and movie theaters, you may get new teens in the library doors.

Con: Gamers bring the games themselves so they may not bring multiplayer versions.

Con: Teens may share equipment, so provide masking tape and markers for everyone to put their name on the games, if applicable, and their devices before they start playing.

Con: Equipment is pocket-size, so make sure that everyone understands the risks in sharing or leaving games unattended.

Idea 6: Borrow Equipment

If you don't have the expertise or the money to buy gaming equipment, try to find someone who does. Sometimes local game stores, computer stores, and even comic book and hobby stores may have tech-savvy adults who would come to your library to offer a program. Many libraries have tested gaming programs by having staff and teens bring in TVs, gaming consoles, and games. If you don't have gaming equipment, you could give this a try.

Pro: Gives teens a place to socialize and play games with their friends.

Pro: Has been a successful program in libraries all over the country.

Con: Equipment could get damaged.

Con: If you are using older TVs, make sure they have a port for the red, yellow, and white AV cables. (You can find adapters at RadioShack.)

Con: Make sure you have the right games for teen appeal and for the console you are borrowing. A few good choices are *Rock Band*, *Guitar Hero*, *Dance Dance Revolution*, *Super Smash Brothers Brawl*, and *Mario Kart*.

Online Game Sites

Puzzles

Falling Sand: http://chir.ag/stuff/sand

Set Daily Puzzle: www.setgame.com/set

SuDoku: www.dailysudoku.com/sudoku

Virtual Jigsaw: www.jigzone.com

Host Sites for Flash Games

Addicting Games (try the flash version of Portal): www.addictinggames.com

Alien Hominid: http://alien-hominid.freeonlinegames.com

All Girl Arcade: www.allgirlarcade.com

Armor Games: www.armorgames.com

Kongregate: www.kongregate.com

MiniClip (try Youda Camper): www.miniclip.com/games

MySpace Games: http://games.myspace.com

WiiCade: www.wiicade.com

XGen Studios: www.xgenstudios.com

Web-Based Strategy Games and Games with a Message

Darfur Is Dying: www.darfurisdying.com

iFiction: www.ifiction.org

Ikariam: www.ikariam.org

Line Rider: http://linerider.com

McVideo Game: www.mcvideogame.com

Ogame: www.ogame.org

Renaissance Kingdoms: www.renaissancekingdoms.com

Sol: www.freeport.de/Sol

Type Racer: http://play.typeracer.com

—compiled by the 2009 Teen Tech Week committee

FREE ONLINE TOOLS FOR SERVING TEENS: FOUR VERBS TO LIVE BY AND GREAT TECHNOLOGIES TO TRY

Mary Fran Daley

With all the technology tools available for little to no money, planning technology programming for teens at the library can be overwhelming. But don't despair! As you begin to plan your Teen Tech Week, remember these four verbs: advocate, communicate, educate, and create.

Advocate

If your teens and their advocates do not know what you are doing at the library, are you really serving them? Step one of great technology programming is getting the word out!

Wow Them with Websites and Work Wonders!

If you do not have a library web page, it is time to get one. Try Weebly.com or Yola.com to set up your no-cost ad-free website. Remember to make one of the pages a news blog with an RSS feed. When your teens subscribe to your RSS, they will get automatic updates in their e-mail or their e-reader about your news postings.

What Do They Want? Why Not Ask Them?

A great way to keep business booming at the library is to fulfill your patrons' needs. If you are not a psychic

This article originally appeared in the Winter 2010 issue of *YALS*.

librarian, get yourself a gmail.com account. Click the item at the top that says, "Documents." Go to "New" then "Form." This opens a survey template. This is your chance to ask all kinds of questions. Once you publish this survey to the Internet, Google will automatically import answers into a nice Google Docs spreadsheet.

Newsletters with Pizzazz, Not Papers

Make a nice newsletter in Word, Publisher, PowerPoint, or as a PDF file in Adobe. Then publish it on www. yudu.com or www.scribd.com. Either way, you will have a beautiful digital product that can be e-mailed and archived on your new website.

Communicate

Teens have a lot of media competing for their attention. If you are lucky enough to get a moment of their time, make it count. Make your messages manageable, accessible, and meaningful.

Hot Off the (Word)Press!

Blogs are a great place to share library happenings, discuss literature, or brainstorm library futures. Weebly. com and Yola.com have built-in blog features, but you can also make a stand-alone blog on Wordpress.com, Blogger.com, Livejournal.com, and many others. Some great blog posts are soapboxes, whereas others are about prompting a great conversation. Experiment to find out what appeals to your teens. Whichever route you go, be sure to enrich your posts with great photographs, video, and audio content.

Show Them What You Mean

Do you need to share something wonderfully tech-y? Does it make any sense when you write it out? Save yourself time and save your teens frustration by expressing exactly what you mean through a screencast. Voicethread.com and Jing.com both have great tools for creating simple videos that will capture anything on your screen that you need to show your teens, including images, videos, and web pages, all while you narrate your cast. Screencasts are great for tutorials and so much more!

Educate

Our teens are growing and learning all of the time. We should be too! There are many virtual venues for learning and teaching.

Weave a Web for Understanding

You could create a simple webliography or links section on your website, but it would not pack nearly as much punch as a Delicious.com or Diigo.com page. These bookmarking tools allow you to collect links, tag them, organize them, and share them more easily. Each has a toolbar you can download directly on to many browsers, and each allows users to subscribe to changes in your bookmarks through RSS.

Wow Them with Wikis

Do you have a lot of content that you need to manage? Do you need help building a site with a lot of content? A wiki is the way. Wikis are pretty much web pages that a team can build collaboratively. Sometimes anyone can edit or comment on a wiki, but many providers allow for monitoring of contributions. Some leading sites include Wikispaces.com, Wetpaint.com, and PBWorks.com. You can build content with text, audio, and video formats, and the community can provide feedback in the comment fields.

Virtually Visit

If you cannot fly your favorite author out for an hour-long program, Skype them in instead. Skype.com is an online portal through which you can talk, chat, and videoconference with just about anyone. Authors and other special guests can visit your teens without the hassle of reservations or a carbon footprint of an airplane ride (and most likely for far less money in these times of smaller budgets and increased expectations).

Create

It does not need to be summer reading time to get creative at your library. There are several ways you can make these fun tools available to your teens. Consider choosing a few for the public computer terminals. Offer classes in others. If you can do nothing else, at least link them to your website so your teens can know about them.

Get Your Groove On!

The teenage years generally involve quite a bit of music (listening to music, dancing to music, getting dissed by your friends for your quirky tastes in music . . .). Albums and bands have given way to iPods and *Guitar Hero*. Although some things about music are still the same, there are many new things in music to explore. One of the neatest tools you and your teens can play with is JamStudio. JamStudio is an online avenue for composing music. Tunes, beats, and various instruments can be arranged in infinite combinations to craft and perfect original compositions. As an added bonus, teachers can apply on behalf of their students for grants that provide complimentary all-access passes that include more features than the regular free version.

Storytime . . . Online

A picture is worth a thousand words. Put your favorite photographs together into a show with some music, and you have more than a thousand words—you have a story. There are more tools than we can count to create and edit images and photographs, so we will limit it to four favorites. FotoFlexer is an awesome site that allows for easy editing of your photographs. You can turn your class photograph into a line drawing or your favorite pet picture into a Warholesque masterpiece. Once you have a groovy photograph collection together, make a music video an Animoto. com. Create a music video with your own photographs and music or choose selections from Animoto's library. Add a few captions and you have got yourself one fancy slide show. Basic free accounts are limited to thirty-second clips, but educators can apply for free accounts for longer videos at http://animoto.com/education. Additionally, Gimp.org offers a more advanced (but still free!) tool for photograph editing and authoring, and Microsoft Photo Story 3 offers the novice videographer more control over their slide shows with image-editing features, soundtracks, and special effects.

Get Your Game On!

Do your teens love video games? Scratch is the fantastic and free video game authorship program from the excellent people at the Massachusetts Institute of Technology. Most people start by creating images, although you can use a number of stock images provided by Scratch. From there you can create little animations with your images. Once you master that, you graduate to making these elements into full-fledged video games. Scratch has numerous recreational and educational possibilities that can be further explored at www.learnscratch.org.

Do Not Wait!

These tools are too fun and life is too short not to try them now. It can be very intimidating to explore new things, especially in the technosphere. Just remember that in most cases if you press the wrong button, your computer will not explode. Start small, then go ahead and try to make your 43-photograph slide show for back-to-school night played to none other than your school marching band's winning performance. Once you try a few of these things, starting a new one is intuitive. It does get easier. Once it gets easier, you will find your flow, and this is where the real fun happens for you and for your teens.

Online Tools

http://docs.google.com
http://scratch.mit.org
http://voicethread.com
www.animoto.com
www.blogger.com
www.delicious.com
www.diigo.com
www.fotoflexer
www.gimp.org
www.gmail.com
www.jamstudio.com
www.jing.com
www.learnscratch.org.
www.livejournal.com
www.microsoft.com/photostory
www.pbworks.com
www.scribd.com
www.skype.com
www.weebly.com
www.wetpaint.com
www.wikispaces.com
www.wordpress.com
www.yola.com
www.yudu.com

NOW IS THE TIME! TEEN TECH WEEK IN A SCHOOL LIBRARY

Kim Herrington

YALSA has sponsored Teen Tech Week (TTW) as a yearly event since 2007. This initiative was established to encourage and enable teens to be "competent and ethical users of technologies," especially those available through libraries. It highlights librarians as "qualified, trusted professionals in the field of information technology." School librarians should challenge themselves to find a way to participate.

When I attended my district's back-to-school meetings in August, I mentioned that I was on the TTW committee this year and asked some of the other secondary librarians whether they had ever celebrated TTW—no one had. Some had never even heard of TTW. The ones who had heard of it complained about the unfortunate timing of the week. We teach in a Texas district, and since TTW is in the spring, it—like many other spring activities—falls prey to the strict focus on state testing. In addition to the unfortunate timing of TTW, other librarians complained that the Internet filter blocked all the sites they might want to show to students and that they doubted that administrators would approve of the promotion of any technology that was not directly related to the curriculum.

The difficulty that many school librarians face in promoting TTW is not a new problem. In February 2008 Frances Jacobsen Harris, a former TTW committee member, wrote about the problem in an article for *School Library Journal*. In "Teen Tech Week, Despite Limited Access," Harris acknowledges the difficulty that school librarians face because in their libraries "technology is highly controlled and restricted."[1] The obstacles she identifies remain obstacles for most school librarians today. Schools continue to block access to social networking sites such as MySpace and Facebook, to prohibit the use of MP3 devices in the classroom, and to restrict the use of blogs and wikis. It is very difficult to overcome these obstacles and especially frustrating when, as one of my school librarian friends put it, schools "seem keen on teachers being up with technology, but ban almost all student technology."[2]

I queried some school librarians about their experience, or lack thereof, with TTW. Only one of them, a high school librarian, had ever done anything for TTW. Three or four years ago, she "bought the posters . . . had a book display of nonfiction/fiction with technology-based themes . . . got together with the [teachers of technology-related courses] and . . . had some student projects available for viewing."[3] Although she could see that the students were interested, she felt "like there should have been something more," but restrictions on student technology use and access to the Internet prevented her from doing more. She pointed out that since then TTW has unfortunately conflicted with spring break or state testing. She ended with this statement: "I love the idea, though, and would like to do more with it." Most of the school librarians that I spoke with echoed her sentiment.

Not all school librarians have been stifled in their efforts to promote TTW. In the first year of TTW, students from a high school library won YALSA's TTW video contest.[4] In the same year, the first-place winner of the TTW display contest was a school librarian.[5] In 2008 high school students won first place and second place in TTW's promotional song contest.[6] And in 2009 two of the twenty TTW mini grant winners were school librarians.[7] Of course, two of twenty is not a very high percentage, but perhaps not very many school librarians apply because of the aforementioned obstacles or lack of technology capabilities in their school libraries.

To those school librarians who have hesitated in the past, I say this school year is a great time to do something for TTW and "to do more with it."[8] Thanks to the Broadband Data Improvement Act, which was signed into law in December 2008, schools that use e-rate funding are now required to teach students "appropriate online behavior, including online interactions with other individuals in social networking websites and in chat rooms and cyberbullying awareness and response."[9] According to my school's Campus Instructional Technology Specialist, schools not only have to "do some type of Internet safety training/lesson" but also have to "document it and be ready to

This article originally appeared in the Winter 2010 issue of *YALS*.

produce the material if audited."[10] Librarians should take advantage of this opportunity and promote TTW as part of this new mandate. Administrators should be more amenable to promotions and activities that can be used to document that the school is in compliance with this new requirement. Administrators, who in the past have said no to students' blogging or participating in a Ning group, might be willing to approve these activities since they can be used to teach students about appropriate online behavior. In addition, at a time when many school librarians fear that their jobs will be cut, positioning yourself as an expert and a leader in online technology according to this mandate might make the difference between being seen as expendable and not.

Even technologically challenged school librarians can do something to celebrate TTW, whether or not it is to be used as proof of compliance with the new law. For example, they could simply create a display of books about old and new technology or fiction books with technology-related themes. They could hand out copies of the YALSA's "Social Networking: A Guide for Teens" brochure, available at www.ala.org/yalsa/handouts. School librarians with more advanced technology skills or access to more advanced technology could have students create YouTube videos or podcasts. YALSA's TTW information page (www.ala.org/teentechweek) includes links to resources, including the brochure mentioned above and the TTW Wiki (wikis.ala.org/yalsa/index.php/Teen_Tech_Week). This wiki includes links to the current and past years' wikis and links to resources. The current year's wiki is a place where participants can share their ideas and experiences.

For the first two years of my school librarian career, I was frustrated in my desire to celebrate YALSA's TTW. Both years the dates coincided with state testing dates, and my school, like most in this state, put everything except state testing on the back burner for a good portion of the spring semester. When I was asked to be on the TTW Committee, I was very excited and immediately started brainstorming how I could do something, anything, for TTW this school year. I hope that other school librarians will join me in showing that the school library is a great place to get connected.

NOTES

1. Frances Jacobson Harris, "Teen Tech Week, Despite Limited Access," *School Library Journal* 54, no. 2 (February 2008): 20.
2. Elisabeth Allison Owens, e-mail message to author, September 23, 2009.
3. Irene Johnson, e-mail message to author, September 23, 2009.
4. "Teen Tech Week Video Contest Winners," *Young Adult Library Services* 5, no. 4 (summer 2007): 55.
5. "Teen Tech Week Winners Named," *American Libraries* 38, no. 6 (June/July 2007): 18–19.
6. "Teen Tech Week Song Contest Winners," *Young Adult Library Services* 6, no. 4 (Summer 2008): 47.
7. "2009 Teen Tech Week Mini Grant Winners," http://www.ala.org/ala/mgrps/divs/yalsa/teentechweek/ttw09/mg09.cfm (accessed November 3, 2009).
8. Ibid.
9. Broadband Data Improvement Act. S. 1492, 110th Cong., Sec. 215, http://www.govtrack.us/congress/bill.xpd?bill=sl10-1492 (accessed September 28, 2009).
10. Sandy Dickerson, e-mail message to author, October 2, 2009.

TEEN TECH WEEK
PROGRAMMING

THIS LIBRARY PROGRAMMING chapter gives options to support Teen Tech Week that include audiobooks for teens, how to run gaming events in libraries, and advice from a library that won a Teen Tech Week Mini Grant.

ALEX, iPODS, AND MY WILDEST DREAMS
Shonda Brisco

It's not often that a librarian has the opportunity to work with a large group of gifted and voracious readers, especially at the high school level. I discovered such a group when I began work this year at Fort Worth Country Day School, a private, college-prep, K–12 school in Fort Worth, Texas. As the new technology librarian for the upper school (grades 9–12), my job included many of the same duties that most high school librarians have, with the exception of additional responsibilities in the areas of technology. This included instruction in web page development, the use of computer application software, and the evaluation and use of instructional databases.

Because my experience had always been in providing students with the opportunities to select and read great literature, I found it difficult to concentrate entirely on just technology. I was always drawn to the observation of students in high school and their lack of time for recreational reading. At a college-prep

school, however, the problem was magnified. With most of our students participating in sports, theater, dance, and community service, all the while trying to maintain their grades, I rarely saw any of them pick up the latest copies of contemporary young adult (or even adult) books. In fact, most of the students only visited the library to use the computers to do research or to pick up a copy of the classroom novel currently being taught—a work usually by, as they call say, great dead men.

When two freshman girls stopped by the library one afternoon to look for something good to read before a long weekend, I had the opportunity to talk with them about the library's collection and their reading preferences. Their comments made me realize that the library was indeed an important part of their lives (especially the public library where they borrowed the latest novels to read during the summer), but that our library was not meeting their expectations

This article originally appeared in the Spring 2006 issue of *YALS*.

of a balanced collection filled with both works they needed and those they wanted.

This new insight made me consider the idea of providing the students with an opportunity to squeeze recreational reading into their lives. As a new librarian, I knew that in some ways ignorance and boldness are often an advantage during the first couple of years at any new school. Because I did not know the perceived reputation or teaching style of any of the high school English teachers, I decided that asking the freshman English teacher to help me with a project that included these students could be done without any second thoughts on my part.

I e-mailed the freshman English teacher to ask if she would be willing to help me create a book club project with her students, and if she thought there would be any others who might be interested in participating. She immediately responded with a very positive note assuring me that most of her students were avid readers and would probably enjoy this type of program designed specifically for them. I then set up a time to meet with her personally, and we discussed the possibilities of involving the students in selecting materials for their book club (which would also be added to the library's collection) and providing additional program ideas to encourage their continued participation.

The next step of selecting a list of possible titles for the students proved to be more challenging than I had initially imagined. In fact, when I submitted the first list of titles with blurbs that included reading levels for students in grades 7–10 (which I figured would provide an acceptable range for most students in high school), her response was, "This is a good list, but do you have anything a bit more challenging?"

I immediately made another appointment to meet with the teacher to discuss the types of books that she had seen the students read, bring to class, or talk with her about privately before or after class. The titles that these students were reading were some of the same titles that I had picked up for my own recreational reading. While these adult titles were not necessarily inappropriate for teens, they definitely made me realize that most of the students were reading adult literature simply because they did not know what else was available for them (and, obviously, we were not providing them with any current options in the library).

Through the LM-NET electronic discussion list, I immediately requested a recommendation of titles for advanced readers in high school and was directed to the Alex list of award-winning titles. As I browsed the lists year by year, I realized that I would not be able to select the titles myself and decided to allow the students to make the decision of which titles they thought they would enjoy reading. After compiling a 36-page list of 306 titles combined with short blurbs about each, I offered the lists to the classes. They then narrowed the list down to 117 titles with enthusiastic notations made by each one about which had to be read first. I decided that regardless of which titles we would later choose to read, all of these titles needed to be added to the collection.

After the list had once again been narrowed down (to a mere thirty-seven titles), I met with the teacher and asked her to help me develop the program that would encourage students to participate and to keep them reading these types of award-winning books. Initially, she was unsure what types of activities we might be able to use to entice the students, but I then asked her to create her wildest-dreams list of activities that she would like to provide if there were no restrictions on the types of programs or activities we could plan. Because so many programs or ideas seem to be squelched before they can be planned or implemented, I knew that many teachers (and librarians) often stop themselves from dreaming big because they are often told no before they even start. My hope was that with her list and my plans, we could create a program that would address most, if not all, of the issues and then be accepted.

Before we moved forward with the list of titles and the wildest-dreams list, I created an online survey that the students would be able to access via the library's website to answer questions relating to their reading preferences. Included in the survey were questions about environment (such as relaxing areas similar to their favorite bookstores that included coffee and food while discussing the books as a group or club), as well as the option of downloading selected titles to their iPods for individual listening between outside activities that often devoured their personal reading time. The survey proved to be another great tool to offer insight into our students' reading preferences and what they felt would help them remain connected to good literature.

We began to create the program using our wildest-dreams list, their book list, and the survey information. We decided that by providing the students with access to both the print and audio titles (via a library account with Audible.com), we would be able to connect with the greatest number of students who were interested in participating. While most of the students had access to portable audio players, we chose to provide iPods through the library. We purchased ten iPod Shuffles for use by those students who were involved in the program and decided to increase those numbers if the program gained interest. We downloaded the titles of those books that were of interest to the students and made them available individually as students became aware of the program and chose to participate. This is a perfect example of how a school library can participate in events like Teen Tech Week—by encouraging students to use nonprint resources that the library already offers.

We purchased ten paperback copies of each upcoming title and made them available for students to check out, and we offered additional copies of the paperbacks for purchase at a discount (made available through our school's Reading Council).

We decided to provide opportunities for the students to participate in the program by promoting it during our daily announcement period and hosting a lunchtime book discussion. Our initial program became known as "Books Sandwiched In" because of the limited amount of time that most of our students had to read for enjoyment and because the discussions were hosted during their lunch periods every month. In addition, many students who did not necessarily dislike reading but could not carry books with them between activities, rehearsals, or sporting events became interested in using the iPods for recreational reading. This, we decided, actually seemed logical for college preparation since most of the students would find themselves in a few years with the option of using their iPods for classroom lectures, reading assignments, and possibly recreational reading. We felt that by teaching them how to access and use iPods for this type of program, they would definitely be prepared for the high-tech access they would face once they entered college.

Enthusiasm for the program has built as the students realized that while we are providing them with options for recreational reading materials, they are making some final choices to share with one another. Our excitement, as educators, has come from the students' willingness to meet with us to give us their reaction to the books that we have chosen for

them and to encourage their friends to participate.

While the program is still ongoing and we have between twenty and forty students participating in reading one of the Alex titles each month, we are still using our wildest-dreams list to provide unique opportunities for the students. Our hope is to involve more teachers in the program in order to expand the group to include sophomores, juniors, and seniors. We also plan to work closely with our school's Reading Council to provide them with the results of our project at the end of the year and to encourage them to use more of the Alex titles for their "One Book, One Community" program, which is held each summer with our students and faculty. Finally, we plan to use our iPod technology to provide RSS feeds of our book discussions for students who read the books but miss the discussion, as well as a quick book review of upcoming titles to entice students to participate in the program via the library's web page, and to check out the print titles from our library.

Our selected Alex Award reading list included the following titles:

Barry, Lynda. *One Hundred Demons.* Sasquatch, 2002

Bodanis, David. *The Secret Family: Twenty-Four Hours inside the Mysterious Worlds of Our Minds and Bodies.* Simon & Schuster, 1997

Boylan, James Finney. *Getting In.* Warner, 1998

Bradley, James, and Ron Powers. *Flags of Our Fathers.* Bantam, 2000

Card, Orson Scott. *Ender's Shadow.* Tor, 1999

Carroll, Rebecca. *Sugar in the Raw: Voices of Young Black Girls in America.* Crown, 1997

Chevalier, Tracy. *The Girl with a Pearl Earring.* Dutton, 2000

Cook, Karin. *What Girls Learn.* Pantheon, 1997

Dominick, Andie. *Needles.* Scribner, 1998

Doyle, William. *An American Insurrection: The Battle of Oxford, Mississippi, 1962.* Anchor, 2003

Durham, David Anthony. *Gabriel's Story.* Knopf, 2002

Enger, Leif. *Peace like a River.* Grove, 2002

Gilstrap, John. *At All Costs.* Warner, 1998

Haddon, Mark. *The Curious Incident of the Dog in the Night-Time.* Doubleday, 2003

Halpin, Brendan. *Donorboy*. Villard, 2004

Haruf, Kent. *Plainsong*. Knopf, 1999

Hosseini, Khaled. *The Kite Runner*. Riverhead, 2003

Jordan, June. *Soldier: A Poet's Childhood*. Basic, 2000

Junger, Sebastian. *The Perfect Storm: A True Story of Men against the Sea*. Harper Mass Paperback, 1998

Kluger, Steve. *Last Days of Summer*. Avon/Bard, 1998

Krakauer, Jon. *Into Thin Air: A Personal Account of the Mt. Everest Disaster*. Villard, 1997

Kruger, Kobie. *The Wilderness Family: At Home with Africa's Wildlife*. Random House, 2001Marillier, Juliet. *Daughter of the Forest*. Tor, 2000

Niffenegger, Audrey. *The Time Traveler's Wife*. MacAdam Cage, 2003

Packer, Z. Z. *Drinking Coffee Elsewhere*. Riverhead, 2003

Patchett, Ann. *Truth, & Beauty: A Friendship*. HarperCollins, 2004

Philbrick, Nathaniel. *In the Heart of the Sea: The Tragedy of the Whaleship Essex*. Viking, 2000

Picoult, Jodi. *My Sister's Keeper*. Atria, 2004

Reed, Kit. *Thinner than Thou*. Tom Doherty Associates, 2004

Senna, Danzy. *Caucasia*. Putnam/Riverhead, 1998

Shepard, Jim. *Project X*. Knopf, 2004

Silverberg, Robert, ed. *Legends: Stories by the Masters of Modern Fantasy*. Tor, 1998

Strauss, Darin. *Chang and Eng*. Dutton, 2000

Sullivan, Robert. *Rats: Observations on the History and Habitat of the City's Most Unwanted Inhabitants*. Bloomsbury, 2004

Thomas, Velma Maia. *Lest We Forget: The Passage from Africa to Slavery and Emancipation*. Crown, 1997

Walker, Rebecca. *Black, White, and Jewish: Autobiography of a Shifting Self*. Penguin, 2002

Winspear, Jacqueline. *Maisie Dobbs*. Soho, 2003

TEEN BOOK DISCUSSIONS GO ONLINE!

Cathy Rettberg

Many libraries are turning to social networking to promote library services and to reach out to their young adult (YA) patrons with online book discussions, an easy method for connecting teens to books and technology during Teen Tech Week. Dialogue can take place in several formats. Blogs and message boards allow readers to see each other's comments and to carry on an online conversation, while e-mail groups allow for interactions to take place between individual members or among the entire group. Both methods can accommodate teens' busy schedules, allowing convenient participation as little or as often as desired. Schools are getting into the action as well, as school librarians encourage recreational reading by offering book discussion blogs. These tend to have more activity during the school year and usually are limited to the school community.

With just a bit of planning, teen librarians can create easy-to-use online book groups while protecting the safety of their patrons. Most sites require free registration and include clear guidelines, with postings monitored for appropriate content. Discussion questions can make good conversation starters, steering the dialogue away from a simple "Did you like this book?" and on to more in-depth exchanges. Most sites include the added fun of avatars—custom images that enable users to project a personality. Links to book reviews or a local library's catalog can also add interest to a discussion site.

Networking sites such as Facebook, Goodreads,

This article originally appeared in the Fall 2006 issue of *YALS*.

and others offer opportunities for teens to join book clubs. By searching either of these sites, teens can locate clubs for particular books or authors, or for general discussions of young adult literature. Several online book discussion sites are profiled below. Check these out if you have teens who are looking for a new opportunity to talk about books, or if you are thinking about designing a site for your library.

Book Divas (www.bookdivas.com)
Young adult and college-age readers can discuss books, read chapter excerpts, and interact with favorite authors at Book Divas. This busy message board offers discussions of some of the latest YA titles, bios of featured authors, and an occasional live chat. Readers may participate in a specialty forum and discuss a particular book, or contribute to a book review message board. Users can upload avatars and create customized profiles. To protect user information, the Book Divas' privacy guidelines encourage parental guidance when young adults create a profile. With over one thousand registered members and forty or more postings each day, the site has discussions to suit all interests.

Grouchy Café: Favorite Teenage Angst Books (www.grouchy.com/angst/favorites.html)
This is one of the older teen reading message boards available, with postings going back to 2002. Participation seems to wax and wane, but the discussions can be lively. Free registration is required in order to post; no guidelines are posted. The message board is intended for use by teens and anyone interested in YA literature. One caution: the site has a substantial amount of advertising, which can be a distraction.

Not Your Mother's Book Club (*http://booksincteen. blogspot.com/*)
This blog was developed to support a book club that meets at a San Francisco bookstore. The online community is intended for use by young adults in grades 7–12, though librarians, teachers, and YA authors are also welcome. A disclaimer notes that comments may not be appropriate for children under thirteen. While the conversation topics vary widely, there are frequent discussions of YA titles, descriptions of author events, and question-and-answer sessions with YA authors.

ALL THUMBS ISN'T A BAD THING: VIDEO GAME PROGRAMS @ YOUR LIBRARY

Beth Saxton

Would you like to attract new teens to your library? Are you wondering how you can reach those teens that only come to the library to camp out on the computers for as long as possible? Would you like to get more boys involved in your activities? Then warm up your thumbs and plan some video game programs.

Programs that capitalize on teen interests are how we maintain relevance in the busy lives of our teens. By taking traditionally solitary activities like reading, writing, and crafting and adding expertise, structure, and community, libraries offer teens enhanced experiences they are unable to create on their own. Giving video games the same consideration can attract new teens to the library and improve your relationship with teen gamers—and Teen Tech Week is an excellent

time to introduce gaming at your library or relaunch your existing gaming program.

Go to the Source

For librarians who are not active gamers, it can be hard to keep up with what the most popular games and systems are in your community. This presents a great opportunity for teen input and leadership in your library. Consider forming a gaming or technology-specific teen advisory board. Seek out your most game-obsessed teens, and be sure to talk to teens who don't usually attend other types of programs. Let them guide your program choices and recommend game-related titles for your collection. Find out what systems they

This article originally appeared in the Winter 2007 issue of *YALS*.

own and what games they are playing, including those for portable systems. Ask them what games they think would attract a lot of players for a tournament. Finally, browse the gaming magazines and websites they read. Your teens are a key resource when planning video game programs.

Equipment

If you are considering a tournament or free-play program, equipment can be one of the major obstacles in planning. For each game station, you will need a television, game system, game, and the correct number of controllers. You will likely need two controllers each for Microsoft Xbox or Sony PlayStation systems and two to four controllers for each Nintendo Wii. Consult the back of the game package for the number of players to be sure. If you are planning to play *Dance Dance Revolution* (DDR) or another game with special equipment, make sure you have enough equipment for each game station. (If your game of choice is DDR, it is highly recommended that you choose the best quality dance mats you can afford.)

There are several ways to procure equipment depending on your library and community. Several libraries have purchased the equipment either out of their budgets or with grant funds, as part of plans for ongoing video game programming. This is the optimal solution if you plan on multiple well-attended events, and your library can afford it.

If this is not an option, then you may be able to solicit help from your local video game store by asking them to cosponsor an event and loan the equipment. Employees at your local store are generally quite knowledgeable about their products. An ongoing relationship with the staff can be a strong asset, especially for librarians who are not gamers themselves. Beyond loaning equipment, these experts can tell you what the most popular games and systems are in your area, help you reach your target audience, and may even be willing to volunteer at your event. The store benefits from the publicity and from your teenagers test-driving games and systems they may decide to buy later.

If you are just starting out and do not expect more than about twenty participants, you can run a tournament on one or two systems that can often be borrowed from library staff. Look into renting additional copies of a game as it can be significantly cheaper than purchasing games for a onetime event. Finally, it may be possible to ask participants to bring in their own equipment. Do this only if you can be sure everyone is aware that the library cannot be held responsible for damage or theft.

Tournaments

A proven way to attract gamers to your library is to hold a tournament. These events can range from informal, after-school competitions with one game system to a large scale, day-long affair with multiple systems. There are several advantages to holding a tournament. First, this type of event offers something patrons would be hard-pressed to organize on their own. Second, the structure of the tournament helps to ensure that everyone gets an equal turn, the most common reason for disputes during free-play programs. Finally, few teens can resist the idea of proving they are the best at anything, especially something as central to their existence as video games.

When planning a tournament, consider the number of playing spots you will have available. The more spots you can offer, the less players will try to entertain themselves with things you would rather they didn't do.

Your choice of game and the time available for your tournament will also influence the format of your tournament. Many popular games have ways to shorten the length of the time it takes to determine a winner. For example, it is possible to adjust the length to half or a quarter of the time in many sports games, and *Super Smash Bros. Melee* offers a sudden-death mode that shortens playing time considerably. Consult the game's manual and gaming websites, or ask your teens for shortcuts to chosen games.

Mario Kart and *Super Smash Bros. Melee*, both for Wii, allow four players to compete simultaneously and finish a game in a relatively short amount of time, making them ideal for tournaments. *Madden NFL* is available for all systems and is incredibly popular with boys, although it has a high learning curve for those unfamiliar with sports video games. For a more active tournament, consider some popular rhythm games. DDR has versions available for all systems and is played on a dance mat on which players step in-sync with arrows on the screen.

When planning your tournament, find teens who are experts at the game you have chosen and ask them to bring their memory cards. Nearly all games have special features that can only be accessed after a certain level of play is reached. To give your players the best experience possible, it is important to make sure all these little extras are available. When possible, avoid single-elimination tournaments and give each player as many chances at the controller as possible. There are several freeware generators to help you create your tournament bracket. Have game-related activities available for participants when it is not their turn at the controller. Board games and a selection of gaming books and magazines are a good start, although many teens will simply choose to watch others compete.

There are several ways to enhance your tournament. Ann Arbor (Michigan) District Library projects key games on a big screen and invites teens to contribute commentary for the featured games. Allowing teens to predict the winner after the first round is fun, and a small prize can be distributed to the best prognosticators. It is a good idea to have a large copy of the tournament bracket posted in the room as well. This ensures all players understand how the tournament works and adds the fun of predicting future match-ups as well.

Free Play

A second option for video game programming is to simply set aside a time for free play. This works especially well as part of a larger program such as an after-school drop-in time, community outreach event, or lock-in. As with a tournament, the more spots you have available for players, the better your program is likely to be received. Games that work well for tournaments also work well for free play. You might also consider collections of classic games and mini-games such as the *Mario Party* series.

Decide in advance how players will take turns. You may choose a set length of time, a single game, or multiple games depending on the games offered. For short multiplayer games like *Mario Kart*, you may consider allowing the winner to keep their seat while rotating the other players.

You'll also want to decide which games will be available and who will be allowed to change the games and have access to the games not being played. Be sure to check the rating of any games your players bring from home and stand firm on the Entertainment Software Rating Board (ESRB) age guidelines. There are plenty of popular and challenging games rated "E" for "Everyone" or "T" for "Teen."

Meet-ups

A third type of game-related programming is to have a portable system meet-up. A meet-up is simply a group of people with a common interest who get together face-to-face. Both Nintendo DS and Sony PlayStation Portable (PSP) allow players to compete across a wireless connection. Many games for iPhone or iPod Touch allow competition as well. If your teens express interest in any of these handheld devices, this is the simplest way to get gamers into the library.

This program has a clear advantage in that there is no equipment to provide and only the amount of space available limits the number who can participate. Participants in this type of program move through the group, playing games and swapping virtual items. Specify one or two specific games for each meet-up so gamers know what to expect. Nintendo DS has many games in which interaction with other players has a significant advantage in game play. For example, players of *Animal Crossing: Wild World* "live" in their hometown but reap high benefits from traveling and accepting tourists. Puppy parents in *Nintendogs* can swap goods and arrange play dates for their furry friends, and Wi-Fi competition adds an extra dimension to staples like *Mario Kart DS* and *Tetris DS*.

The biggest disadvantage to this type of program is that teens must have their own systems to participate; however, if your teens have expressed interest in meet-ups, this should not stand in your way of offering this type of program. Remember that you are trying to fill a specific need with this program, and other events will fill the needs of the teens who can't participate this time.

Video Games and Traditional Library Programming

There are many options for integrating gaming into more traditional types of library programming, in addition to the game advisory group. This is an area, however, where it is crucial to have teen input. Your own attempts may backfire, leaving teens with the impression that the library can make even video games boring.

Form a video game discussion group at your library in addition to your book discussion group. Attendees can discuss titles they have played and enjoyed, elements of what makes a good game, the best games they've played, sources of video game information, and the issue of violence in video games. The discussion group may also complete world-building exercises. Many libraries put together publications featuring teens' creative writing and artwork. This idea can be adapted by inviting gamers to write for a video game magazine instead. Allow the gamers to decide what types of things should be included and if they are going to limit content to console games or include table and computer games as well. They may want to include teen-generated game reviews, playing tips and tricks, or articles about gaming topics. You can even assign a reporter to cover your own tournaments.

Career-related programs are another place to capitalize on the popularity of video games. Seek out professionals in your community who have careers related to the gaming industry, including programmers, designers, marketers, or small-business people. Invite them to give presentations and ask their advice on books related to their area of expertise. Professional organizations, colleges, and universities are a good starting point to make these kinds of contacts. This is another way to involve your local game store.

Game Over

Librarians holding video game programs report that they have no more—and often fewer—behavioral issues at game programming events than any other kind of event. Many have reported better library behavior overall among game program participants, thanks to improved relations with the librarians and teens who feel a sense of ownership of the library. Many teens who initially became involved in the library through gaming events have gone on to attend other library programs as well. Adopting any of these options for video game programming can have great benefits for both your teens and the library.

Additional Resources

Gallaway, Beth, and Alissa Lauzon. "I Can't Dance without Arrows: Getting Active @ Your Library with Video Game Programs." *Young Adult Library Services* 4, no. 4 (Summer 2006): 20–25.

Helmrich, Erin, and Eli Neiburger. "Video Games as a Service: Hosting Tournaments at Your Library (No MARC Records Required)." *Voice of Youth Advocates* 27, no. 6 (February 2005): 450–53.

Levine, Jenny. "Gaming and Libraries: Intersection of Services." *Library Technology Reports* 42, no. 5 (September/October 2006).

Websites

Bracket Maker (www.bracketmaker.com)

DDR Freak (www.ddrfreak.com)

Entertainment Software Rating Board (ESRB) (www.esrb.org)

Game FAQs (www.gamefaqs.com)

Game Spy (www.gamespy.com)

Nintendo (www.nintendo.com)

PlayStation (www.us.playstation.com)

Xbox (www.xbox.com)

GAMING IN LIBRARIES 2.0

Katherine Makens

Many libraries now offer gaming programs for their teens that involve console games and sometimes MMOGs (massively multiplayer online games). These programs give teens a very positive and educational experience in the library and usually generate a good turnout. However, these programs are often similar to gaming events that teens could find elsewhere. The library is not the only place where gaming can become a social event.

The question is: How can we apply Library 2.0 concepts to make gaming events that are truly unique to a library setting? There have been several takes on this idea. In some libraries, the teens run the gaming programs, decide what games to have, compete in

This article originally appeared in the Summer 2007 issue of *YALS* library teams, or post their comments about games in general or library tournaments on their library's blog. Another possibility would be to provide a program that shows teens how to make the games that they are playing and allow teens to really control the content. This article will be an examination of one library's experiments with finding a viable option for such a program.

In 2006 North Regional/BCC Library of Broward County (Florida) Libraries tried testing several programs for a video game design for teens. Since the library had a license for Flash, we tried a small experiment showing ActionScript to a small group of teen volunteers. This was quickly abandoned as a summer program since it was too labor-intensive for staff and not workable for a large group.

The next experiment was with a piece of shareware called Game Maker (www.gamemaker.nl). Game Maker has a basic version available for free or a full, paid version. This software does allow for surprisingly sophisticated game design for the money. However, it is not intuitive to use and requires at least one person on staff to learn the software very, very well for an ongoing summer program. It also takes a very long time for teens to learn enough to create a really satisfyingly complex game from start to finish. This proved to be difficult with a large group of teens. The solution we opted for was to give teens a ready-made game and then show the teens how to alter or "mod" the game in interesting ways. This was a less stressful option that let teens get something quickly that they had made on their own, but didn't require the time and skills to create an entire game independently from start to finish.

Because the summer program from last year had shown that there was community interest in video game design, we wrote and were awarded a grant for Multimedia Fusion 2 and a subscription for online classes from the Youth Digital Arts CyberSchool (www.ydacs.com) for the summer of 2007. The goal of the grant is to provide an enjoyable video game design program for teens that will teach them useful skills, expose them to a career that otherwise they would not have access to, and to test these products for possible systemwide use in Broward County Libraries. The program will take place at three branches over the summer. By the end, these teens should be able to create a game with Multimedia Fusion 2.

In 2008 we held a contest for the best game at each of the three locations, chosen by the teens themselves. However, this could be extended to having teens create games to teach other teens different library skills. A contest could be held to see who can create the best game that promotes the library. Staff who learn how to design games can create games to teach other staff new skills or to test current skills in a fun way that does not require an individual instructor for each session. Although it takes awhile to design a game, the library can save money in the long run since once the game is created, there is no longer a need for an individual instructor for each class session. There are myriad possibilities for what could be accomplished with a successful game design program that truly incorporates Library 2.0 concepts and lets our teens generate their own content—and lets the librarians generate their own games as well.

BENDING CIRCUITS AND MAKING MUSIC: TEEN TECH WEEK IN DOWNTOWN MINNEAPOLIS

Camden Tadhag

The table in the back of Teen Central resembles a computer graveyard; plastic casings, circuit boards, and wires are strewn across the table's surface while a group of young people use pliers and other tools to pull strange groans and wails from the circuits. Library-sponsored cyborg torture? Nope! These teens are participating in a circuit-bending workshop.

In 2009 Teen Central at the Hennepin County Library Central in Minneapolis, Minnesota, was honored to be awarded a Teen Tech Week Mini Grant, sponsored by YALSA and the Verizon Foundation. The grant provided funds for one-on-one training at the Science Museum of Minnesota, where I learned the basics of this unusual and creative activity. The

This article originally appeared in the Winter 2010 issue of *YALS*.

remaining grant money funded a Teen Tech Week circuit-bending party.

Circuit-bending is the process of using electronic sound-making circuits to create sounds and music that the circuits were not designed to create. Electronic music-making toys for children are the most common instruments; they contain simple circuits and are designed to make various noises, be they polka beats or mooing cows. Initially developed in the 1960s, circuit-bending remains on the cutting edge of electronic music; artists such as Blur and Peter Gabriel include circuit-bent instruments in their work.[1] Circuit-bending offers an opportunity to demystify technology hardware and experiment with music and creativity.

What is great about circuit-bending is that you can run this activity on your own. Experts are a fantastic resource, and if your budget can cover it, I strongly recommend hiring an expert circuit-bender to lead workshops. But if that's not an option, you can learn the necessary skills and lead a workshop on your own. You do not even need to be highly tech-savvy. Provided that the sight of a circuit board does not cause you to hyperventilate and you are willing to experiment, this is a skill that is within your reach. I strongly recommend *Circuit-Bending: Build Your Own Alien Instruments* by Reed Ghazala as a starting point. It covers electrical components, tools, instrument decoration, and more, all with a wonderfully irreverent tone. It also includes step-by-step instructions for making specific circuit-bent instruments, so if you can find the appropriate raw materials, you can create a fully functional instrument for demonstration without all the trial and error.

Materials Needed

Tools
You will need screwdrivers in many sizes and types, especially one with a Phillips head. Look for screwdrivers with long necks to reach the screws. A set of tiny jeweler's screwdrivers is essential for the interior screws. You will also need wire cutters and wire strippers. Needle-nose pliers, though not essential, are useful for maneuvering into tighter spaces. I suggest skipping the soldering iron; permanent connections are not strictly necessary and it takes some practice to use the iron safely and successfully.

Supplies
Various supplies all serve the same basic purpose—to connect points on the circuit board. Play-Doh is the simplest tool, and some connections can be made with your hand, but ideally you also want electrical components. Test leads (lengths of wire with alligator clips at each end) are the easiest to use, but simple pieces of insulated wire will also work. LEDs, or light-emitting diodes, add a visual component to the experimentation. You should also collect various kinds of switches—push button (e.g., computer power button), toggle (e.g., light switches), and potentiometers (e.g., volume controls). Purchasing resistors, capacitors, and transistors is optional; although they can make some pretty cool sounds if you find the right connection points, it is more difficult to locate those connection points. These supplies can be purchased at low cost from a surplus store.

Your most essential raw materials, however, are children's toys. For these, I suggest a thrift store, or if you do not have a budget, try asking teens and your coworkers to bring in electronic toys they no longer need. You want toys that make music, especially those that can play a continuous tune, like the background beats on a toy keyboard. Be sure to bring batteries and a screwdriver (for those pesky childproof battery cases) to the store so you can make sure the toys actually work. Some stores do not mind if you switch out batteries in the aisles; others require you to bring toys to the cashier or customer service desk before removing batteries. Check with store staff to ensure you are following the correct procedures.

Space
Your ideal workshop space will be well lit and contain a large table with space for tools and supplies in the center. It is useful to provide heavy objects (some nice vampire romances or fantasy epics will work!) against which the teens can prop the top half of their toys. The wires that are linked between the top and bottom halves of the plastic casing are usually too short for the two halves to be laid flat.

The Workshop

I organized the workshop around three sections. First, we took apart the toys and I explained, in very general terms, how the toys work and how electricity passes along the circuit. I had the teens explore the circuits and test what noises their toys made under normal circumstances. Second, we moved on to experimenting with simple connections. Play-Doh is the best place to start; it triggers sounds very easily, and the teens can change the sounds by mashing the Play-Doh around. For more accurate pinpointing, we used insulated wires with alligator clips. Last, I had the teens select a few connections that produced interesting sounds and experiment with the more complicated components. The potentiometers were particularly popular because they gave the teens more control in creating various sounds.

Lessons Learned

Every new program has its own learning curve. Here are some tips based on my experience of running a circuit-bending workshop.

Set Realistic Goals

Having each participant create their own circuit-bent instrument is a complicated, time-consuming, and expensive proposition that does not lend itself to a casual setting. Unless you have a small group of very enthusiastic teens in a closed setting, it is probably too much to take on for your first program. Luckily, the experimental nature of bending circuits lends itself to a more casual atmosphere. Teens can use Play-Doh and wires to test out different connections and see what sounds they can make without creating any permanent connections. This also allows you to reuse the electronic toys for multiple programs and participants.

Test Your Toys

It is best to take apart every one of the toys ahead of time. Because the toys are machine-made, it often takes quite a bit of work to loosen up the screws. The process requires patience that your teens may not have during the program. Also, it allows you to weed out any toys that have internal problems or simply will not open. Just be sure to put the toys back together again before your program so the teens can still have fun taking things apart! Claiming one toy as your own permanent circuit-bending tool during your initial tests allows you to map out cool sounds for easy demonstration. If you have the time and inclination, you can even solder a few permanent connections to show your teens.

Plan for the Screws

It sounds a little silly, but this was one of the biggest problems I ran into. Ghazala suggests putting the screws on the magnetic portion of the speaker, which is a perfect solution when you are working with one or two toys. When you have six to ten rambunctious teens working on toys at the same table, however, things get a little more complicated. My suggestion: When you take the toys apart ahead of time, use a digital camera to take a picture of one of each kind of screw in the toy and note how many of each you need to put the toy back together. When you collect the dozens of screws that will end up under and around your workspace, you can use the pictures to match each toy with the correct screws.

Get Teen Buy-in

For some teens, the idea of taking something apart and messing with the insides will be an easy sell, but for others it may be hard to visualize what circuit-bending is all about. See if a local circuit-bending artist would be willing to do a demo for your teen advisory group or bookmark some circuit-bending performances on YouTube to give teens a clearer picture. Make connections with the activities your teens are already enthusiastic about, like remixing and creating beats for hip-hop and electronica or creating eerie background music for anime music videos. If you have access to a microphone, try to work a recording element into your plan so teens can follow through on those ideas.

Be Safe

Whenever you are working with circuit boards, keep in mind that there is often lead in the solder used to attach components on a circuit board. You and your teens should wash your hands thoroughly after circuit-bending. Any snacks should be served before circuit-bending begins and put away before you break out the toys. Do not try to scavenge circuit-board parts from discarded electronics if it involves cutting into or chipping away at any soldered connections.[2]

Conclusion

Our "Party Like It's Teen Tech Week" event was a huge success with our regular crowd and with many teens who had never before visited Teen Central. Many newcomers attended because the program was highlighted on a local morning news program. Some of the most enthusiastic circuit-benders were actually younger siblings and relatives who accompanied the teen attendees. The circuit-bending aspect of the party was designed to tie in with existing programs in the library, so teens were able to move from one activity to the next and get a sense of the programming available at Teen Central. Our teen advisory group set up a Wii *Super Smash Bros. Brawl* tournament. Our Teen Tech Squad interns created a temporary local-area network on which to test open-source multiplayer games.

Our program gave teens leadership opportunities, exposed young people to technology, and encouraged interest in the library. The skills and equipment used in the program are being adopted by our Teen Tech Squad interns for use in our monthly Open Tech Lab, where teens work with a variety of open-source software and do-it-yourself electronics to increase their technology skills and express themselves creatively. We are very grateful for this opportunity to extend the technical literacy skills of our teens and engage them in exciting, enjoyable programming.

NOTES

1. Reed Ghazala, *Circuit-Bending: Build Your Own Alien Instruments* (Indianapolis: John Wiley, 2005), 4–6.
2. Brittany Forks, *Kilobyte Couture* (New York: Watson-Guptill, 2009), 19.

MARKETING, OUTREACH, AND PROMOTION FOR **TEEN TECH WEEK**

IN THIS CHAPTER, you'll find tips for using pop culture to market to teens and taking your marketing online where the teens are, and an interview with Stephen Abrams on what kind of technology teens will want at your library. Along with marketing and promotion tips, learn how to reach out to teens with special needs and potential partners to make this your best Teen Tech Week yet!

WHAT TEENS WANT: WHAT LIBRARIES CAN LEARN FROM MTV

Erin Helmrich

Sometimes I wonder if I can handle one more glamorous day in the library—the swarms of teens begging me for a booktalk, the gangs of popular kids wishing they could be on my teen advisory board—it gets to me. Can't I just go back to the days when only dorks and losers used the library? I wish this were my life. I am a pop culture addict with a "big picture" problem. I dream of a day when a rap star is the reason teens use my library. I dream of a day when "Got Library Card?" is the new celebrity cause—when someone sings about their mom taking them to the library instead of serving milk. Someday my dream will come true, but first we must change the way we think. What do teens want? We struggle to answer this question in a million different ways and with a million different "solutions." The answers are all around us, but because we often insist on a "library model," we don't always look in the right places. Consider a different approach and choose a new viewpoint.

This article originally ran in the Spring 2004 issue of YALS.

In 2003 I attended the "What Teens Want: Marketing to Teens (ages 12 to 17) Using Music, Movies, and the Media" conference. I figured that a conference hosted, sponsored, and presented by the likes of *Adweek*, the WB network, *Teen Vogue*, and *Billboard* might provide some interesting perspectives. The true audience for this conference was account executives in marketing, advertising, licensing, and brand management in industries like publishing, apparel and accessories, fashion, retailing, entertainment, telecommunications, and so on.

I had been eyeing this conference ever since it was originally scheduled in 2001—that year it was planned for November, was eventually canceled, and has been in renegotiations ever since. As a teen librarian with a pop culture fixation, this conference was a perfect fit. What harder "sell" is there than the notion that the library can be a cool place?

MTV Is Doing Something Right

As an MTV baby from its inception, I was thrilled when I found out that the kickoff keynote was none other that Brian Graden, then-president of entertainment at MTV and VH1 (and close personal friend of *South Park* creators Trey Parker and Matt Stone). Under Graden's direction, MTV had some of its highest ratings with *The Osbournes, Cribs, Making the Video, Jackass,* and *Total Request Live.* If this were not proof of Mr. Graden's innate understanding of "what teens want now," then the electrifying and inspirational talk he gave would be. Mr. Graden spoke about teens today with a passion and enthusiasm that was contagious. A few of his main points:

- The technological divide will only widen. The more technologically savvy that teens become, combined with a complete lack of savvy among many adults, the harder it will be for adults to tune in to their world and learn what drives them.
- Teens today are much more adept at cutting and pasting their style, their identity, and their ideals with past/present, punk/prep—challenging us to the max.
- There is no sense of right or wrong—only gray. The Internet is their geography—a world where there are no rules, false identities are the norm, and downloading almost anything takes just the press of a button. In a world of reality TV based on lies, teens today are more likely to see the spin; they learn to play all sides.

Graden spoke at length about the combination of research and focus groups with pure inspiration, art, and ideas to come up with the magic that is MTV. Shows on MTV burn very fast—as they are expected to—but it is this ephemeral and elusive quality that drives the network's success. Ultimately, Graden's main recommendation is to be "in" the teen experience as much as possible. Listen to their music, watch their TV shows: not only will the teen themes reveal themselves, but you will be reminded of the emotional search, which stays constant no matter what generation it is.

Breaking the Code

Want to be as up to the minute as H&M? Then Irma Zandl is your woman. And it will only cost you tens of thousands of dollars! Her presentation, "Values, Attitudes, and Lifestyles: Through the Psychographic Lens," was mind blowing. Corporations pay Zandl Group more than $15,000 a year for six bimonthly "hot sheet" reports. Zandl's (www.zandlgroup.com) New York–based consulting and research boutique specializes in young consumers from tweens through young adults. With a consumer panel of teens numbering in the thousands, Zandl's anthropological approach is dead-on. Using their interests and attitudes as guideposts, Zandl can divide teens into various categories. These categories are by no means finite or universally applicable, but they do offer a baseline from which to build. Keep in mind that these categories change often—Zandl produces a "hot sheet" six times a year in order to keep her clients as up-to-date as possible, so use this information wisely, but don't count on it twelve months from now!

Teen Tech Savvy

Don't become roadkill on the tech highway! How many of us use e-mail, chat, or text messaging to market the library to teens? Maybe those flyers you put out in the teen area just aren't cutting it anymore. According to a Harris Interactive and CTIA (a wireless trade association poll), four out of five teens own a mobile phone. Billions of text messages are sent every month—on everything from homework questions to note passing and flirting. Technology has allowed today's teens to be free agents in choice. Camera phones, interactive TV, downloading music, text messaging—teens have seamlessly integrated technology into their lives. Technology is part of the social currency of being a teen: from voting on *American Idol* to chatting with the stars of their favorite shows, teens use technology in ways that we aren't even aware of—a divide that will only increase with each new generation.

Reel Life

Done well, there are few mediums that can replicate the full-range of emotions and senses involved in living the way that film can. The directors of critically acclaimed "teen" films spoke at the conference. Catherine Hardwicke, the cowriter and director of *Thirteen* and director of *Twilight*; Stacy Peralta, cowriter and director of *Dogtown and Z-Boys*; and Justin Lin, cowriter and director of *Better Luck*

Tomorrow; all shared their stories. Hardwicke was a particularly inspiring speaker. Her story about how she came to write *Thirteen* with her then-teenage friend (and star of the film) Nikki Reed was the one compassionate voice heard at the conference. Hardwicke touched on the real-life issues that affect teens' lives, and she challenged those in attendance to take a more humane approach to the conference's topics.

Real Teens

One of the only other youth advocates I met at the conference was Kate Dunlop Seamans, onetime editor of *TeenInk*. Ms. Seamans coordinated a fantastic teen panel featuring local Santa Monica high school students. While the twelve teens answered questions about cell phone ring tones, contests, music, and movies, what was most enjoyable was listening to their humor and candor—the ways in which they expressed their individuality while also identifying themselves as part of their generation. Proof that teens do heed message advertising, the teens noted that they liked "The Truth" anti-smoking ads. They responded to the provocative and edgy style of the ads, but also trusted the message.

Now What?

Librarians need agents. Hey, if milk, meat, and bread need to advertise themselves, why shouldn't we? Competition is what drives the private sector, and to a greater extent every year, institutions like the YMCA and the library are no longer a given in the crowded marketplace. At a time when taxpayers are making tough choices about funding, we cannot afford to take our communities for granted. "They'll never close the library!" Why not? Many, many people live full lives without using their local library. Has your library proven its worth to the taxpayers?

What's your favorite commercial? Do you cry during Hallmark ads, sing along with the Gap ads? Don't you feel better about all of your cotton clothing now that you know that it's the "fabric of our lives"? Good advertising is a powerful thing. Like the www.thetruth.com ads, a library marketing campaign can be cool and authentic while also communicating important information. Why are all library promotions about reading? Our summer *reading* programs, Teen *Read* Week, the *Read* posters. Is reading the only way our communities can enjoy the library?

Step out of your comfort zone, throw out the old rules, and try something new. Instead of surveying your teens about their library usage or asking them what they want from the library, ask your teens who they are.

- Never stop asking—because it never stops changing.
- Integrate teen pop culture into your information seeking: what's popular often reveals a deeper truth about the audience it attracts.
- Change your approach: the library is a "brand" that you have to sell.
- Explore opportunities to integrate more technology into your publicity and promotion to teens. If you're lucky enough to have an in-house techie (or techie department), work with them to come up with creative ways to use emerging technologies with teens.
- Participate in the process yourself: send a text message from your cell phone if you never have before or IM a friend the next time you're online.

The next time you're at the mall—look closely—notice the signage, displays, use of color and fonts, and imagine incorporating some of these ideas into the library setting. Take a closer look at commercials and advertising for teens. What are some of the techniques they use to grab teen money? Watch MTV for an hour—study the shows, the ads, the music, the aesthetics. How can you replicate the MTV experience in the library?

Lastly, for those of you who mourn the "loss" of more traditional library service or those of you who have a problem using consumerism as a tool to serve teens, consider this: Libraries can either move forward and embrace the changes that are coming our way, or they can become irrelevant antiquities. I, for one, would rather be a participant in the revolution and not a casualty of it.

ADVOCATING FOR TEENS' TECHNOLOGICAL NEEDS: A Q&A WITH STEPHEN ABRAM

YALSA Technology for Young Adults Committee

The YALSA Technology for Young Adults Committee (TYAC) hosted a session featuring Stephen Abram at the 2006 ALA Annual Conference in New Orleans. Abram is past president of the Canadian Library Association, past president of the Ontario Library Association, and past vice president of innovation for SirsiDynix. We took the opportunity to ask Abram a few questions about serving this generation of young adults.

TYAC: What are the essential library services we should be offering to millennials?

Abram: "Essential" is a difficult word. Thinking skills, information literacy training, and great collections are essential. However, I suspect that "essential" really refers to understanding what technologies actually align with millennial skills and behaviors and enhance learning and development. So, in that context, "essential" would include the following:

- Advanced web access with decent broadband speed. You can't support all learners if your access is worse than most of their peers' home systems. Wireless is becoming essential. Rural and remote areas are not exempt from this.

- Place few limits on the browser's functionality. Try to avoid thinking that control trumps exploration.

- Use instant messaging (IM) with students, peers, teachers, and fellow librarians. E-mail is so last century. IM is a mainstream technology.

- Blog. Both ways. Leave comments on.

- Develop learning portals that support the curriculum. Partner between public and school libraries. We're in the same business and serve the same users. Serve parents as well as teens for homework helper applications.

- Ensure that there is community adoption of electronic content sources, "Best of the Web"

lists, streaming media, online courseware, and so on. Then make the world aware of these services. Go beyond just marketing article databases.

- Support community-wide experiments to understand the roles played by new technologies like gaming, iPods, and iTunes.

TYAC: What is the best thing we can do to advocate for our teen library customers?

Abram: Again, "best" is such a situational word. Every child or learner is different and every school and community has different strengths, challenges, and initiatives. That said, of course I have an opinion! So here goes . . .

- Advocate for light (or even no) filtering. Teens can't learn how to deal with the world of information if they never see examples of the range.

- Advocate for tools that align with teens' comfort levels. For example, disabling IM on library PCs just makes the library appear dysfunctional or, worse, lame.

- Advocate for tools and technology that support the full range of learning styles. Our text-based collections are totally necessary, but many (maybe most) learners need interactivity, visuals, and sound. Public library and school PCs that don't support these formats or restrict their use are misaligned with the needs of teens.

- Advocate to teens in their spaces. Learning happens in social environments as much as in formal environments. So, review how you might work with or be present in such environments as MySpace, Facebook, or Second Life. In 2006, MySpace was headed to be the most visited site on the web, with 2.5 times the traffic of Google.

- In public libraries, reduce friction points that

This article originally appeared in the Summer 2006 issue of *YALS*.

add nothing to the user experience. Do we really need to have so many rules that disrupt our image with teens? Consider building a teen advisory council and even have them develop training sessions for your staff.

TYAC: In your article "Born with the Chip," you discuss collaboration as a key characteristic of the way NextGens learn. How can we as librarians capitalize on this trait?

Abram: Kids are educated in what is essentially a collaboration-oriented environment. They do much of their work in teams; they carry their high comfort levels with collaboration into their social and work lives. Librarians can capitalize on this by offering services that support teens' collaboration behaviors. This means more than being comfortable with one IM client. You can't just choose one—like MSN, AIM, or Yahoo! You need to support all of them. Use clients like Trillian and Pidgin, or web-based services like Meebo that aggregate the major IM services and clients. Then you're cooking with gas. Libraries that have adopted full or limited IM reference are seeing the payoffs. Next, add collaboration services—like professional virtual reference that lets you track transcripts and mine the data for insights into user behaviors, or simple co-browsing software like Jybe. Public libraries can offer information literacy training using live meeting software to align with school-based programs that use Blackboard or other courseware. Lastly, review your physical space. Are there too many carrels and too few round tables? Can the tables support group technology? Are there social spaces? Are the spaces built to control sound and limit annoyances for other users? Are teens given a respectful distance for privacy, or are they treated to a fishbowl environment?

TYAC: What are the implications of the self-service model for traditional librarian-delivered services?

Abram: Self-service is a huge opportunity. There is not a librarian or library worker in the world today who will tell you that they have enough hours to accomplish everything they need to do. So why would we continue to waste time buried in non-value-added tasks that can be automated to free up our time to do programming that makes an impact? Self-checkout, circulation tools on PDAs, RFID, PC booking software, online holds, e-reserves, and e-book circulation all offer the opportunity to serve more patrons at lower costs. Then we can focus on what is actually strategic. What programs engage the kids and bring them into the library? How many messages can we deliver at once? When a library offers a "Rock the Stacks" local band night after hours, it isn't really just about the teens and music. You engage teens in the library, improve your relationship with current and future users, and even circulate a few items. No one leaves without a transformed opinion. The same things happen when libraries have gaming collections and gaming events. Some of our traditional services are fantastic. Some are musty. Rita Mae Brown wrote that insanity is doing the same things in the same way that we have always done and expecting different results. If we want better results, we have to experiment with some new ideas.

TYAC: What are some ways the "Librarian 2.0" can facilitate communication between millennials and reluctant librarians and administrators?

Abram: Call them on it. Ask if the library is serious in gaining the attention of the largest demographic cohort in history. This generation of millennials is larger than the boomers—and it's growing through immigration. All other markets are shrinking. Are libraries ready to leave them behind? What about when they're voting for library budgets? This is an amazing generation of smart, talented kids. Here are a few techniques that can help with the journey to respecting this major group of users:

- Have a teen advisory board. Don't just pick friendly, local users. Make the board reflect your community of teens. Listen to them; don't just talk at them. Don't be defensive. Respect their experience.

- Demonstrate that you listen. Take action on what they say about their needs. Be open about changing some of your rules.

- Have annual panels of teen users interact with all staff. I have done this many times, and it never ceases to transform opinion.

- Play with their tools. Just play. You'll start to understand. Don't kill understanding with policies, committees, and the like before you understand the overall dynamic. Don't study the tools to death, though. That's not your goal, either. Lose control for just a little while and start to learn anew.

- Assign staff to talk to a half dozen teens in the family or neighborhood. Bring these viewpoints back to the ranch for brownbag sessions. Ask questions that explore teen behaviors rather than judge them.
- Serve as an example and role model—blog, IM, podcast. Model the behaviors and share them. Change will happen.

TYAC: How can we retain the "magic of librarianship" virtually or through digital devices?

Abram: A lot of the conversations over the past few years have covered our "bricks" and "clicks" strategies. I have added "tricks" to this conversation. The magic of librarianship cannot be allowed to go away in the virtual world. That means more virtual reference, more IM, more "Ask a Librarian" buttons. These things are necessary for survival and evolution. We also need to understand what our "magic" is. Some librarians spend a great deal of effort defining themselves as information professionals—people who deliver information and organize it. I prefer to think that it's a means to an end. I like to think librarians are "question" professionals. We improve the quality of the question and everything else flows from that. As we create new and revitalized experiences in our physical and virtual presences, we generate the magic that creates the knowledge-based society. Teens will experience more of this new world than we will. It's incumbent on us to lay a great foundation.

PARTNERSHIPS FOR TEEN TECH WEEK
Stephanie Iser

YALSA's Teen Tech Week (TTW) initiative urges librarians serving teens to act as qualified, trusted professionals in the field of information technology. While teen librarians may be knowledgeable of teens' technology needs, a lack of financial support can roadblock quality teen tech programs and services. One way of addressing this financial issue is to look outside the library doors for a potential partner. By partnering with local businesses and organizations that have access to new technologies, the library can gain resources needed to run a successful technology-based program.

Benefits of Partnering

One of the main reasons for partnering is the potential gain in resources for programs and services. For example, a library might not have the money to purchase multiple gaming systems for a teen video game club, but there may be a local gaming store that would be willing to demonstrate the Nintendo Wii or Xbox 360. Another resource that can be gained is the expertise of the partners. As in the gaming example, the store representatives probably know quite a bit about gaming systems and can make qualified recommendations to teens.

Community building is another benefit of partnering with local businesses and organizations. Through partnerships for teens, young adult library services' visibility is raised within the eyes of the partners and affiliates. When the partnership offers a new resource that wouldn't otherwise be available, there also is a possibility of recruiting new teen patrons that are interested in these new services.

Even with all the benefits of partnering, there are a few drawbacks. Partnerships require time and effort on behalf of both parties, which could amount to several meetings to plan and finalize the programs. Plans may need to be approved by several levels of management. With careful planning and advanced preparation, however, these drawbacks can have less of an impact.

Partnership Success Examples

Local businesses can provide financial support, advertising, and technical expertise for your array of teen tech programs. Theresa Woldermann, librarian at Old Bridge (New Jersey) Public Library, which won the 2007 TTW contest for best program, found that the local Apple store was a good candidate for this type of partnership. She got the idea from her teen advisory board during a brainstorming session, during which

This article originally appeared in the Winter 2008 issue of *YALS*.

most ideas thrown onto the table were "tech-ier" than library staff and teens could handle alone. Through discussion, the teens found they had something in common—all could not live without their iPods, yet few had actually created a podcast. One of the teens suggested that the library approach the local Apple store for help with a podcasting class.

On the advice of the teens, Woldermann spoke with the local Apple store's assistant manager. The meeting resulted in two teen programs: "Podcasting Basics" and "iLife 101." The library provided the meeting space while the Apple store provided the expertise and equipment. Theresa found that working with the Apple store gave the Teen Tech program a higher credibility with the community's brand-conscious teens. While the library benefited from the Apple store's knowledge of podcasting, the Apple store received free publicity for products.

One way of gaining teen interest is to feature a speaker of notoriety. Kathie Burns, school librarian at the Arnold O. Beckman Library Media Center in Irvine, California, gained teen approval when she worked with a reporter from the local county newspaper to present "Latest Tech Gadgets for Teens." After a series of phone calls and e-mails, reporter Tamara Chuang, also known as the "Gadgetress," agreed to do a presentation during a school lunch period that had an audience of around seventy-five teens.

In addition, the Irvine Police Department provided service by presenting "What You Don't Know Can't Hurt You: MySpace, YouTube, and Online Gaming," which also attracted a large audience. Kathie mentions that her Teen Tech Week programs would not have been possible without these partnerships.

It's no myth that school and public libraries can do amazing things when working together. For the 2007 TTW celebration, I partnered with a school librarian to provide a gaming program at the local high school. Michelle Lowe, librarian at Central High School in Kansas City, Missouri, mentioned that many of the students didn't have public library cards and would sometimes use this as an excuse for not completing research assignments. In response to this issue, we brainstormed methods for using TTW to get students signed up for cards. After a few meetings, we had a plan: We would host a free gaming session during a school lunch period of TTW, but students had to have a public library card to be admitted.

Through this collaboration, the school librarian

was able to provide students with a video game program that she would not otherwise be able to offer, as gaming equipment is not typically in the budget for school library media centers. In return, I received free publicity for the library's TTW event that took place the very next day. These mutual benefits were the result of the brainpower of two librarians as opposed to one.

Tips for Partnering

If you are considering a tech partnership for teens, here are a few tips:

- **Think locally.** Start at the local level when approaching community organizations and businesses. For example, a call to central head-quarters might not get you very far, but a visit to the local store is more personable and will likely receive better results.

- **Be flexible.** There may be a few policies that make it impossible to get the donations you'd really like. Find out what is available, and be sure to send a thank-you note.

- **Share a common goal.** Be sure that the partnership actually benefits the teens in your community. Don't waste time with partners that want to take without giving anything in return.

- **Plan ahead.** Begin developing the partnership at least two months before the service or program is scheduled. It could take a handful of meetings to make larger partnerships come to fruition, and there may be more than one level of management involved in the approval process.

- **Try and try again.** What works for one person will not work for the next, as policy tends to vary from region to region and store to store. For example, in one community the local gaming store might be more than willing to set up a monthly gaming event for teens, while another may be understaffed and unable to donate time.

- **Be positive.** Remember, you are representing the library and the needs of teens in your community. Every potential partner is worth the effort, because the request for support raises visibility of teen services in the eyes of community organizations and local businesses.

Through teen tech partnerships, libraries can gain the support and resources they wouldn't otherwise have to run successful Teen Tech Week events. Relationships with organizations and businesses also raise the visibility of teen library services within the community. More partnership and program ideas for Teen Tech Week can be found on the YALSA wiki at http://wikis.ala.org/yalsa/index.php/Teen_Tech_Week.

MARKETING THE HOMEWORK CENTER DIGITALLY

Suellen S. Adams

Libraries across the country are creating a wide variety of web-based and in-library homework help centers. Some are manned by adult volunteers, others by student tutors who help younger students. Librarians are virtually always involved in creating and promoting the centers. These centers may handle everything from remedial tutoring to hands-on assistance in planning, organizing, researching and writing papers, and other types of literacy instruction. Whatever the mission or goal of your particular center, it is not enough to design and build it, whether face-to-face, web-based, or both. Building it does not ensure that "they will come."

Marketing is a joint process between service providers and clientele. It is no longer a matter of having an "us and them" relationship, but of having "us and us" as partners in the marketing process. Of course, much more is involved. But the point is that marketing is more than just believing that we have a wonderful product and trying to convince others of this so that they will use it. Therefore, we must not only make users aware of the services the homework center offers, but ideally give them a voice in the process, so that we can actually make the service work for them.

We must first determine who the customers are for our service. Then, since they exist in a rich context, we must evaluate that context. Students and librarians are the first people we think of when developing a homework help center, but there are others we also need to reach—parents, school personnel, and the community at large, for instance. To a greater or lesser degree, most of these people are increasingly "plugged in" to digital technologies. So how can we go about using technology to reach these groups?

Reaching our customers, particularly teens, can be a challenge, especially if we wish to attract those who do not already frequent the library. We often think of reaching our customers via local businesses such as banks and grocery stores, where parents might see flyers or other publicity, or in places where teens spend time, such as teen centers, youth clubs, the mall, and after-school activities. These channels remain, but they clearly leave out an important part of the teens' context—the digital part.

We already know and use traditional publicity tools such as brochures, press releases, bulletin boards, and giveaways. But we need also to consider nontraditional means, such as social networking applications. The following are some ways to teach stakeholders, most importantly teens, through technology:

- E-mail and electronic discussion groups
- Web pages
- Blogs
- Social networking sites

E-newsletters for all sorts of groups and businesses have become popular in recent years. This innovation allows us to convey the same information to roughly the same audience as traditional paper newsletters for a smaller cost, since we no longer must consider printing costs and bulk mail rates. On the other hand, however, is another whole set of technological and design issues. As Christine Sevilla reminds us, e-newsletters, especially those in a text-only format, can have the same design problems as the paper variety.[1] Sometimes writers try to make them more pleasing by using html formats, but not every e-mail application deals well with these formats, and some users do not like them. Some e-newsletters are sent as attachments, which can result in technical issues.

Because so many businesses and organizations now use e-newsletters, many customers have their

This article originally appeared in the Winter 2010 issue of *YALS*.

e-mail boxes cluttered with such mail and they go directly into the junk mail, where they are not opened at all. Exacerbating this problem is the temptation to send mass e-mailings and to send more frequent e-newsletters, which may just increase the number of deletions by customers.

If the library wishes to send frequent updates, and if the customers wish to receive them, an electronic discussion list or blog targeted toward a certain customer population may be a better choice. In either case, those who really desire the information can subscribe and there is often a mechanism for response. This capability for customer response is a very useful part of many digital technologies and will help us fine-tune our service and its promotion.

Blogs are sites with regular entries of commentary, descriptions of events, or other material. Entries are commonly displayed in reverse-chronological order so readers can see the latest news but can also scroll down or link to archives of interest. Typically the blog will contain text and images, sometimes including videos, links to other pages, or other content. A vital aspect of maintaining a blog related to your homework help center is the interactive ability for readers to leave comments that is nearly always a feature of blogs. This gives us clues about who has interest and what they think. Be aware, though, that once a blog has been started, it must be kept up. Once the content becomes stale or outdated, the readers will not come back and the comments that could have helped strengthen the service will dry up. Someone must be assigned to keep the blog updated and follow the comments on a frequent basis.

Most libraries now have web pages that can be put to good use in promoting new services. A "See What's New" button with the homework help center logo could be linked to a page specifically about the center, for instance. And a library blog of any type should certainly be linked from the library page. Web pages of various municipalities can also serve as an entry to your web page. If the local school district approves, perhaps a link could be added to the schools' web pages leading to the library page or the homework help center page. School websites are a particularly good way to reach teens and their parents. Both may visit these sites for items such as school newsletters, schedules of events, contact information, and so on. If your information is prominent and inviting enough, this placement can raise awareness of your center and increase its use.

One way to think about social networking sites such as MySpace and Facebook is this: from time immemorial, people have learned things by word of mouth through their connections. Even now, one of the most commonly sought and trusted sources of information is the peer group, and this is true whether one is a parent, a child, a teen, a scientist, or an engineer. Information reported by a friend or colleague often carries more weight than a formal source. That is an unhappy thought for many librarians, but it need not be. The energy of informal communication can be harnessed online.

In social networking online, we are purposely trying to create networks of people with whom we can share thoughts and who will, in turn, share information about our services with the rest of their networks. When using social networks, there are some important points to remember:

- We must take care to behave within our social networks as we would if we were dealing with people face-to-face. Just as a positive interaction or a negative interaction in person will make a difference in the information you pass on to others, so will a comparable interaction online.

- It is important to remember the proper uses of the social network. As one expert commented, "Social networking sites are back-and-forth communication forums, not broadcast media. Annoy or abuse people and they'll tell the world."[2]

- Social networks, like any kind of personal relationship or network, require personal attention, and that means taking time. It is not enough to put up a MySpace page or a Facebook group and leave it for people to find. If you cannot be current, it may not pay to do it at all. Someone must update it often to keep others coming back for new content.

- It is important to follow the links and comments left by people responding to your content, making more personal connections by commenting there, checking their networks to see who you might contact, and so on. This is wonderful way to reach teens, but it is a labor-intensive process.

Finally, when considering any of these technological strategies, particularly blogging and social networking solutions, remember that it is unwise to jump in because it is "the thing." All of these things sound glitzy and cool, but that may not be enough of a reason to make use of them. We must weigh the time and cost against the impact it will have on reaching our customers.

NOTES

1. Christine Sevilla, *Information Design Desk Reference* (Menlo Park, CA: Crisp Publications, 2002), 182.

2. Bobbette Kyle, "Online Marketing through Social Networking Sites (Part 2)," 2008, http://www.website marketingplan.com/online/socialnetworking2.htm (accessed June 10, 2009).

TECHNOLOGY FOR EVERY TEEN @ YOUR LIBRARY
Vikki C. Terrile

Few teen librarians would argue the importance of technology in library services to young people. Today's library calendars are packed with gaming and computer programs; library websites proudly link to teen-generated podcasts and social networking pages; and more and more libraries are adding text alerts to their options for staying in contact with library users. But, as recent posts on the YALSA blog have pointed out, it may be that teens with special needs are being inadvertently left out of this new frontier.[1] Approaching accessibility can be intimidating, especially for those who don't think of themselves as particularly tech-savvy, but there are more than enough resources available to help any librarian make sure all teens can enjoy the technology that today's libraries have to offer.

According to the U.S. Census Bureau, 8.5 percent of Americans age fourteen and under and 10.5 percent of fifteen- to twenty-four-year-olds have some type of disability provided for under the Americans with Disabilities Act (ADA), defined as "a physical or mental impairment that substantially limits one or more major life activities."[2] Another source shows that in 2006 a total of 2,997,346—or roughly 12 percent of teens between the ages of twelve and seventeen—received special education services in the United States and outlying areas. This number reflects any student receiving services for a disability included in the Individuals with Disabilities Education Act (IDEA). IDEA lists the categories of disability as mental retardation, hearing impairments including deafness, speech or language impairments, visual impairments including blindness, emotional disturbance, ortho-

pedic impairments, autism, traumatic brain injury, other health impairments, multiple disabilities, deaf-blindness, specific learning disabilities, and developmental delay. But each state has its own criteria to determine if a student is eligible for services under a particular disability.[3] This means that easily one in ten of our potential teen library users has a special need that can affect how they use the library.

The ADA requires that libraries provide equitable access to all services for people with special needs. This includes reasonable accommodations for technology, though there is continuing debate over how this applies to websites.[4] Learning about assistive and adaptive technologies can be intimidating; a good place to start is the Association of Specialized and Cooperative Library Agencies (ASCLA) Tool Kit tip sheet on assistive technology (and the many other tip sheets in the Tool Kit) for an overview of what the different products offer.[5] William Reed, assistant head librarian at the Cleveland Public Library for the Blind and Physically Handicapped, also suggests looking at resources like the World Wide Web Consortium's (W3C) Web Accessibility Initiative, Section 508, and the U.S. Access Board for a better understanding of accessible technology (see the Accessibility Resource Guide in the sidebar).[6] Barbara Huntington, youth and special services consultant at the Wisconsin Department of Public Instruction, believes that public libraries should offer services such as accessible workstations, electronic and technology tools (adapted keyboard, trackballs, switches, Braille printers, scanners, and adaptive software), accessible program or meeting

This article originally appeared in the Winter 2009 issue of *YALS*.

aids (microphones and real-time captioning), and accessible library web pages, in addition to accessible formats for media, including recorded, Braille, and large-print books, closed-captioned videos, and materials in languages other than English.[7] Sharon Rawlins, youth services consultant at the New Jersey State Library, adds that while adaptive technology may be expensive, libraries should have at least one computer equipped with some type of screen reader software (which converts print into speech) or have a Kurzweil machine (which converts text to speech or Braille).[8]

Many of the areas where teen librarians focus their technology programming can pose real difficulties for teens with disabilities, even with assistive hardware. In his post to the YALSA blog, Joseph Wilk refers to a recent article about how lack of captioning and narration on many websites are limiting use by people with visual and hearing impairments.[9] This can also affect teens with learning disabilities. For example, while social networking sites remain hugely popular with teens, many of these sites lock out users with certain types of disabilities before they can even open an account. These sites use CAPTCHA, a visual verification code shown as a display of distorted letters and numbers that cannot be deciphered by software, to ensure that people, not computers, are trying to set up accounts. This technology works so well, in fact, that screen reader programs cannot interpret the code, so for users with vision impairments, dyslexia, or other learning difficulties, trouble interpreting the graphic can prevent them from going beyond the sign-up page.[10]

Since this information made web headlines in January 2008, Facebook and Google have added an audio option to CAPTCHA, but CAPTCHA may show up unexpectedly in other places that teens visit on the Internet. Of course, anyone who has tried to buy tickets online has run into that window of weird characters (Ticketmaster does offer an audio verification option), but during Virtual Library Day on the Hill at the ALA Annual Conference 2008, we found that many elected officials use CAPTCHA (without an audio option) to authenticate the electronic messages they receive. Reed also points out that few social networking sites are alt-tagged: equipped with descriptive text as an alternative to images that is read by screen readers and search engines. One way around these problems is for adaptive technology users to use the different features (like blogs or instant messaging) separate from the larger site so teens with special needs can be creative about how they use these features.[11]

Video game programs continue to gain popularity, allowing teens to play in a social setting they don't get at home on their couch. Elizabeth Burns, youth services consultant at the New Jersey Library for the Blind and Handicapped, says that some of the most popular games at her library are accessible for teens with specials needs; the Nintendo Wii sports games work well for teens with visual impairments, especially boxing, baseball, and bowling.[12] Huntington says a teen who uses a wheelchair and has good use of his hands can participate in a *Guitar Hero* program quite easily.[13] There are many resources on the web for gamers, educators, and game designers about using and building accessible games, such as the notes from a June 2008 presentation to MIT's Gambit game lab that offers practical insight on the issues facing gamers with disabilities.[14]

Today's teens are technologically resilient, making them able to figure out a way to get to the information and services they want even if it is not obviously accessible. If your library's adaptive technology tools are only on computers designated for adult use, look for creative ways to ensure that teens have access to those machines in ways that are comfortable for them. You could also invite teens who use adaptive or assistive technology to show other teen and adult patrons (and staff members!) how it works.[15] Reed suggests that simply asking teens with special needs how they use technology or having them test Library 2.0 tools and utilities for accessibility will not only increase their access but can improve access awareness within the library.[16]

Having a strong virtual presence is important for all libraries that support teen services, so work with your teens to create virtual services that are as teen friendly as they are accessible. Look at how you can have audio options for print information or alternative text and captioning for pictures and video. If you are fortunate enough to have an IT department or webmaster, they should be included in conversations with the teens so that they can understand the teens' needs and offer technologically sound suggestions. If you are directly responsible for maintaining your library's teen web pages, consider having the teens themselves work on creating the transcripts and captioning, for example, of the podcasts and videos they produce.

Once your library's teen web page is fully accessible, it can become a true gateway to all your services. For teens with adaptive technology at home, virtual programs can eliminate transportation and mobility barriers. An online book discussion may facilitate participation for a variety of teens who might not join in at the library—for example, teens with speech problems, those in a hospital with a long-term illness, or even teens in juvenile detention.[17] Newsletters, e-mail updates, and a frequently updated website are all easy ways to let teen library patrons know about new virtual programs in addition to what is happening in-house. These tools can also be effective ways to receive feedback about what you are offering. Consider adding a virtual component to your teen advisory board so that teens who cannot or do not come into the library can have more of a voice in planning library services.[18]

When considering access, don't forget to think beyond technology to the many other programs and services you offer teens. Physical teen spaces and collections should also be as welcoming and inclusive as possible, even if you do not think there are teens with special needs in your community (there are!). Rawlins says things like high-interest and low-reading-level books, large-print teen books, audiobooks, and e-books for teens, as well as shelving and computers that are easily accessible, are all things that will make the library easier to use for a variety of teen consumers.[19] Make sure all patrons know that Talking Book Libraries provide services to anyone who has difficulty reading print (including patrons with physical and reading disabilities) for free. This is also a good time to consider your library's policies and procedures to make sure they are not unintentionally alienating teens or anyone else with special needs. Consider using universal design as your service model. This concept, borrowed from the building industry, shifts the focus from adapting existing or adding extra services for people with special needs to creating an array of services that will be more easily used by all consumers. According to Rachel Gould, children and youth services librarian at Perkins Braille and Talking Book Library, program and outreach plans that use a universal design approach and integrate multiple intelligences and diverse learning styles will benefit all library users, including those with special needs, without singling anyone out.[20]

There may be some barriers to teens' library use that you are not even aware of—things that teen customers perceive as unwelcoming. Burns points out that valuing print above other formats is a common example of this; excluding audiobooks from summer reading tells teens who listen to books that they are not welcome.[21] "Truly realize that there are many ways to read," says Gould. "Listening to books is not any less valuable than reading print."[22] Of course, the biggest barrier to access may be the attitudes of staff. The fact that you are not seeing teens with special needs from your community in your library may be an indicator that somewhere along the way teens received a message that they are not welcome.[23] If you hear from teens that this is the case, bring their concerns to your administration to see what can be done to improve the behavior of staff. Consider whether this is an issue with teens in general, people with disabilities, or some combination of the two.

Through outreach efforts and a commitment to the participation of a wide and diverse population of your teen community, you will learn what matters to them and may also discover what has happened (or not) to make them feel welcome in the library and at programs. Use what you learn to inform your work with staff to ensure that all patrons—including teens and people with special needs of any age—are welcome and can have equal access to the materials and services that your library offers.

NOTES

1. Joseph Wilk, "When It Comes to Teens, Don't Forget Accessibility," YALSA blog, July 8, 2008, http://yalsa.ala.org/blog/2008/07/08/when-it-comes-to-teens-tech-dont-forget-accessibility (accessed September 3, 2008).

2. Erica Steinmetz, *Americans with Disabilities: 2002 Household Economic Studies*, Current Population Reports (Washington, DC: U.S. Census Bureau, 2006), www.census.gov/prod/2006pubs/p70-107.pdf (accessed September 3, 2008).

3. IDEAdata.org, "IDEA Part B Child Count (2006)," table 1-1, www.ideadata.org/arc_toc8.asp#partbCC (accessed April 14, 2008).

4. Jim Blansett, "Digital Discrimination," *Library Journal* 13 (August 15, 2008): 26.

5. ASCLA, "Tip Sheet 11: Library Accessibility: What You Need to Know," ed. Monique Delatte, www.ala.org/ala/ascla/asclaprotools/accessibilitytipsheets/default.cfm (accessed September 3, 2008).

6. William Reed, personal communication with author, May 27, 2008.

7. Barbara Huntington, personal communication with author. May 23, 2008.
8. Sharon Rawlins, personal communication with author, June 4, 2008.
9. Wilk, "When it Comes to Teens, Don't Forget Accessibility."
10. AbilityNet, "State of the ENation Reports," www.abilitynet.org.uk/enation85 (accessed May 16, 2008).
11. Reed, personal communication.
12. Elizabeth Burns, personal communication with author, June 13, 2008.
13. Huntington, personal communication.
14. Kestrell, "Reading in the Dark—Notes on Accessible Games Presentation at MIT," June 16, 2008, http://kestrell.livejournal.com/431444.html (accessed September 3, 2008).
15. Burns, personal communication.
16. Reed, personal communication.
17. Huntington, personal communication.
18. Rachel Gould, personal communication with author, June 13, 2008.
19. Rawlins, personal communication.
20. Gould, personal communication.
21. Burns, personal communication.
22. Gould, personal communication.
23. Burns, personal communication.

ACCESSIBILITY RESOURCE GUIDE

General Information

Youth with Special Needs: A Resource and Planning Guide for Wisconsin Public Libraries, http://dpi.wi.gov/pld/ysnpl.html. A resource and planning guide intended to provide guidance and practical suggestions to ensure that all youths with special needs have appropriate, convenient, and equitable access to materials and technology at public libraries.

New Jersey State Library, "Equal Access to Information: Libraries Serving People with Disabilities," www.njstatelib.org/LDB/Disabilities/dsequa2.php#programs. Information for libraries serving people with special needs.

Collaborative Summer Library Program (CSLP), www.cslpreads.org/diversity/diversity.htm. Resources and information from the CSLP Diversity Committee on creating a more inclusive community of summer readers.

Accessibility

American with Disabilities Act (ADA) Home Page, www.ada.gov. Information and technical assistance on the ADA.

Section 508, www.section508.gov. A website for federal employees and the general public about Section 508, which requires that federal agencies' electronic and information technology be accessible to people with disabilities.

"Think Accessible before You Buy," www.ala.org/ala/mgrps/divs/ascla/asclaprotools/thinkaccessible/default.cfm. An ASCLA Tool Kit on accessible technology for libraries.

United States Access Board, www.access-board.gov. The Access Board is an independent federal agency devoted to accessibility for people with disabilities.

The Web Accessibility Initiative (WAI), www.w3.org/WAI. WAI is working with organizations around the world to develop strategies, guidelines, and resources to help make the web accessible to people with disabilities.

~Avatar Me!

An avatar is a computer user's representation of him- or herself. They allow you to be more anonymous online. Here are sites where you can make an avatar for free:

DoppelMe (www.doppelme.com)

Gala Dream Avatar (www.tektek.org/dream)

Lego Head (www.reasonablyclever.com/blockhead)

Otaku Avatar Maker (www.moeruavatar.com/index_en.shtml)

Portrait Illustration Maker (http://illustmaker.abi-station.com/index_en.shtml)

Yahoo Avatars (http://avatars.yahoo.com)

Try these virtual doll makers to create images of your friends or favorite characters:

Doll Makers (http://elouai.com/doll-makers.php)

DollzMania (www.dollzmania.com)

Edit an existing photo online:

Photo editing made fun (www.picnik.com)

—The 2009 Teen Tech Week Committee

APPENDIX A
YALSA WHITE PAPERS

WHITE PAPER NO. 1: WHY TEEN SPACE?

Kimberly Bolan Cullin, MLS, Library Consultant

This paper provides an overview of and commentary on teen space development and its implicit bearing on the strategic vision, planning, and development of facilities design for twenty-first-century libraries. Attention will be drawn to key success factors such as why teen space is important as well as to current and future priorities and best practices related to library facilities for teenage users. This paper will help you understand the importance of teen space within your community and organization, and address issues that shape the quality of a teen customer's experience with your library.

Background

Over the past twelve years, there has been a transformation in library facility design for teens. Traditionally speaking, common practice has been to ignore dedicated space for teens or to create boring,

Accepted by the YALSA Board of Directors, June 2007

unfriendly facilities with little attention to adolescent needs and wants. Libraries have generally been designed without teen customers in mind, driven by librarian, administrator, and architect personal likes and ideas. Today more and more schools and public libraries are working to accommodate thirteen- to eighteen-year-olds, moving away from the previously described "traditional" approaches to creating more efficient, innovative, appealing, and teen-inspired spaces.

Position

As libraries continue to move forward, organizations of all types, sizes, and budgets must realize that warm, inviting, comfortable, and user-centered environments are integral in attracting teenage users and transforming the role and image of the library. Such environments are essential in encouraging positive use of libraries for recreational activities, learning, and education.

Whether building a new library, renovating an existing facility, or working on a minor facilities revamp, the primary key success factor is understanding why teen space is critical. Developing dedicated, attractive, motivating, and teen-oriented space provides a way to

- create a positive, safe environment for studying, socializing, and leisure activities
- outwardly and interactively acknowledge teen customers and their needs by supporting adolescent asset development; creating an environment that encourages emotional, social, and intellectual development; and building a sense of teen belonging, community involvement, and library appreciation
- expand your customer base by appealing to users and non-users, creating a wider variety of customers from diverse social groups, backgrounds, and interests
- effectively market library services by drawing teens into the physical library space, leading them to other library services such as materials, programming, and so on
- increase current and future library supporters: the future of libraries are tomorrow's adults and, believe it or not, these are today's teens

Other key success teen space factors include the following:

- Making teen participation and input a priority as well as a regular practice throughout the planning, design, implementation, maintenance, and marketing of the space and related teen library services.
- Appropriately sizing a teen facility based on a library's community/student population (ages 13–18). Libraries must reevaluate space allocations in their overall facilities and scale them according to demographics, not personal bias. In public library facilities, the ratio of a teen area to the overall library should be equal to the ratio of the teen population to the overall population of that community.
- Developing a well-thought-out plan for improvement, including short-term and long-range planning for current and future teen space and services.

- Getting buy-in and support from all stakeholders, including teens, staff, faculty, administrators, and the community.
- Creating a truly teen-friendly space that is comfortable, colorful, interactive, flexible in design, and filled with technology. It is important to keep in mind that "teen-friendly" is not synonymous with unruly, unreasonable, impractical, or tacky.
- Thinking about what teens *need*, not about what adults *want*. Don't make assumptions or let personal biases impact decision making, whether selecting furniture, shelving/displays, flooring, lighting, paint color, signage, and so on. Items should be welcoming, have visual impact, be versatile, and encourage positive, independent use of the facility.

Conclusion

Making libraries appealing and important to teens is not an impossible task. Library facilities design is one integral step in attracting teen customers and redefining libraries of the future. Looking at teen facilities design in a new light, letting go of antiquated ideas, reevaluating traditional ways of "doing business," and emphasizing customer needs and wants are essential first steps in moving forward in the world of twenty-first-century libraries.

References

Bernier, A., ed. *Making Space for Teens: Recognizing Young Adult Needs in Library Buildings.* Scarecrow Press, forthcoming.

Bolan, Kimberly. "Looks like Teen Spirit." *School Library Journal* 52, no. 1 (November 2006): 44+.

———. *Teen Spaces: The Step-by-Step Library Makeover.* 2nd ed. ALA Editions, 2009.

Jones, Patrick, Mary Kay Chelton, and Joel Shoemaker. *Do It Right: Best Practices for Serving Young Adults in School and Public Libraries.* Neal-Schuman, 2001.

Search Institute. "The 40 Developmental Assets for Adolescents (Ages 12–18)." 2007. www.search-institute.org/content/40-developmental-assets-adolescents-ages-12-18. Accessed June 14, 2007.

WHITE PAPER NO. 2: THE VALUE OF YOUNG ADULT LITERATURE

Michael Cart

To ask, "What is the value of young adult literature?" is to beg at least three other questions:

1. What is meant by "value"?
2. What is meant by "young adult"?
3. What is meant by "literature"?

To answer these questions, in turn:

1. "Value" is defined, simply, as "worth." When used in juxtaposition with the term "young adult literature," it invites an assessment of how worthwhile, important, or desirable that literature is—measured, as we will see below, in terms both of its aesthetic success and its personal impact on readers and their lives.

2. "Young adult" is officially defined by YALSA as meaning persons twelve to eighteen years of age. Unofficially, however, it is acknowledged that "young adult" is an amorphous term that is subject to continuous revision as demanded by changing societal views. Since the early 1990s, for example, it has (again, unofficially) been expanded to include those as young as ten and, since the late 1990s, as old as twenty-five (or even, some would argue, thirty).

3. "Literature" has traditionally meant published prose—both fiction and nonfiction—and poetry. The increasing importance of visual communication has begun to expand this definition to include the pictorial, as well, especially when offered in combination with text as in the case of picture books, comics, and graphic novels and nonfiction.

Often the word "literature" is also presumed to imply aesthetic merit. However, because young adults have, historically, been accorded such scant respect by society—being viewed more as homogeneous problems than as individual persons—the literature that has been produced for them has, likewise, been dismissed as little more than problem-driven literature of problematic value. Accordingly, the phrase "young adult literature" has itself been dismissed as being an oxymoron.

The Young Adult Library Services Association takes strenuous exception to all of this. Founded in a tradition of respect for those it defines as "young adults," YALSA respects young adult literature as well. A proof of this is the establishment of the Michael L. Printz Award, which YALSA presents annually to the author of the best young adult book of the year, "best" being defined solely in terms of literary merit. In this way, YALSA values young adult literature—*as literature*—for its artistry and its aesthetic integrity.

But to invoke the Printz Award is to invite one last definition: this time of the very phrase "young adult literature," for—like "young adult"—this is an inherently amorphous and dynamic descriptor. Narrowly defined, it means literature specifically published *for* young adults. More broadly, however, it can mean anything that young adults read, though it must—of necessity—have a young adult protagonist and address issues of interest to this readership. This broader definition is demonstrated by YALSA's annual selection of what it calls "Best Books for Young Adults," a list that often includes books published for adults and even, sometimes, for children.

Whether young adult literature is defined narrowly or broadly, however, much of its value is to be found in how it addresses the needs of its readers. Often described as "developmental," these books acknowledge that young adults are beings in evolution, in search of self and identity; beings who are constantly growing and changing, morphing from the condition of childhood to that of adulthood. That period of passage called "young adulthood" is a unique part of life, distinguished by unique needs that are—at minimum—physical, intellectual, emotional, and societal in nature. By addressing these needs, young adult literature is made valuable not only by its artistry but also by its relevance to the lives of its readers. And by addressing not only their needs but also their interests, the literature becomes a powerful inducement for them to read, another compelling reason to value it.

Yet another of the chief values of young adult literature is to be found in its capacity to offer readers an opportunity to see themselves reflected in its pages. Young adulthood is, intrinsically, a period of tension. On the one hand, young adults have an all-consuming need to belong. But on the other, they are also inherently solipsistic, regarding themselves as being unique, which is not cause for celebration but, rather, for despair. For to be unique is to be unlike one's peers—to be "other," in fact. And to be "other" is to not belong but, instead, to be an outcast. Thus, to see oneself in the pages of a young adult book is to receive the blessed reassurance that one is not alone after all, not other, not alien, but, instead, a viable part of a larger community of beings who share a common humanity.

Another value of young adult literature is its capacity to foster understanding, empathy, and compassion by offering vividly realized portraits of the lives—exterior and interior—of individuals who are *un*like the reader. In this way, young adult literature invites its readership to embrace the humanity it shares with those who—if not for the encounter in reading—might forever remain strangers or, worse, irredeemably "other."

Still another value of young adult literature is its capacity for telling its readers the truth, however disagreeable that may sometimes be; for in this way, it equips readers for dealing with the realities of impending adulthood and—though it may sound quaintly old-fashioned—for assuming the rights and responsibilities of citizenship.

By giving readers such a frame of reference, it also helps them to find role models, to make sense of the world they inhabit, to develop a personal philosophy of being, to determine what is right and, equally, what is wrong, and to cultivate a personal sensibility. To, in other words, become civilized.

So what, finally, is the value of young adult literature? One might as well ask, "What is the value of breathing?"—for both are essential, even fundamental, to life and survival.

WHITE PAPER NO. 3: THE BENEFITS OF INCLUDING DEDICATED YOUNG ADULT LIBRARIANS ON STAFF IN THE PUBLIC LIBRARY
Young Adult Library Services Association with Audra Caplan

Background

The Young Adult Library Services Association adopted a strategic plan in 2004. That plan included a Core Purpose and a Vivid Description of the Desired Future. The Core Purpose is "to advocate for excellence in library services to the teen population." The first bullet below the description states: "There will be a young adult librarian in every public and secondary school library." The group of practitioners who developed both of these statements understood that advocating excellence in library service for teens goes hand in hand with the provision of a dedicated young adult librarian in each location that serves teens.

Position

Why is it important to have young adult librarians on staff?

Because a significant percent of the American population is composed of adolescents and many of them are library users. There are over 30 million teens currently in the United States, the largest generation since the baby boomers, and, according to a 2007 survey of young people conducted by a Harris Poll for the Young Adult Library Services Association (YALSA 2004), 78 percent of these teen respondents have library cards. Not surprisingly, participation in library programs by youths under age eighteen has been rising steadily over the past decade, from 35.5 million per year in 1993 to more than 51.8 million in 2001 (Americans for Libraries Council 2006). We also know that while 14.3 million kindergarteners through twelfth graders are home alone after school every day (Afterschool Alliance 2006), three-quarters of Americans believe it is a high priority for public libraries to offer a safe place where teens can study and congregate (Public Agenda 2006). Unfortunately, many communities do not provide after-school or weekend activities that can engage teens, despite the understanding that successful, well-prepared young adults are essential to fill roles as contributing members of a vital society and that teens need responsive and responsible venues in which to develop into successful, contributing members of society.

Why can't generalist library staff serve the teen population as well as young adult librarians?

Because librarians especially trained to work with young adults are age-level specialists who understand that teens have unique needs and have been trained especially to work with this particular population. As books like Barbara Strauch's *The Primal Teen: What New Discoveries about the Teenage Brain Tell Us about Our Kids* have shown us, teens' brains and bodies are different from a child's or an adult's. As a result, their behavior, interests, and informational and social needs are not the same as those of children or adults.

The Chapin Hall Center for Children, www.chapinhall.org, completed a study in 2004 on "Teens in the Library." In the area of staffing, the first statement related to improving youth services in libraries is that "dedicated staff are essential to effective youth programs." Across all of the sites studied by Chapin Hall and the Urban Institute, senior administrators and librarians agreed that "youth programs require a staff person whose priority is to manage the program." Library services that best address teen needs and interests are the professional priority of young adult librarians.

Why provide staff and services specifically for teens?

Dedicated library services for teens improves the library as a whole. Armed with knowledge and understanding of adolescent behavior, interests, and needs, young adult librarians create programming and build collections appropriate to the concerns of young adults and develop services based on knowledge of adolescent development. They are experts in the field of young adult literature and keep up with current teen trends in reading, technology, education, and popular culture. They provide reference services that help young adults find and use information, and they promote activities that build and strengthen information literacy skills. They know the benefits of youth participation and understand that it is essential in order to offer excellent service to teens, encouraging teens to provide direct input to library service through activities such as teen advisory groups and volunteer or paid work in libraries. They also collaborate with other youth development experts in the community and with agencies that provide services to teens.

According to key findings from the Wallace Foundation's "Public Libraries as Partners in Youth Development (PLPYD)," public libraries selected for this program were challenged to "develop or expand youth programs that engaged individual teens in a developmentally supportive manner while enhancing library services for all youth in the community." Based on the experiences of the PLPYD sites, the findings conclude that "Public Libraries have the potential to design youth programs that provide developmentally enriching experiences to teens and have positive effect both on youth services and the library more broadly."

Young adult librarians build relationships with teens and help other staff to feel comfortable with them. One of the findings from a study by Chapin Hall indicated that staff prejudice in relation to teens broke down when staff can be mentored to develop relationships with teens. Youth development principles were credited with changing the general culture of the library by providing an "important new language" for library administrators that helped the library to establish a new leadership role in the area of youth development and in the community. In an era when libraries must clearly articulate their importance to the larger community, the role of youth development agency increases the public library's value as an institution and also makes good economic sense for the community.

A 2007 survey conducted by the Harris Poll for YALSA asked young people what needed to happen in their local library in order for them to use it more often. One in five respondents said they would use their library more if "there was a librarian just for teens." One-third of respondents said that they would use the library more if the library had more interesting materials to borrow and events to attend.

The young adult librarian acts as a significant adult in the lives of many young people, thereby meeting one of the seven developmental needs of teens: positive social interaction with peers and adults (Search Institute).

Conclusion

Why employ young adult librarians?

The practical reasons are listed above. On a fundamental level, the goal is to provide excellent service to a large but unique segment of the population, teens. Young adult librarians are essential to providing the best service to young adults in libraries, and they are essential to keeping libraries viable and up-to-date by translating knowledge about cultural trends into programs, collections, staff engagement with youths, and collaborative efforts in the broader community. So the answer is simple—employing young adult librarians is the smart thing to do.

References

Afterschool Alliance. 2006, November 13. "7 in 10 Voters Want New Congress to Increase Funding for Afterschool Programs, Poll Finds." Press release.

Americans for Libraries Council. 2006. "Learning in Motion: A Sampling of Library Teen Programs." www.publicagenda.org/files/research_facts/long_overdue_teens_fact_sheet.pdf. Accessed December 28, 2007.

Chapin Hall Center for Children. 2005. "New on the Shelf: Teens in the Library." www.chapinhall.org/research/report/new-shelf. Accessed September 27, 2008.

Harris Interactive, Inc. 2007. "Youth and Library Use Study." American Library Association. www.ala.org/ala/mgrps/divs/yalsa/HarrisYouthPoll.pdf. Accessed September 27, 2008.

Jones, Patrick. 2003. *New Directions for Library Service to Young Adults*. ALA Editions/Young Adult Library Services Association.

Public Agenda. 2006. "Long Overdue: A Fresh Look at Public and Leadership Attitudes about Libraries in the 21st Century." www.publicagenda.org/files/pdf/Long_Overdue.pdf. Accessed December 28, 2007.

Public Library Association. 2007. *2007 PLDS Statistical Report*. PLA.

Spillett, Roxanne. 2002, October 3. "When School Day Ends, Danger Begins for the Young." *Atlanta Journal-Constitution*.

Strauch, Barbara. 2003. *The Primal Teen: What New Discoveries about the Teenage Brain Tell Us about Our Kids*. Doubleday.

Wallace Foundation. N.d. "Public Libraries as Partners in Youth Development (PLPYD)." www.wallacefoundation.org/GrantsPrograms/FocusAreasPrograms/Libraries/Pages/PublicLibrariesasPartnersinYouthDevelopment.aspx.

YALSA. 2004. "Competencies for Librarians Serving Youth: Young Adults Deserve the Best." www.ala.org/ala/mgrps/divs/yalsa/profdev/youngadultsdeserve.cfm.

WHITE PAPER NO. 4: THE IMPORTANCE OF YOUNG ADULT SERVICES IN LIS CURRICULA

Don Latham, on behalf of the Young Adult Library Services Association

Abstract

This white paper discusses the importance of educational programs for training young adult librarians within schools of library and information science (LIS). It describes the evolution of library services to young adults as well as education for young adult librarians. It identifies the various competencies needed by young adult librarians in the twenty-first century and situates these competencies within the larger context of LIS curricula. Finally, it concludes by emphasizing the value of young adult library services courses both for professionals-in-training and for young adults.

Background

American libraries have a long and proud tradition of providing services to young adults (defined by the Young Adult Library Services Association as young people ages twelve to eighteen). The Brooklyn Youth Library opened in Brooklyn, New York, in 1823, nearly seventy-five years before psychologist G. Stanley Hall introduced the concept of "adolescence" into the popular parlance (Bernier et al. 2005). In the twentieth century, the profession saw a burgeoning in young adult services in libraries, particularly in the period following World War II. As a result, in 1957 the

American Library Association established the Young Adult Services Division (now the Young Adult Library Services Association) as a separate entity from the Children's Library Association (Bernier et al. 2005). Over the years, the profession has produced a number of outstanding librarians and advocates for young adult services, among them Margaret Edwards, the young people's librarian at Enoch Pratt Free Library in Baltimore (Bernier et al. 2005), and Michael Printz, a school librarian in Topeka, Kansas (YALSA n.d.), both of whom now have young adult book awards named for them.

Concomitant with this growth in library services for young adults has been a growth in programs for educating young adult librarians. Some of the earliest of these included the Pratt Institute in Brooklyn, Case Western in Cleveland, and the Carnegie Library of Pittsburgh's Training School for Children's Librarians (Jenkins 2000). Now most schools of library and information science offer at least one course in young adult resources and/or services, and many offer multiple courses. A search of the Association for Library and Information Science Education (ALISE) membership directory reveals that approximately 13 percent of ALISE members identify "young adult services" as one of their teaching and/or research areas (ALISE 2007).

And, indeed, the need for young adult services in libraries is greater than ever before. According to the U.S. Census, the number of young people ages ten to nineteen increased from approximately 35 million in 1990 to over 40 million in 2000 and to nearly 42 million by 2007 (U.S. Census Bureau 2008). In addition to the increasing numbers of young adults, there has been an explosion in information technologies, a proliferation of resource formats (and user preferences), and a growing emphasis on the importance of information literacy (Jones et al. 2004), all of which have presented both exciting opportunities and formidable challenges for librarians who serve young adults.

Position

The Young Adult Library Services Association (YALSA) is committed to the philosophy that "young adults deserve the best." Recognizing the varied knowledge and skill sets needed to provide exemplary services to young adults in the twenty-first century, the division works to promote a rich and diverse educational experience for students preparing to become young adult librarians as well as other information professionals who will work, at least in part, with young adults.

Toward that end, in 2003 the division adopted a set of core competencies for young adult librarians, in which seven areas of competency are identified: Leadership and Professionalism, Knowledge of Client Group, Communication, Administration, Knowledge of Materials, Access to Information, and Services (YALSA 2003). LIS schools can foster these competencies through various means: by offering courses devoted specifically to young adult resources, services, and programming; by incorporating discussion of young adult users and their information needs into other courses, such as reference services, media production, research methods, and information policy; and by encouraging students to gain valuable experiences outside of the classroom, through such things as internships in young adult services and membership in professional associations like YALSA and the American Association of School Librarians (AASL).

The most important competency, because it is that from which the other competencies follow, is knowledge of young adults, and LIS curricula should incorporate that topic into various courses. Knowledge of young adults includes understanding the developmental needs of teens and recognizing that these needs can be different for different teens. It also includes an understanding of the diversity among teens and an appreciation of the information needs of teens from various cultural and ethnic backgrounds. And it involves a recognition of the special needs of "extreme teens," that is, those teens who do not fit the mold of the "typical teen" perhaps because of their educational situation, their living situation, and/or their sexuality (Anderson 2005). Knowledge of young adult users and their information needs is complemented by an understanding of how to conduct user needs assessment, so research methods should be an integral part of education for young adult librarianship.

LIS curricula should also provide education in the myriad resources that are available to today's young adults. Libraries traditionally have promoted reading, and that is still a core mission. But it is also the case that teens now engage with various forms of media in addition to print: movies, television, games (especially computer games), music, and, of course, the Internet. Young adult librarians should be conversant with the seemingly infinite variety of materials now available in order to meet the needs and preferences of the clients they serve.

Today's young adults are not only consumers of media, but also producers. Most are avid computer users, engaging in social networking, creating their own digital videos, participating in gaming, texting, instant messaging—and often doing several of these things at once! Young adult librarians certainly should be trained in the use of information technology to create and deliver information services, but they should also be educated to understand the broader cultural implications of how and why teens use technology and how this is changing the way that teens interact with and process information.

Closely related to the use of technology as a way of accessing and interacting with information is the concept of information literacy. Young adult librarians should be educated to understand what information literacy is and how to promote information literacy skill development among teens. Information literacy— which may be defined as the ability to access, evaluate, and use information ethically and effectively—has received much attention both in the K–12 and higher-education environments in the twenty-first century (see, for example, the standards developed by the American Association of School Librarians 1998 and the Association of College and Research Libraries 2000). Such skills are seen as increasingly necessary for success in school, the workplace, and life. The teenage years are a crucial time in the acquisition of the numerous complex skills related to information literacy, and young adult librarians can play an important role in ensuring that teens are successful in developing these abilities.

Designing effective programs to promote resources, technology, and information literacy among teens provides a way to bring together these three pillars of young adult services. LIS schools should offer courses in various types of programming as well as the marketing of services to teens. After all, today's teenaged library users will become tomorrow's adult library users—and, hopefully, library supporters. Some will even become tomorrow's librarians.

Conclusion

For these reasons, the Young Adult Library Services Association affirms the value and importance of young adult services in LIS curricula. Educating young adult librarians for the twenty-first century represents a commitment to helping young adults become lifelong readers, lifelong learners, and lifelong library users.

References

American Association of School Librarians/Association for Educational Communications and Technology. 1998. *Information Power: Building Partnerships for Learning*. Chicago: American Library Association.

Anderson, S. B. 2005. *Extreme Teens: Library Services to Nontraditional Young Adults*. Westport, CT: Libraries Unlimited.

Association of College and Research Libraries. 2000. "Information Literacy Competency Standards for Higher Education." www.ala.org/ala/mgrps/divs/acrl/standards/informationliteracycompetency.cfm. Accessed December 18, 2008.

Association for Library and Information Science Education (ALISE). 2007. "Directory of LIS Programs and Faculty in the United States and Canada—2007." www.alise.org/mc/page.do?sitePageId=55644&orgId=ali. Accessed December 18, 2008.

Bernier, A., M. K. Chelton, C. A. Jenkins, and J. B. Pierce. 2005. "Two Hundred Years of Young Adult Library Services History." *Voice of Youth Advocates* 28:106–11.

Jenkins, C. A. 2000. "The History of Youth Services Librarianship: A Review of the Research Literature." *Libraries & Culture* 35:103–40.

Jones, P., M. Gorman, and T. Suellentrop. 2004. *Connecting Young Adults and Libraries: A How-to-Do-It Manual for Librarians*. 3rd ed. New York: Neal-Schuman.

U.S. Census Bureau. 2008. "Resident Population by Age and Sex: The 2009 Statistical Abstract." www.census.gov/compendia/statab/cats/population/estimates_and_projections_by_age_sex_raceethnicity.html. Accessed December 18, 2008.

Young Adult Library Services Association (YALSA). 2003. "Young Adults Deserve the Best: Competencies for Librarians Serving Young Adults." www.ala.org/ala/mgrps/divs/yalsa/profdev/yacompetencies/competencies.cfm. Accessed December 18, 2008.

———. n.d. "Who Was Mike Printz?" www.ala.org/ala/mgrps/divs/yalsa/booklistsawards/printzaward/whowasmikeprintz/whomikeprintz.cfm. Accessed December 18, 2008.

TEENS AND SOCIAL NETWORKING IN SCHOOL AND PUBLIC LIBRARIES: A YALSA TOOL KIT FOR LIBRARIANS AND LIBRARY WORKERS

What are social networking technologies? They are software that enables people to connect, collaborate, and form virtual communities via the computer and the Internet. Social networking websites are those that provide this opportunity to interact via interactive web applications. Sites that allow visitors to send e-mails, post comments, build web content, or take part in live audio or video chats are all considered to be social networking sites. These kinds of sites have come to be collectively referred to as Web 2.0 and allow users to interact and participate in a way was previously possible.

Social Networking Defined

The following definitions of social networking tools should help you explain to your community what it is all about.

blog: A web page where you can write journal entries, reviews, articles, and more. Blog authors can allow readers to post their own comments. No web design knowledge is needed to create a blog.

microblog: A blog that is made up of short posts usually only of 140 characters or less.

podcasts: Audio files available for download via subscription, so you can automatically download it to a computer or MP3 player (like an iPod).

RSS: A way for subscribers to automatically receive information from blogs, online newspapers, and podcasts.

social networking: In the online world, this refers to the ability to connect with people through websites and other technologies, like Facebook and discussion boards.

tagging: Refers to the ability to add subject headings to content in order to organize information in a meaningful way and to connect to others that tag similar content in the same way.

virtual worlds: Allow for real-time communication and collaboration with people from all over the world. Each person in a virtual world uses an avatar as a virtual representation of him- or herself.

wiki: A collaborative space for developing web content. No web design knowledge is needed to create a wiki.

How Online Social Networking Facilitates Learning in Schools and Libraries

Social networking technologies have many positive uses in schools and libraries. They are an ideal environment for teens to share what they are learning or to build something together online. The nature of the medium allows teens to receive feedback from librarians, teachers, peers, parents, and others. Social networking technologies create a sense of community (as do the physical library and school) and in this way are already aligned with the services and programs at the library or school.

Schools and libraries are working to integrate positive uses of social networking into their classrooms, programs, and services. By integrating social networking technologies into educational environments, teens have the opportunity to learn from adults how to be safe and smart when participating in online social networks. They also learn a valuable life skill, as these social networking technologies are tools for communication that are widely used in colleges and in the workplace.

Literacy and Social Networking

Social networking tools give teens meaningful ways to use and improve reading and writing skills. All social networking software requires teens to read and write. Reading and writing skills are used when a teen

- creates a profile on a social networking site
- posts or comments on a blog
- writes about an idea on Twitter
- adds or edits content on a wiki
- searches for social content
- consults peers online as a part of research

This is why these technologies are referred to as the "read/write web."

Developmental Assets and Social Networking

When schools and libraries help teens use social networking tools safely and smartly, they also help teens meet their developmental assets as defined by the Search Institute (http://www.search-institute.org).

- When teens learn how to use blogs, wikis, Facebook, and MySpace within an educational context, they learn about *boundaries and expectations*.
- When teens are able to use social networking tools in learning, they have a *commitment to learning*.
- When teens have the opportunity to communicate with peers, experts, authors, and so on via online social networking, they develop *social and cultural competence*.
- When teens work with adults and peers on developing social network sites and teaching others how to use these sites, they are *empowered*.
- When teens have a voice in the future of the school or the library, they gain a sense of *personal identity* and value.
- When teens see how librarians and teachers use social networks, they are presented with *positive role models*.

How Can You Use Social Networking with Teens?

Here are a few examples of how teens are being introduced to the positive uses of social networking technologies:

- A school uses blogging software to publish its newspaper. The blog format allows for timely publication and the ability to make updates easily. This format also allows for comments from readers and easy navigation to archived stories. Publication costs are minimal (no color print costs!), and there is no limit to the length of the paper, allowing for more student participation. See http://waylandstudentpress.com/.
- An author creates a blog or Twitter account as a way to reflect on the reading and writing experience. Teens who enjoy the author's work keep up on what the author is writing and thinking through the blog. The author's blog is used as a research source and as a way to communicate with the author about books, reading, and writing. See http://www.twitter.com/barrylyga and http://halseanderson.livejournal.com/.
- A school librarian works with teachers to encour-

age student reading. As a means of getting students actively involved in their own reading, the librarian creates a VoiceThread where students discuss books in which they are interested. See http://voicethread.com/share/164125/.

- A public library creates a Facebook page as a way to connect with teens ages fourteen and older. The page includes information on programs and services at the library in which teens can take part. Teens who are not traditional library users learn about and use the library through the Facebook page because they are familiar and comfortable with the technology. Teens make the library one of their Facebook friends and then are reminded of the library whenever they log onto their page.

- A public library works with its teen advisory groups to create video reviews of favorite books, movies, and games, and posts them on YouTube. As a result, teens get a chance to articulate what they like and don't like about materials and have a chance to express their views to a global audience. See http://www.nypl.org/books/sta2009/.

- A student creates a MySpace site for an author she needs to study. As she gathers information, she enters it into the writer's MySpace profile. She uses the blog function to post stories or poems she analyzes. Before long, other MySpace authors and poets (some real, some not) befriend her author. They comment on what is written and lead the student to more resources. The student has to adopt the persona of her author and imagine what the author's responses might actually be. See http://tinyurl.com/2zah77.

- A library creates a Facebook application so teens are able to search the library's catalog from within their own Facebook profile page. This enables teens to quickly and easily access library content and brings the library to these teens in the place where they feel comfortable already. See http://www.facebook.com/apps/application.php?id=2353074921.

- A high school creates a social network via Ning as a way to create a space for teens to connect with each other, faculty, and administration. See http://rcarams.ning.com/.

- A teacher uses Google Docs for a writing assignment so that students can easily access their documents from outside of the classroom and collaborate with classmates on their writing. See http://www.google.com/educators/p_docs.html.

- Teens take lyrics from a favorite song and paste them into Wordle. They then get to analyze the language used in the song and consider what the repetition and use of words implies about the lyric's meaning. See http://www.wordle.net/gallery/wrdl/262858/Stairway_to_Heaven.

Educating the Community about Online Social Networking

In the media there are many examples of how social networking has played a dangerous role in teen lives. However, positive examples of how this technology supports teen literacy skills and developmental growth are not always so readily accessed. For that reason, librarians should play an active role in educating parents, teachers, and other members of the community about the positive benefits of social networking in teen lives. The following examples of how you can educate your community provide a starting point. When planning, be sure to enlist your teen advisory group (TAG), teens that spend time in your library, or teens in the community to help you plan and implement the ideas suggested below.

- Convert online resource guides and pathfinders to a wiki format so that students and teachers can collaborate on these resources. Wikis give users of information the chance to add their own ideas about tools and resources that they have found to be useful in the research process.

- Create and distribute brochures and post information online about what your library is already doing to ensure that children and teens are safe online. Include information about Internet filters and Internet Acceptable Use Policies that your library has.

- Invite parents and educators to a workshop where they can learn about a variety of social networking tools. In the workshop have librarians and teachers discuss how these tools are being integrated positively in the classroom and library. Have teens with well-designed Facebook and MySpace profiles, YouTube content, Flickr pages, and so on demonstrate the positive ways they use social networking tools.

- Host Do-It-Yourself Days for adults to learn how to use social networking sites and tools successfully. After an introduction about what social networking is and why it's an important part of a teen's life, teens from your TAG could work with adults on using the tools in a way that enhances their own lives. Teens might show adults how to set up a blog that showcases a hobby or special interest, a MySpace or Facebook page to keep in touch with friends, a Flickr account so they can share family photos, an IM account to conduct live chats with family members overseas, and so on.

- Create an online demo or class that gives adults the chance to test out and discuss social networking technologies at their leisure and in a somewhat anonymous setting. Make the demo available from your library's website. Use your TAG to help develop the demo.

- Use social networking technologies as an access point for your library's services. Create a MySpace or Facebook page as a place for adults and teens to learn about programs and materials. Set up a blog where adults and teens read about what's going on in the library and can add comments about programs, materials, and so on. Develop a book-list wiki where adults and teens can add titles of books on specific themes.

- Inform—perhaps via an audio or video podcast—educators, parents, and community members about how social networking tools allow for schools and libraries to integrate technology in meaningful ways, with and for teens, at low (or no) cost. Information could include overviews of the technologies, interviews with teens about their use of technology, interviews with experts in technology and teen development who discuss how the technologies support teen growth and literacy development, and so on.

- Create and distribute an information sheet for adults providing information about the positive aspects of social networking, Internet safety tips, and annotated lists of resources. You can also post the information on your library's website, blog, wiki, Facebook, or MySpace page.

- Sponsor a scholarly presentation or series of presentations for local educators and concerned adults by experts in the field of developmental assets, teen print literacies in the world of technology, and social networking. Ask speakers to focus directly on how social networking technologies have positive benefits for teens.

- Create your own social network with Ning: http://www.ning.com. Invite teens, parents, school faculty, and administrators to join the network as a way to learn how the tools work and to discuss issues related to social networking in teen (and adult) lives.

- Host an evening that focuses on how social networking is being used in higher education and business. Invite faculty from a local college or university to talk about how they use social networking technologies with students to facilitate the teaching and learning process. Invite business leaders to talk about what social networking technologies their employees must know how to use in order to be successful in their jobs.

Educating Teens about Online Social Networking

You can help teens use social networking technologies successfully and safely by sponsoring programs and services that focus on these technologies. The following examples are available to help you get started. Show these examples to your teen advisory group (TAG) and see which one(s) they feel are important to offer in your community. Have your TAG help plan and carry out the event(s). Remember that social networking sites often have minimum age requirements and be sure to honor those.

- Offer a class to teach teens how to use the blogging site wordpress.com. As teens set up their blog, you can facilitate a discussion about Internet safety issues, the importance of guarding against identity theft, online etiquette, and so on.

- Host Do-It-Yourself Days for teens where they learn about a variety of social networking technologies. You might have a day for photo-sharing technologies, another day for bookmarking sites, another day for friend building, and so on. During each of the sessions, you can talk with teens about how to make decisions about safe use of these technologies.

- Work with teens to produce audio and video podcasts on topics of interest. They might review media and books, talk about what's going on in the community, booktalk, and so on. As a part of the podcast process, have teens write outlines of the content they want to cover and talk with them about whom they want to make the podcast available to.

- Create a library book and media wiki with teens as a means for recommending resources to library patrons. Train teens on how to update the content of the wiki, and talk about how to evaluate the quality of information in wikis and other types of resources.

- Take photos at the library, and have teens upload and tag them on Flickr or another photo-sharing site. As a part of the uploading and tagging process, discuss safety and privacy concerns with teens and decide whether or not the photos should be private or public. As they tag the photos, ask them to consider what the best ways are to describe content in order for friends or the public (if the photos are made public) to find them.

- Work with teens to create a wiki, podcast, or web page about Internet safety aimed at children. Post the completed resource on your library's website.

- Have teens create Delicious.com social bookmarking accounts for collecting resources they can use in school research. The teens can network with classmates and peers in Delicious.com in order to learn about resources their peers have uncovered that support learning on a particular topic. Use Delicious.com networking as a jumping-off point for a discussion of evaluating information quality. See http://www.delicious.com/.

- Use Flickr as a platform for creative writing exercises with teens. Upload your own or teens' photos to Flickr, and then have teens tell a story with the photos through captions that they add.

- Invite a technology expert in to talk with teens about how social networking tools work.

- Give teens the chance to connect with favorite authors, artists, musicians, and so on via MySpace, Twitter, Facebook and personal blogs. Teens can search for the pages and blogs using common search tools and then comment on the blogs and sites of those with whom they connect.

- Build a library MySpace or Facebook Fan page with teens. Have teens meet to plan the page, including what it should look like and include. Work with them to build the site, and develop guidelines for blogging, commenting, and making friends on the site. As a part of this project, talk with teens about how to decide whether or not to accept those who want to friend them on MySpace or Facebook. Add value to your MySpace or Facebook presence through links to online safety and library resources. Make it possible for teens to add your catalog search on their MySpace or Facebook accounts.

Social Networking and Legislation

As social networking has developed, many laws regarding restrictions have been considered on both the federal and local levels. There are many sites currently used by adults and teens that would be blocked in schools and libraries if legislation prohibiting access to social networking sites was instituted. These include the following:

- Photo-sharing sites like Flickr.com, which patrons use to share photos with family members who are far away
- Health-related sites like PsychCentral.com, which allow users to get important medical questions answered during live chat sessions
- Educational sites like LegalGuru.com, which allows users to get free legal advice
- Library reference sites, where patrons can get questions answered via instant messaging that use AOL, Yahoo, or other commercial services

Tips for Talking with Legislators about Social Networking

Even though librarians are respected members of the community, the competition for the attention and time of elected officials is great, as is the competition for funding. It is important that librarians reach out to elected officials and educate them about the needs of libraries and library patrons.

Before You Visit

- Do your homework. Find out what legislation is pending and be aware of what it says and where the person you are going to talk to stands on the issues related to social networking.

- Gather personal stories relating to the issue from your teen library patrons and their parents to share with the legislator.

- Visit or contact your legislator as soon as you hear about pending legislation.

- Find out about legislation on the ALA website at http://capwiz.com/ala/home/.

- Find out about federal social networking legislation at Open Congress: www.opencongress.org.

When You're Ready

- Communicate via phone, fax, or in person. If you're hoping to meet with a legislator in person, set up an appointment in advance. (By the way, don't be disappointed if you end up communicating with someone from the legislator's staff.)

- Be polite, respectful, professional, and friendly.

- Introduce yourself, identify your job title, and state your purpose.

- Stick to the point: communicate *one* message—the benefits of social networking for teens.

- Use specific examples from your own work with teens to illustrate your point. If you're meeting the legislator in person, you might even be able to take a well-spoken teen and/or parent with you who can talk about the benefits of social networking.

- Ask for action. For example, ask the legislator to vote against any legislation that attempts to restrict or ban social networking sites in libraries. Or ask the legislator to support any legislation that supports social networking and Internet access, like the E-rate.

- Offer to provide additional information about social networking. Take such materials with you if you're meeting the legislator in person.

- Listen carefully and courteously.

- Invite the legislator to visit your library. Provide a calendar of events.

- Remember to say "thank you."

Additional Resources about Online Social Networking and Libraries

For Librarians and Educators

American Library Association (ALA) wikis: ALA hosts an array of wikis that focus on technology in libraries in general and with teens specifically. These include

- YALSA (http://wikis.ala.org/yalsa)
- Teen Tech Week (http://wikis.ala.org/yalsa/index.php/Teen_Tech_Week)

Steve Hargadon, *Tapping into MySpace Minds*, http://www.stevehargadon.com/2007/01/tapping-into-myspace-minds-with-chris.html.

Steve Hargadon talks with Chris O'Neal about the impact of social networking on education.

Internet Safety Technical Task Force, *Enhancing Child Safety and Online Technologies*, http://cyber.law.harvard.edu/pubrelease/isttf/.

The final report of the Internet Safety Technical Task Force highlights how socioeconomic conditions have an impact on the safe use of technology by children and teens.

Mizuko Ito, *Kids' Informal Learning with Digital Media* (Catherine & John D MacArthur Foundation, 2008), http://digitalyouth.ischool.berkeley.edu/report.

A report following a three-year study that focuses on how young people use digital media for learning, information gathering, and content creation.

John Palfrey, *Born Digital: Understanding the First Generation of Digital Native* (Basic Books, 2008).

A look at challenges and positive ramifications of technology use by digital natives.

Pew Internet and American Life Project—Teens, http://pewinternet.org/topics/Teens.aspx.

The Pew Internet and American Life Project frequently releases reports on teen use of technology.

Will Richardson, *Blogs, Wikis, Podcasts, and Other Powerful Web Tools for Classrooms*, 2nd ed. (Corwin Press, 2008).

Richardson explains how and why social networking can be used in the library and classroom.

Dan Tapscott, *Grown Up Digital: How the Net Generation Is Changing Your World* (McGraw-Hill, 2008).

Tapscott looks at what the world is like for those who have grown up with technology as a part of their daily lives.

Joyce Valenza. *NeverEnding Search*, http://www.schoollibraryjournal.com/blog/1340000334.html

The blog of high school library media specialist, Joyce Valenza, that frequently covers teens and social networking.

YALSA Blog, http://yalsa.ala.org/blog.

The YALSA blog often includes posts about social networking and teens.

YALSA, *30 Positive Uses of Social Networking*, http://www.leonline.com/yalsa/positive_uses.pdf.

Ideas from librarians about how social networking can be integrated into schools and libraries successfully. Use these ideas to educate your colleagues, peers, and government officials about how social networking plays a positive role in teen lives.

For Teens

Federal Trade Commission, *Social Networking Sites: Safety Tips for Tweens and Teens*, www.ftc.gov/bcp/edu/pubs/consumer/tech/tec14.htm.

The Federal Trade Commission's short and useful list of reminders for staying safe on social networking sites (and online in general). Includes a list of resources for finding out more.

That's Not Cool, http://www.thatsnotcool.com/.

Your cell phone, IM, and social networks are all a digital extension of who you are. When someone you're with pressures you or disrespects you in those places, that's not cool.

For Parents and Caregivers

Family Online Safety Institute, http://www.fosi.org/cms/.

Identifies and promotes best practices of technology.

GetNetWise, http://www.getnetwise.org/.

Sponsored by the Internet Education Foundation, GetNetWise provides resources and information to help educate adults about young people's privacy and safety online.

SafeTeens.com, http://www.safeteens.com/.

A site with information about how to keep teens safe online that includes blog posts on topics of current interest as well as links to helpful resources.

For Everyone

i-SAFE, www.isafe.org.

Provides resources about Internet safety. There's a different section of the site for parents, educators, kids and teens, and law enforcement. There are free online tutorials for young people and adults as well as printable newsletters and other resources.

National Center for Missing and Exploited Children, *NetSmartz Workshop*, www.netsmartz.org.

Provides resources about Internet safety. There's a different section of the site for parents, educators, kids, teens, press, and law enforcement.

YALSA's Ultimate Teen Bookshelf highlights must-have teen materials for libraries. The Ultimate Teen Bookshelf, with titles listed at www.ala.org/teenbookshelf and available as a PDF download, was developed in conjunction with President Barack Obama's "United We Serve" initiative.

The list includes fifty books, five magazines, and five audiobooks. Subscribers to the YALSA-BK electronic discussion list suggested titles for the Ultimate Teen Bookshelf, which were vetted by Pam Spencer Holley, former YALSA president and author of *Quick and Popular Reads for Teens* (ALA Editions, 2009), and Judy Sasges, district manager for Sno-Isle Libraries in Marysville, Washington, a 2002 Printz Award committee member, and a 2010 YALSA Nonfiction Award committee member.

Librarians can use this collection to ensure they have quality materials to attract teens; parents and teens can use it to find interesting books and materials to keep reading skills sharp between school years.

During the summer months, it is critical for young people to continue to read and visit the library. Studies consistently show that teens who do not read over the summer lose important reading skills, beginning the next school year at a disadvantage. The Ultimate Teen Bookshelf is a great place to get started finding terrific reads for teens.

Books

1. *Acceleration* by Graham McNamee
2. *Alanna: The First Adventure* by Tamora Pierce
3. *All Things Bright and Beautiful* by James Herriot
4. *American Born Chinese* by Gene Luen Yang
5. *Among the Hidden* by Margaret Peterson Haddix
6. *Beauty* by Robin McKinley
7. *Black and White* by Paul Volponi
8. *Blizzard!: The Storm that Changed America* by Jim Murphy
9. Bone series by Jeff Smith
10. *The Book Thief* by Markus Zusak
11. *The Chocolate War* by Robert Cormier
12. *The Chosen* by Chaim Potok
13. *The Diary of a Young Girl: The Definitive Edition* by Anne Frank
14. *Ender's Game* by Orson Scott Card
15. *Fallen Angels* by Walter Dean Myers
16. *Fat Kid Rules the World* by K. L. Going
17. *Feed* by M. T. Anderson

18. *The First Part Last* by Angela Johnson
19. Fruits Basket series by Natsuki Takaya
20. *The Golden Compass* by Philip Pullman
21. *The Graveyard Book* by Neil Gaiman
22. *The Guinness Book of World Records*
23. Harry Potter series by J. K. Rowling
24. *The Hitchhiker's Guide to the Galaxy* by Douglas Adams
25. *The House of the Scorpion* by Nancy Farmer
26. *The Hunger Games* by Suzanne Collins
27. *I Know What You Did Last Summer* by Lois Duncan
28. *I Know Why the Caged Bird Sings* by Maya Angelou
29. *If You Come Softly* by Jacqueline Woodson
30. *The Killer's Cousin* by Nancy Werlin
31. *Lock and Key* by Sarah Dessen
32. *Looking for Alaska* by John Green
33. *Make Lemonade* by Virginia Euwer Wolff
34. *My Heartbeat* by Garret Freymann-Weyr
35. *A Northern Light* by Jennifer Donnelly
36. *The Outsiders* by S. E. Hinton
37. *Persepolis: The Story of a Childhood* by Marjane Satrapi
38. *The Pigman* by Paul Zindel
39. *The Princess Diaries* by Meg Cabot
40. *Rules of the Road* by Joan Bauer
41. *Saving Francesca* by Melina Marchetta

42. *Sleeping Freshmen Never Lie* by David Lubar
43. *Son of the Mob* by Gordon Korman
44. *Speak* by Laurie Halse Anderson
45. *Staying Fat for Sarah Byrnes* by Chris Crutcher
46. *Stuck in Neutral* by Terry Trueman
47. *Twilight* by Stephenie Meyer
48. *Uglies* by Scott Westerfeld
49. *The Wee Free Men* by Terry Pratchett
50. *Weetzie Bat* by Francesca Lia Block

Magazines

1. *Game Pro*
2. *Seventeen*
3. *Rolling Stone*
4. *Shonen Jump*
5. *Mad*

Audiobooks

1. *The Absolutely True Diary of a Part-Time Indian* by Sherman Alexie (Recorded Books)
2. *Bloody Jack* by L. A. Meyer (Listen and Live)
3. *The Killer's Cousin* by Nancy Werlin (Brilliance)
4. *To Kill a Mockingbird* by Harper Lee (Caedmon)
5. *Wintersmith* by Terry Pratchett (HarperAudio)

PUBLICITY TOOLS

Each year, YALSA creates publicity tools for librarians to use to get the word out about Teen Read Week and Teen Tech Week. You can adapt the materials here, including press releases, proclamations, and letters to the editor to use to promote these events in your library.

To find themed publicity materials, check the Teen Read Week website (www.ala.org/teenread) and the Teen Tech Week website (www.ala.org/teentechweek) each year.

Press Releases

You can use the templates here to create your press releases, but be sure to keep these tips in mind:

- Address the *who*, *what*, *where*, *when*, *why*, and *how* in the first paragraph.

- E-mail or fax your release 10–14 days in advance of the release date. Check with your local newspaper or TV or radio station for their preferred format.

- Remember to include library contact information (contact name, title, department, telephone number) in all your releases.

Sample Press Release (Teen Read Week)

For Immediate Release: [Date]

Contact: [Name, organization, and phone number]

[Headline:] [Library/school name] celebrates Teen Read Week™!

[Library name] will celebrate Teen Read Week™ during [week, year] with special events and programs aimed at encouraging area teens to read for the fun of it. Thousands of libraries, schools, and bookstore across the country will hold similar event to encourage teens to read for the fun of it.

Teen Read Week™ is the national adolescent literacy initiative of the Young Adult Library Services Association (YALSA), a division of the American Library Association.

"Teens have more activities to fill their free time than ever—web videos, social networking sites, video games, after-school activities, athletics—and increasingly high expectations in the classroom," says [librarian's full name]. "It's important that we show them that reading is something that's fun and relaxing that they can do for free. And that reading for fun can translate into better performance at school."

In addition, [librarian's last name] hopes to show parents and other concerned community members what the library can offer by hosting special programs and events during Teen Read Week™. [Describe the programs and provide contact information for readers who want to learn more].

"Many families have learned to make do with less as a result of the economy and have flocked to the library," says [librarian's last name]. "Teen Read Week™ is a great time to make sure teens and their families know about all the free services the library can offer them and to reach out to teens who aren't regular users and encourage them to come see what they can find here."

Parents of teens are encouraged to celebrate Teen Read Week™ at home as well. [Librarian's last name] offers these ideas:

- Visit the public or school library with your teen to attend a program or to check out books.
- Set aside time each night for the family to read.
- Give books or magazine subscriptions to your teen as a gift or reward.
- Share your favorite book with your teen.
- Go online with your teen to learn about new books or authors. A good place to start is YALSA's Book Awards and Booklists page: www.ala.org/yalsa/booklists.
- Join a book discussion group at the school or public library.

Teen Read Week™ is held annually during the third week of October. An updated list of sponsors and supporting organizations can be found at www.ala.org/teenread.

Sample Press Release (Teen Tech Week)

For Immediate Release: [Date]

Contact: [Name, organization, and phone number]

[Headline:] Get Connected @ Your Library® during Teen Tech Week™

Local teens will be tuning in at the library as [school/library name] celebrates Teen Tech Week™ [week, year]. They join thousands of other libraries and schools across the country who will get connected during Teen Tech Week™. Teen Tech Week™ is a national initiative of the Young Adult Library Services Association (YALSA) aimed at teens, their parents, educators, and other concerned adults.

The purpose of the initiative is to ensure that teens are competent and ethical users of technologies, especially those that are offered through libraries. Teen Tech Week™ encourages teens to use libraries' nonprint resources for education and recreation, and to recognize that librarians are qualified, trusted professionals in the field of information technology.

[Librarian, administrator, or staff person's full name here] explains: "Getting teens into libraries is essential. Offering a variety of technologies and providing top-notch education about these resources is key in getting them in the door. Once they're in the door, anything is possible."

Recent studies from Pew Internet and American Life Project show that, on average, eight- to eighteen-year-olds spend more than six hours per day using technology including TV, DVDs, video games, audio media, and computers. "Teen Tech Week™ is a way for librarians and educators to collaborate with and educate teens about technology," says [librarian, administrator, or staff person's last name here]. "Over the last several years, the library's role in increasing technology literacy has become more and more important, equal to that of reading literacy."

Teens are encouraged to celebrate Teen Tech Week™. [Name of librarian, administrator, or staff person] hopes to attract a wide variety of teenagers and increase teen technology literacy locally by offering a series of programs including: [Insert a bulleted list of the programs and services being offered. Provide contact information for readers who want to learn more.]

Teen Tech Week™ is held annually the second week of March. For an updated list of sponsors and supporting organizations, visit www.ala.org/teentechweek.

Proclamations

Teen Read Week Sample Proclamation

- Whereas, the ability to read and process information is a basic survival skill in our global information society;

- Whereas, the reading proficiency of teens has remained stagnant over the last thirty years;

- Whereas, the number of students who can read but choose not to do so is increasing;

- Whereas, the most effective way to improve reading skills is to read regularly and often;

- Whereas, too few teens think reading is a valuable tool for enjoyment and relaxation as well as for schoolwork;

- Whereas, regular daily reading for the fun of it creates the reading habit for life;

- Whereas, parents, teachers, librarians, and all concerned adults can serve as role models by reading for fun themselves;

- Therefore, be it resolved that I [name, title of official] proclaim [dates] Teen Read Week™ in [city, state] and encourage teens to read for the fun of it.

Teen Tech Week Sample Proclamation

- Whereas, the ability to read and process information online is a necessary skill for success in our global information society;

- Whereas, 71 percent of teens report that the Internet is their primary source for completing school projects;

- Whereas, multiple studies have shown that the majority of teens lack the critical thinking skills and technical expertise to use the Internet and other electronic resources effectively;

- Whereas, teens' use of nonprint resources has increased dramatically in recent years;

- Whereas, the library offers teens and their families free access to multiple types of technology, including but not limited to Internet access, gaming, audiobooks, research databases, online homework help, DVDS, and music;

- Whereas, the library is a trusted resource for accessing information;

- Whereas, librarians are information knowledge professionals who can quickly sort through the glut of information in print and online and find what patrons need;

- Whereas, librarians are uniquely suited to show teens and their families how to safely and ethically use the many types of technology available at the library;

- Therefore, be it resolved that I [name, title of official] proclaim [dates], Teen Tech Week™ in [city, state] and encourage teens and their families to get connected at the library.

Sample Letters to the Editor

Teen Read Week

Letter from a Teen:

I'm _____ [age] years old, and I wanted to make sure everyone knew about something really important in our town: the library. Lots of students go there for help with homework or to do research for school projects, but the library has a lot more than that! They have cool programs like _____ [name of event you've been to here] and they're free. They have all kinds of stuff to read like magazines, stories, graphic novels, manga, and more.

My favorite book from the library is _____ [italicized title of book here]. Even if you don't like to read, I bet if you look hard enough or ask a librarian for help, you'll find something good. And at a time when my parents and everyone else is trying to spend less money, the library is the perfect place to go.

My library also has computers I can use for homework, to keep in touch with my friends and family, and to play games and relax.

[Date] is Teen Read Week™. I'd like to tell other teens who may not be using the library that they should definitely check it out. There is more to do here than they may think, and there are people here who can help you get your questions answered. Also, parents should go to the library too! They can see all of the resources the library has for the whole family.

My librarian, _____ [name], says that the theme for Teen Read Week™ is "read for the fun of it." I do like to hang out with my friends, play video games, go online, and all kinds of stuff. But I think that reading can be good when you want to relax or have some time by yourself, and I like that I can get books for free from the library and that people there can recommend interesting books to me.

So, don't forget to read a book for Teen Read Week™, and go check out the library. You'll see teens there, and they'll be having a good time.

Letter from a Parent:

The library is an important part of the community for my family. It truly has something for everyone, and its resources are free to the public. As the parent of a teenager, this resource means a lot.

My teen uses the _____ [library name] for homework and school projects, but also for quite a lot more. The library provides interesting and age-appropriate programs like _____ [name of event your teen has attended recently], where my teen learned _____ [describe activity], all for free. It offers a wide array of reading materials for my teen, including magazines, newspapers, classic stories, graphic novels, how-to books, and more. I know that the librarians there have chosen the books carefully and that they can help me find books that aren't just interesting for my teen, but appropriate as well.

[Date] is Teen Read Week™, a national literacy event sponsored by the Young Adult Library Services Association. I'd like to encourage other parents to make a trip to the library with their teenager to check it out. There are more great resources and events than you may think, and there are trained professionals who can help you get your questions answered. Plus, it is a safe place for teens to have fun and do something positive.

My librarian, _____ [name], informed me that the theme for Teen Read Week™ is "read for the fun of it." I read that the National Assessment for Educational Progress found that students who reported reading for the fun of it score better on standardized tests. So I'll be taking my teen to the library for Teen Read Week™ and for other weeks, as a way to encourage him to read and also to provide him with a place where he can relax, be with friends, and learn.

Teen Tech Week

Letter from a Teen:

I'm _____ [age] years old, and I read all kinds of articles and hear reports on TV about how the Internet is unsafe or how teens steal music online. But most teens are not irresponsible when it comes to technology, and one important reason why are the librarians at my library, _____ [name of school or public library].

Libraries are not musty old buildings filled with shushing librarians. I like to read, but one thing I really love about my library is all of the technology I can use there for free. I get on the computers to do my homework, to keep in touch with my friends and family, and to play games and relax. [Date] is Teen Tech Week™.

I'd like to tell other teens who may not be using the library that they should definitely check it out. There is more to do here than they may think, and there are people here who can help you get your questions answered. Also, parents should go to the library too. If they're worried about their teens and the Internet, a librarian can show them how to use things like Facebook in a way that keeps us safe. They can check out DVDs and CDs for us to use, for free.

I love to hang out with my friends, play video games, surf the Internet, and listen to music. I don't think many kids realize you can do all this at the library. The library is a great (and safe) place to relax with friends, do homework, or have some time by yourself. And the librarians are there to help you learn all about the best way to use all this stuff.

Letter from a Parent:

Even though my children are educated, I worry a lot about my teenagers, especially when it comes to technology. I worry about predators that might lurk online. I worry my kids won't know how to do actual research for their school projects, but will just "Google" something instead or find answers on disreputable websites. I see them downloading music, and I just hope they know how to do it legally.

But I worry a lot less after talking to the librarians at _____ [name of school/public library]. Libraries are a safe place for my teens, and I want them to learn how to navigate all these new things that pop up online. I know they're teaching my kids to use all of the Internet safely and responsibly. They answer all my questions and are more than happy to demonstrate how Facebook works or how my teens can get online homework help.

But my teens use the _____ [library name] for more than school projects and to show their nervous parent that they're safe online. Our library provides interesting, age-appropriate, and free programs like _____ [names of technology-specific events your teen has been to]. The library offers a wide variety of technology and has staff that are knowledgeable. With all the new technologies, it's difficult to keep up as a parent, so it's good to know that there are adults who are on top of all the new trends and can assist my child in a positive way. Plus, my teen can check out DVDs or CDs for free, play video games with friends, and get online to read magazines or websites, all for free.

[Date] is Teen Tech Week™, a national initiative aimed at teens, their parents, educators, and other concerned adults. The purpose of this initiative is to ensure that teens are competent and ethical users of technologies, especially those that are offered through libraries. I'd like to encourage other parents to make a trip to the library with their teenager to check it out. There are more great resources and events than most parents would think, and there are trained professionals who can help you get your questions answered. Plus, it is a place where teens can engage in positive activities.

INDEX